55
WAYS to the Wilderness in

SOUTHCENTRAL
ALASKA

D0974078

55 WAYS to the Wilderness in

SOUTHCENTRAL ALASKA

FIFTH EDITION

HELEN D. NIENHUESER

JOHN WOLFE JR.

THE MOUNTAINEERS BOOKS

Published by
The Mountaineers Books
1001 SW Klickitat Way, Suite 201
Seattle, WA 98134

First edition 1972. Second edition 1978. Third edition 1985. Fourth edition 1994. Fifth edition: first printing 2002, second printing 2004.

Published simultaneously in Great Britain by Cordee, 3a DeMontfort Street, Leicester, England, LE1 7HD

Manufactured in the United States of America

Project Editor: Laura Slavik
Editor: Uma Kukathas
Layout: Jennifer LaRock Shontz
Mapmaker: Marge Mueller, Gray Mouse Graphics
Photographers: All photographs by the authors unless otherwise credited

Cover photograph: *Portage Glacier, Trip 20* Photo by Helen Nienhueser
Frontispiece: *Golden birch, Trip 21* Photo by Nancy Simmerman
Dedication page: Photo by Callie Lustig

Library of Congress Cataloging-in-Publication Data
    Nienhueser, Helen.
    55 Ways to the wilderness in southcentral Alaska/by Helen D. Nienhueser and John Wolfe Jr. — 5th ed.
        p. cm.
    Includes index.
    ISBN 0-89886-791-6 (pbk.)
    1. Hiking—Alaska—Guidebooks. 2. Cross-country skiing—Alaska—Guidebooks. 3. Boats and boating—Alaska—Guidebooks. 4. Alaska—Guidebooks. I. Title: Fifty-five ways to the wilderness in southcentral Alaska. II. Wolfe, John, Jr. III. Title.
    GV199.42.A4 N54 2002
    796.51'09798—dc21

Hans Van der Laan
November 17, 1937–April 12, 1971

To Hans

Who still lives in the hearts of his family and friends and who, through his part in this book, shares with others his love of Alaska's mountains and valleys and his devotion to excellence.

You cannot stay on the summit forever; you have to come down ... so why bother in the first place? Just this: what is above knows what is below, but what is below does not know what is above. One climbs, one sees. One descends, one sees no longer, but one has seen. There is an art of conducting oneself in the lower regions by the memory of what one saw higher up. When one can no longer see, one can at least still know.

—**Rene Daumel,** Mount Analogue

CONTENTS

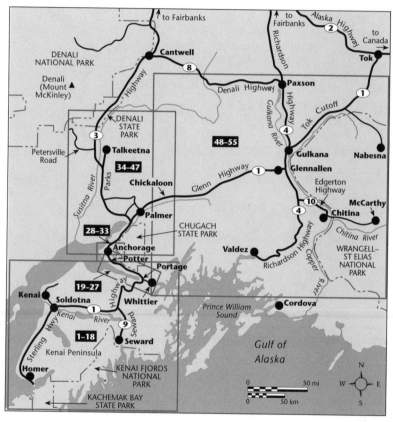

Inset boxes refer to section maps.

MAP LEGEND

——①——	highway	●	town or community	◇	text reference
———	road	✕	mine	▪3	trip number
+++++++++++	railroad	Ⓢ	start of trail	) (	pass
- - - - - - -	primary trail	→	direction of travel	→←—	bridge
– – – – – –	secondary trail	⌂	cabin	∿	stream or river
··············	primary route	⌂	yurt	∿╫╫∿	waterfall
·············	secondary route	▟	trail shelter		lake or body of saltwater
—·—·—	powerline	⬆	ranger station		marsh
●—●—●	ski lift or tram	▪	building	▲ 5,000 ft	mountain summit
▪—▪—▪	ore tram	▲	campground		glacier
—·-·—	land unit boundary	⟁	campsite		
		⌇	picnic area		

ACKNOWLEDGMENTS

This book may list just two authors, but it is a group effort in many ways. We authors split up the trips and do not hike most of them together, so we frequently have other companions along—for good company, help in getting the directions straight, safety in numbers, photo subjects, and second opinions. Primary among these are our spouses, Gayle Nienhueser and Gretchen Nelson, and John's children (Helen's grandchildren), Avery and Rebecca Wolfe, all of whom not only participated willingly on the trail but also continually had their home schedules altered for them by the writers in their families.

Others who contributed repeatedly or substantively as hikers, reviewers of specialty sections in the Introduction, child care providers, or sounding boards (or some combination) for this edition include Dave Wolfe and Lynn Palmquist; Ali Iliff; the Mark and Jeanne Larsen and Cami and Mark Dalton families; Jill Fredston; Larry Aumiller; David Imus; Thomas Hunt, M.D.; Verna Pratt; Lynn Spencer; Julie Graham; Dick and Liska Snyder; Linda Smith; Alison Hedberg; Nina Faust; Frank Cook and Bonnie Cudnohufsky; Matt Kinney; Nancy and John Nelson; Tucker Spohr; Gary Snyder; Christine Clapp; Becky Jermaine, Nancy Gehm, Jeannie Woodring, and Patti Sandvik.

Agency personnel were routinely overflowing with ready assistance—Kenai Fjords and Wrangell–St. Elias National Parks, Alaska Division of Parks and Outdoor Recreation, USDA Forest Service, Matanuska-Susitna Borough, and Kenai National Wildlife Refuge.

There are many photographs in this edition by folks other than the authors—all donated. The names of the photographers, many of them professionals or serious hobbyists, appear with the photos. We appreciate their skills.

There is one debt of gratitude that goes way back. Nancy Simmerman was the photographer for the first and fourth editions. She was co-author for the second and third editions. Although most of her photographs have now cycled out of the book, much of her research and some of her words still appear in these pages. She has been a strong force in the book since its inception.

Finally, we acknowledge the efforts of the Mountaineering Club of Alaska and its members who originally compiled 30 Hikes in Alaska (Seattle: The Mountaineers Books, 1967). Bill Hauser edited that initial volume, which was the basis for the first edition of this book in 1972. Contributors to 30 Hikes included Bob Spurr, Hans Van der Laan, John Wolfe Sr., J. Vin Hoeman, Nicholas Parker, Carol and Dave DeVoe, Gary Hansen, Rod and Gwynneth Wilson, Bill Hague, Ron Linder, and Helen Nienhueser.

PREFACE TO THE FIFTH EDITION

ALASKA WILDLANDS: THEY'RE WHO WE ARE

"... best of all, the rich silence of the mountains." This kind of language has been associated with the Turnagain Pass Ski Tour (Trip 18) since the first edition of 55 Ways, in 1972. For this edition, sadly, we took it out. The reason? Noise.

I was in Turnagain Pass on a late winter, blue-sky day with my daughters, 8 and 5, for their first-ever "mountain tour" (a short way up the Center Ridge route). The area is as visually stunning as ever, but in recent years powerful snowmobile engines have created a continual background hum. During my daughters' first experience, revs and whines frequently pierced the air. This in an area considered a model because it designates one side of the valley "motorized" and the other "nonmotorized." But it is clear, with machines so powerful and popular, that even this "solution" leaves those who value quiet out in the cold. I am disappointed that our children apparently will not have the opportunity to know the "rich silence of the mountains" at Turnagain Pass.

Other trips in this book are threatened by helicopter landings, low-flying airplanes, all-terrain vehicles, and snowmobiles. Machines create intrusive noise, especially, but in some cases also leave visual scars. To ensure that all land is not overrun by these vehicles, we must work together to foster in our children a deep appreciation of quiet, natural landscapes, so they will grow up to defend their natural quiet. True appreciation comes not from slick woods and wildlife websites but from overcoming nature's adversities large and small through one's own initiative, being in the mountains not so much for thrill as for peace.

Lynn Spencer, friend, environmental planner, and trail groomer for the Nordic Skiing Association of Anchorage, champions the notion of being in the wild instead of doing, and of teaching children these values. She grew up the third of four siblings raised on a homestead between Kenai and Soldotna. Her father, Dave Spencer, came north in 1948 to manage the Kenai Moose Range—now the Kenai National Wildlife Refuge—and ultimately to manage all Alaska refuges. He passed away in 2000 as we began work on this fifth edition. Lynn reminisces about how her father dragged his children out on canoe trips, hiking trips, and skiing trips, as my parents did, and reflects on how the kids were unappreciative at the time and reluctant to admit to having fun:

Dad was very much a woodsman. We went out camping and skiing when we were pretty little. [Often], the weather was horrible. It was pretty grim (jeans, soggy Army surplus chicken feather sleeping bags)...wet and miserable. Dad just had this dry sense of humor, even in the grimmest situations. He made us all laugh.

We'd go cross-country skiing out into the swamps (from the homestead)—just in the evening, in the moonlight. He'd take us canoeing. My dad was a silent Quaker by upbringing. He'd dip his paddle. He'd let us glide and just listen.

Each one of those little experiences—not only was it valuable, but from where we sit now, we look out and we see the natural world and we know what it is. It's not just something out there; it's who we are. We need the silence, we need the quiet; we need to go to those places where we can stop and hear the sounds and just be. There's a lot of doers of things. I like to go where you can still hear and see. My father, when he was dying, he wasn't afraid. He was so closely involved with the natural world. He'd seen life happening over and over again.

It is critical that our society continue to raise kids as the Spencer parents raised theirs—to seek and appreciate silence, wilderness, and wildlife—and that adults who have never known these things be introduced to them. That is why I write this book, and why I work with the Alaska Mountain and Wilderness Huts Association. It takes a lot of effort in modern society to step out of the day-to-day routine and experience the backcountry. It takes a Herculean effort for a working family with small children. To expand a community that values the rich silence of the mountains, however, the effort is worthwhile.

—*John Wolfe Jr., Anchorage, 2001*

ALASKA WILDLANDS: HOW ARE WE DOING?

The best reason for writing a guidebook to Alaska's wild places is to develop a constituency for protecting these areas. We've seen many changes in Alaska since the first edition of this book, and it is appropriate to ask: how are we doing? The answer: there is a large constituency, and important protective steps have been taken, but we are nevertheless seeing the erosion of Alaska's wilderness.

The bright spots are the protected lands—the state and federal parks and wildlife refuges that did not exist when I began work on this book in the 1960s. Although many preferred the freedom of the Alaska wilderness we found here before the discovery of oil, oil brought more people, and wilderness cannot survive the unregulated inundation of people, especially when that inundation is assisted by technology (e.g., snowmobiles). Thus, protecting the lands as parks and refuges has been an important step toward preserving some of the wilderness that drew many of us here in the first place. The regulations that follow park and refuge designation, and that limit our freedom to do whatever we want on these lands, are the price we pay for our increasing population and exploding technology. Alaska's wilderness would fast disappear without such protection.

The forces of change leading to the erosion of Alaska's wilderness are the same here as in the rest of the world: population growth, exploding technology, and our thirst for energy. These forces led to three milestones in Alaska's recent history: the Alaska Native Claims Settlement Act of 1971; the construction of the Trans-Alaska Pipeline in the 1970s; and the Alaska National Interest Lands Conservation Act (ANILCA) in 1980, which established more than 100 million acres of parks and wildlife refuges.

These three milestones reflect compromises made by the three major actors on the Alaska stage: Alaska's indigenous people, development interests, and conservationists. The discovery of oil at Prudhoe Bay precipitated these compromises. Before the oil pipeline could be built, the claims of Alaska's indigenous peoples had to be addressed. And, before a workable compromise could be achieved on the Native claims, a mechanism was built into the Claims Act that led to ANILCA and creation of many new parks and refuges. The battles have been fierce and divisive, as Alaska struggles to find the right balance among these three major interests.

The same forces and actors are at work across the globe, particularly in developing nations. Development provides jobs and the kind of lifestyle we enjoy in the United States—but it too often has negative impacts on the environment and on the culture of indigenous people.

But in two respects, Alaska is different. First, development of Alaska is taking place at a time when American values have undergone a fundamental shift. Most of us no longer see wilderness as something to be conquered. Rather, we see wild lands as a valuable repository of beauty, peace, silence, and wildlife, places fundamental to our American culture. Second, Alaska's population remains relatively small, and our climate is likely to keep it that way. Therefore, the pressures for development are not as strong as in developing nations. We have an opportunity, still, to find the right balance among these three interests. In doing so, we have the potential to be a model for others.

WHAT NEEDS TO BE DONE?

The biggest contributors to the erosion of wilderness, in southcentral Alaska at least, are exploding technology and population growth. In winter it is nearly impossible to find quiet natural places. Snowmobiles are almost entirely unregulated and, except for Anchorage and parts of Chugach State Park, they are almost everywhere. Today's powerful machines are able to get to places the old ones could not, introducing conflict into new areas. In summer the burgeoning tourist industry keeps small planes buzzing over much of southcentral Alaska's backcountry.

The Alaska Legislature is not, currently, a stronghold of people who value natural quiet or other wild values of Alaska's lands. Any move by a state agency to bring balance to the winter recreational scene is met by retaliatory legislation, affecting the agency's authority, budget, or both.

On the other hand, though snowmobiles are mostly unregulated, there are few places designated for their use. It would surely help to designate some places for recreational snowmobiling and groom some trails. A cooperative planning process by state agencies, local governments, user groups, and private property owners is needed to achieve this.

Airplane noise is an even more difficult problem, but this much seems predictable: continued unregulated growth will lead, sooner or later, to restrictions. It behooves the air taxi operators and the tourism industry to limit themselves.

All-terrain vehicles are also unregulated on public lands outside of parks, and those who hike the Peters Hills, Hicks Creek, or Syncline Mountain will see firsthand the results.

As Thomas Jefferson told us, "the price of liberty is eternal vigilance." We must monitor management of public lands, especially "multiple-use" lands managed by the Alaska Department of Natural Resources, the Bureau of Land Management, and the U.S. Forest Service. Bureaucrats occasionally need to be reminded that, under state and federal law, multiple use does not mean that all uses must be allowed to occur simultaneously on the same parcel. We must lobby for adequate funding for state land management agencies. The Alaska Division of Mining, Land, & Water is not funded to do on-the-ground management. The Alaska Division of Parks and Outdoor Recreation does not have money for maintenance. We must urge the Legislature to adopt a fiscal plan that includes adequate funding for state responsibilities and new revenue sources—even if it means paying some taxes, as in other states.

There are some areas of state land that need protected status, though the current legislative climate makes that difficult. Two areas that have long been on wish lists are Hatcher Pass (Trips 43 and 44) and Keystone Canyon (Trip 54).

WHAT CAN YOU DO?

Get involved! Because of our small population, one person can make a big difference in what happens in Alaska. Know which agency manages your favorite trails. This book lists the managing agency in the information block at the top of each trip description. Ask to be placed on the managing agency's mailing list for notice of planning or proposed development. To support funding requests, write letters to legislators for state agencies and to Congress for federal agencies.

To understand the issues each agency deals with, you must understand the mandate under which each agency operates, as set out in law. The mandate will determine the extent and type of conflict that may affect the land through which these trails pass. Twenty-five of these trips are in state park units, which are managed by the Alaska Division of Parks and Outdoor Recreation for purposes of recreation. Thirteen of these trails are in Chugach National Forest, which the U.S. Forest Service manages for multiple use. All or parts of ten trips are on public-domain lands managed by the Alaska Division of Mining, Land, & Water for multiple use.

The remaining trips are managed by the U.S. Fish and Wildlife Service (Kenai National Wildlife Refuge), Wrangell–St. Elias National Park and Preserve, Kenai Fjords National Park, and the Alaska Department of Fish and Game. The appendix lists addresses of these agencies and of conservation groups. To help you understand current issues, join conservation organizations. And write letters! They matter, and letters are better than emails.

We must not lose the wild character of Alaska. We must work together to find the right balance between development and the environment and between technology-assisted recreation and quiet, human-powered recreation. The two kinds of recreation are not compatible in the same place at the same time except at very low levels of use. Alaska should be big enough to accommodate both uses, even on lands managed for multiple use.

If we keep a global perspective as we think about Alaska's future, perhaps our wild places will take their place among our most precious assets because they are so rare. Help decide the future of these areas. Don't take these special places for granted!

—Helen D. Nienhueser, Anchorage, 2001

Upper Palmer Creek valley (Trip 15), September (John Wolfe Jr.)

INTRODUCTION

BACKCOUNTRY TRAVEL IN SOUTHCENTRAL ALASKA

This book is a guide to routes and trails that lead to some of southcentral Alaska's finest wild and beautiful backcountry. The trick, especially in southcentral Alaska, with its proliferation of brushy alder and willow, is getting above brushline. *55 Ways to the Wilderness in Southcentral Alaska* describes numerous access routes to high country, making the best use of existing trails. In this book we've tried to create a pleasant balance among different kinds of trips—some through woodlands, some across tundra, a couple by canoe, a few with good mountain biking, and winter excursions for playing in the snow.

This book also offers trips for all skill levels. The novice who has never before ventured out of the city will enjoy starting with Trips 2, 19, 33, 35, 37, and 41. The bulk of the book describes good, solid trips of such beauty and variety that they are worth doing every few years. Some of the descriptions—for example, those for Trips 44, 48, and 51—offer longer routes or variations. These lead far from the road system, require a minimum of 3 days, and assume that the traveler can successfully plan and execute an extended wilderness trip.

Alternate routes and destinations are given in most of the trip descriptions and in Trip Summary Tables on pages 42–51. When all are tallied, this book might be more accurately titled *160 Ways to the Wilderness in Southcentral Alaska*. Although we field-check trips every few years, conditions may differ from those described. Signs are erected or fall down, and maintenance on routes improves or is discontinued. A few hikes follow unmarked trails created and maintained only by public and animal use. Such unofficial routes can change annually. Those with limited backcountry experience should only venture into areas without marked trails in the company of more experienced companions. When possible, we incorporate changes and corrections in new printings. If you find changes or errors, please contact us in Anchorage at (907) 279-4663 (John) or (907) 277-9330 (Helen).

The following paragraphs are a basic introduction to hiking in southcentral Alaska—reminders for the experienced and information to start visitors and new residents on their way.

TRAIL MANAGERS AND SOURCES OF INFORMATION

Many trips described here are in the Kenai National Wildlife Refuge, Chugach National Forest, Chugach State Park, other units of the state park system, Kenai Fjords National Park, or Wrangell–St. Elias National Park and Preserve. Insofar as possible, the trail descriptions are accurate, but up-to-date information can be obtained from land managers. Addresses and phone numbers are listed in the appendix.

Each agency has its own regulations to protect the areas it manages. In the Kenai National Wildlife Refuge and Chugach National Forest, fire building and camping are unrestricted, although open campfires outside established campgrounds may be prohibited during high fire danger periods. Chugach State Park has no restrictions on camping but allows campfires only in established firepits or on the gravel bars of Eagle River and Eklutna Lake.

Chugach State Park personnel encourage backcountry travelers to file a trip plan at the park office or the Eagle River Nature Center. Budget cuts have led to the imposition of user fees for parking and campground use. An annual pass may be purchased at the Alaska Department of Natural Resources Public Information Center (see Appendix, p. 245), or day-use fees may be paid on site.

The Alaska Division of Parks and the U.S. Forest Service maintain a number of public-use cabins, several associated with trips described here. See the appendix for information on how to rent these. Be sure to carry your use permit with you.

Mountaineering: The Freedom of the Hills, sixth edition, edited by Don Graydon and Kurt Hanson and published by The Mountaineers Books, 1997, contains additional information about many of the topics discussed here. *A Naturalist's Guide to Chugach State Park*, by Jenny Zimmerman (Alaska: A.T. Publishing and Printing, 1994), contains a wealth of information about the geology, plants, animals, and birds of Chugach State Park.

HIKING WITH CHILDREN

Experienced hikers take children along on almost all the trips in this book, but some hikes are too long or difficult for the average child. Try out the easier hikes on your children first. Babies can go almost anywhere in a pack. From three years old and up, children are tougher physically than mentally. Little guys can manage a few miles a day with play breaks and an occasional piggyback ride (for variation, not usually because of true exhaustion). Children five and older can easily cover 4 to 5 miles a day and often more.

Most important is that a trip has variety—a stream or lake to play in, rocks to climb on. Canoe trips combine short hikes on the portages with time on the water, and kids love them. Contrary to popular opinion, many children find climbing uphill more interesting than flat trails, but too much of anything will do in a youngster. To keep things interesting, pick up a "magic stick"—you carry one end; they take the other. Trade off leads. Use it for follow-the-leader around a tree. Give a boost when needed. Or keep the pace moving with leap-frog hide 'n' seek, where kids go a bit ahead

Sharing a kid-size summit (Trip 41), September (John Wolfe Jr.)

and "disappear" while hapless parents "search" for them until they pop out behind and charge ahead to hide again. Always carry favorite nibble foods. Join forces with another family to ensure your child has a playmate.

Parents should set their sights low and worry less about destinations than they normally would, gradually teaching young ones that a steady pace pays off with the reward of reaching a lake or a summit. See the Trip Summary Tables on pages 42-51 for suggested trips for kids. And ignore the protests at home when you suggest a hike; kids love it once they're out.

EQUIPMENT

Although the market pushes gear enough to fill your pack and empty your wallet ten times over, the beauty of hiking is how little you really need. That said, it is important to recognize that a short distance from the road you are, for all practical purposes, in the wilderness. You must be self-sufficient, with proper clothing, food, camping equipment, and navigation aids. *Mountaineering: The Freedom of the Hills*, the classic backcountry how-to book, lists Ten Essentials to be carried at all times: extra clothing, extra food, sunglasses, a knife, matches, fire starter (e.g., candle), a first-aid kit (in Alaska, leave the snakebite kit at home), a flashlight (not necessary early June to late July), a map, and a compass. *The Freedom of the Hills* and other books detail equipment needs. We focus here mostly on general guidelines and needs for southcentral Alaska.

Know your gear and its limitations (Trip 44) (John Wolfe Jr.)

Clothing

Don't be hoodwinked into thinking you have to have high-tech clothes to go for a walk. Good judgment in knowing the limitations of your clothes is more important than owning expensive duds. Invest most in durable raingear. Waterproof-breathable fabrics are expensive and generally better for winter than for summer rainstorms. Even in midsummer in the mountains, take gloves, a warm hat, coats or sweaters, and raingear. In Alaska's cool and sometimes rainy climate, synthetics are generally better than cotton for backcountry hiking because they dry quickly and don't absorb water into the fibers. Cotton jeans are a particular problem if they are wet.

Footwear

Some swear by traditional leather hiking boots, others by running shoes. The goal is protection—you need healthy feet to get you home again. Avoid blisters by making sure shoes are comfortable and by taking tape or moleskin for use immediately at signs of hot spots. If you have weak ankles, make sure you have boots with maximum ankle support. Many of these trips take you to country where you'll want to leave the trail and explore. For this, ensure that boots have a decent edge and a solid, non-flared heel that you can plunge into a hard snow or rough scree (gravel) surface. Rocky terrain suggests a boot with a beefy toe box for additional protection.

Gear for Fall-Winter-Spring

Some clothing associated with winter is necessary for fall and spring travel, especially up high: mittens with windproof shells; extra wool socks; synthetic long underwear and overpants; wind pants; and a face mask. Gaiters, worn over boot tops, keep the snow out and help keep feet warm.

Midwinter trips require a thick parka and insulated pants, not so much for while you're moving but in case you or a partner have an accident and need to sit in the cold for a long time. Many loose-fitting layers of clothing allow for fine-tuning body temperature at different levels of activity.

Winter hiking or snowshoeing boots with a rubber foot, nylon or leather upper, and thick liners are generally fine if not too sloppy on your foot. Some Alaskans use military surplus "bunny boots," which are very warm but clunky. If using snowshoes, be sure bulky boots will move freely in the toe opening.

Skis and ski boots are marketed for specialty niches. Many people do fine without four pairs of skis for different purposes, but it may take a sympathetic sales person to help you find a pair of all-around touring skis: medium width, with good side-cut for turning and either a waxable or no-wax base, constructed well to reduce danger of breakage on the trail. Climbing skins help in the mountains when you expect to ski up for much of the day and then ski down. Some very beefy backcountry ski boots are available. Most people do fine with boots that provide comfort and good support, that flex easily at the toe, and that are of medium weight. Consider insulated overboots.

LEAVE NO TRACE

We hike to find wilderness, but in hiking we leave tracks that diminish wilderness. We all have heard about "minimum-impact camping," but it means more than carrying out litter. It is a state of constant awareness. The phrase "leave only footprints, take only pictures" rings in our memories, but in fragile areas, even leaving "only footprints" has caused erosion. It is up to each of us to realize that, when tiny tundra roots rip underfoot, we must look for a better place for our next footstep.

These concepts can be summed up in a three-word directive that's easy to remember: Leave No Trace. This is not only common sense but is the name of an education program developed by the National Outdoor Leadership School (NOLS) in cooperation with federal land managers nationwide. The ethic? Make it hard for others to see or hear you, and Leave No

Trace of your visit. There are Leave No Trace (LNT) training books, master courses, and booklets for different environments. But the core principles, based on LNT for kids, are these:

- **Know before you go!**
  Know what you're getting into, and take the Ten Essentials (see "Equipment," earlier in the Introduction) and other equipment necessary for the area. Plan for a small group (up to six) or self-sufficient subgroups of this size that can travel together during the day.

- **Choose the right ground!**
  Use the prepared trail, where there is one, and where there is no trail at all, spread out so as not to create one. Use existing camp-sites, or, where there are none, camp 100 Big Steps or more from water and trails and then on the most durable surfaces available (rock, sand, and snow are best). Spend only a night, maybe two, at any one site. Place cooking and sleeping areas 100 Big Steps apart or more (see "Moose and Bears," later in the Introduction).

- **Trash your trash!**
  If you pack it in, pack it out—but don't pack much in to begin with. Bury feces 100 Big Steps from water, and carry used toilet paper and tampons out in a baggie. Further protect water by washing yourself and dishes away from lakes and streams, not in them.

- **Leave what you find!**
  Good campsites are found, not made. Avoid digging dirt, cutting trees, picking flowers, or removing artifacts at camp or along the way.

- **Burn wisely!**
  Take a camp stove to reduce forest fire risk and the visual "traces" of fire: broken and sawed limbs and sterile black holes on the ground. It's best to build fires only at campgrounds.

- **Keep wildlife wild!**
  Stay well away from birds and animals, and keep people food for people. See also "Moose and Bears," later in the Introduction. Keep dogs home or under true control so they don't stress or kill wildlife (even squirrels).

- **Do unto others!...**
  Keep your fun clean and quiet, remembering that other hikers and nearby landowners may be out there with you. Respect Alaska Natives and others whose culture depends upon subsisting off the land.

"Leave No Trace: Alaskan Tundra" (text available at *www.LNT.org*) is a great booklet. Inside the front cover, it reads: "The principles and practices discussed here are meaningless as a set of rules and regulations. They must be based on an abiding respect for and appreciation of wild places...." Such respect and appreciation come from experience on the trail. So go—accepting that you will sometimes "leave a trace," but always striving to "leave no trace."

Boiling water on a camp stove (Trip 3) (Gretchen Nelson)

DRINKING WATER

Drinking from Alaska's lakes and streams is dangerous. The most serious threat in Alaska's backcountry is the microorganism *Giardia lamblia,* which causes giardiasis ("beaver fever"). An emerging threat is *Cryptosporidium,* or Crypto. Both are carried in the feces of many mammals, including humans, so it is a matter of time until Crypto, now present in some Alaskan waters, becomes a problem. Water used by beavers is particularly suspect. *Giardia* and Crypto cysts survive best in cold water and may be found in any surface water. Both giardiasis and cryptosporidiosis cause diarrhea and cramps, and both are potentially dangerous diseases for some people.

Boiling is the most effective treatment. The Centers for Disease Control and Prevention advises that to kill *Giardia* and Crypto cysts water should be boiled for at least 1 minute, and 3 minutes at 3,000 feet or above. If other contaminating organisms might be present, boil at least 20 minutes. To remove *Giardia* and Crypto by filtration, look for a pore size of 0.2 microns or less and an *absolute* (not *nominal*) pore size of 1 micron or less. Not all handheld backpacking filters are equally effective, and filters that remove *Giardia* may not remove Crypto. Chemical methods of disinfectant *do not work* on Crypto and are less effective on *Giardia* than boiling or filtering, although they are effective against bacteria. Iodine-based treatments are more effective for *Giardia* than chlorine-based treatments, though iodine causes health problems for some people. The longer the contact time, the more effective iodine is: it is 90-percent effective with 30 minutes' contact time at 50°F and 99- to 99.9-percent effective with 8 hours of contact time.

MOSQUITOES

Although generally not as much of a problem in southcentral Alaska as in the interior, mosquitoes are annoying. But at least Alaskan mosquitoes do not transmit diseases! Peak mosquito season in southcentral Alaska is the end of June and the first part of July. Mosquitoes can be thick in marshy lowlands but are rarely a problem on breezy alpine ridges.

Most Alaskans carry insect repellent during summer, but many of these should be used cautiously. Only repellents with the chemical N,N-diethyl-meta-toluamide (deet) have tested as effective against mosquitoes, but deet is absorbed by the blood and can have side effects, occasionally serious ones. These include skin irritation and neurological problems such as confusion and irritability.

Experts advise using repellents with low concentrations of deet. Some sources recommend 30-percent deet repellents, and others recommend concentrations of 40 percent for adults. Do not use deet on children under two, and use it sparingly on children under six. For any child, deet concentrations should not exceed 10 percent. Apply deet-based repellents sparingly and only on exposed skin. Trapping the repellent under clothing can increase the possibility of side effects. Deet should not be sprayed on the face, inhaled, or ingested. Avoid putting deet-based repellents on the fingers and hands of children, so they won't swallow any of it.

Alternatives to using deet repellents on your skin include spraying clothing only, especially cuffs, collars, and waistbands, and wearing long sleeves, long pants, head nets, and even gloves. Deet is safe on cotton, wool, and nylon but may damage spandex, rayon, and acetate. Clothing treated with many deet-based repellents also becomes more flammable. Avoid hair sprays, colognes, and perfumes, which attract mosquitoes. Also avoid alcohol and foods high in serotonin such as bananas and nuts. Some sources recommend avoiding the use of yellow, white, and tan clothing in heavily infested mosquito areas. Some people find that frequent applications of citronella-based repellents work for them, although *Consumer Reports* (June 2000) did not find these effective against mosquitoes. Oily sunscreen is said to keep mosquitoes from getting a grip on your skin. Finally, stick to the ridges in peak mosquito season!

PLANTS

Although Alaska is free of poison ivy and poison oak, it does have a few plants that should be avoided. These include stinging nettle, devil's club, poison water hemlock, baneberry, poisonous mushrooms, and cow parsnip. The general rule is: do not eat berries or mushrooms that you cannot positively identify as edible. Musky smelling cow parsnip is found below the alpine zone everywhere in southcentral Alaska and is usually harmless, but its sap can make the skin of hikers or mountain bikers crashing through it sensitive to sun on bright days, and the resulting sunburn can lead to massive ugly blisters. Avoid this by wearing long sleeves and pants or by washing at a stream once you leave the parsnip zone. The Cooperative Extension Service (see Appendix for address) publishes and sells a useful booklet on plants called "Wild Edible and Poisonous Plants of Alaska" (1993).

Flower of cow parsnip, one of Alaska's few problem plants (Dick Snyder)

MOOSE AND BEARS

One of the nicest events on a wilderness outing is seeing wildlife. Most sightings are occasions for photos and opportunities to observe the habits of Alaska's fascinating animals. Moose and bears, however, must be treated with distant respect.

Most moose will move away from or ignore a hiker or skier. Cow moose, however, are protective of their calves and can be dangerous. Expect a cow to be nearby whenever you see a calf. Stopping to take a picture is not a good idea.

Bears, either black or brown (grizzly), can be dangerous, but rarely attack humans. With sensible precautions, humans are safer in bear country than in many cities.

Although bears rarely attack, it is important to understand why they sometimes do to know how to avoid attacks. Predacious attacks are extremely rare. Almost all attacks are defensive because the bear is surprised. A defensive attack is more likely to occur if you are between the bear and its food source, or a female is protecting her cubs from a perceived threat.

To avoid a surprise encounter, *make noise* when traveling in bear country. Sing loudly, clap your hands, shake pebbles in a can or metal canteen, beat on a pot with a spoon, or blow on a noisemaker. Some people use bells tied to pack, waist, or boots. Making noise is especially important in deep brush or terrain where surprising a bear is more likely. A party of four to six people is safer than a single person because the larger group makes more noise and is more intimidating to a bear. At night use a flashlight. Stick to open routes. If you are walking downwind, you are less likely to surprise a bear, because animals will more easily smell and hear you.

Avoid bears' food caches and food sources. If you smell something dead and rotten, *go some other way.* If you see an animal carcass, *leave the area the same way you came.* A bear may be sleeping nearby. If you see a number of magpies, eagles, or ravens, they may be feeding on a bear's food cache; avoid that area. If possible, do not walk along a stream or a lake when its shore is littered with dead salmon; if you must do so, be especially alert. Be alert in berry season; berries are important to a bear's diet, and bears will leave salmon streams for berries.

If you encounter a bear cub, assume its mother is nearby and *leave the vicinity.* If the cub sees you and is curious, talk to it firmly to get it away from you. Move away slowly. Try to avoid getting near a sow and her cub.

Given sufficient warning and an avenue for retreat, most bears will move away from humans. Constantly be alert for bear signs (bear trails, tracks, droppings, or diggings), and for the bear itself. If you spot a distant bear, avoid an encounter by changing your route or by sitting quietly (if it remains unaware of you) until it has left the area.

Grizzly and cubs hunting for salmon (Gayle Nienhueser)

Camp or rest at least 25 yards away from a bear trail or salmon stream. If you cannot get that far away from a river, camp on a gravel bar in the river or in as open a spot as you can find (but be aware that rivers can rise quickly from rainstorms, including rain upstream, so be cautious in choosing a gravel bar campsite). If bear signs are abundant, reduce food odors in camp by cooking dinner in one place and then moving to another at least half an hour away to camp. In any camp establish a cooking area 100 yards or more from the tent. Do not keep *any* food in your tent. Cache it in a tree (16 feet above ground in brown bear country) or, if no trees are available, 100 yards or more away from the campsite. Keep all food well wrapped in resealable plastic bags. Better yet, carry and store food in bear-proof containers made of PVC with screw-in caps. These are available at sporting good stores in Alaska and fit inside many backpacks. Mothballs in small net bags (discarded panty hose work fine) attached to the outside of food caches may discourage animal raiders. Pile pots and pans on top of the food cache; if an animal gets into the cache, the tumbling pots may scare it off or the noise may alert you so you can scare it away. Do not carry especially odoriferous foods such as bacon, smoked salmon, or peanut butter. Never feed wildlife. In Alaska it is illegal to feed bears, foxes, wolves, and wolverines, either intentionally or by leaving food within their reach.

Do not wipe food off your hands onto your clothes. Before going to bed, wash your hands and face carefully and brush your teeth to remove food odors. Do not use scented deodorants, perfumes, or skin creams. Bears may be attracted by any strong odor, and bears have excellent noses!

If, despite trying to avoid bears, you meet one, what should you do? If it has not seen you, attempt to get out of sight, giving the bear plenty of room to avoid an encounter. If the bear has seen you, *do not run.* This might trigger a bear's chase response, and you cannot outrun a bear. Let the bear know you are human. Talk to it in a normal voice. Wave your arms. Walk slowly backward, facing the bear and talking sternly, much as you would to a large, menacing dog. Do not drop your pack or anything else with food in it, as that rewards the bear. If the bear continues to follow you, stop and hold your ground. It may just be trying to figure out what you are. Continue waving your arms and talking to the bear. Bang pots and pans or use other noisemakers. The closer a bear purposefully approaches, the stronger your response should be.

If a bear actually charges you, stand your ground, wave your hands, and yell; it discourages actual contact. Increase your apparent size by standing shoulder to shoulder with your companions and waving a jacket. Keep talking to the bear; shouting is appropriate, but don't shriek. Even without this vigorous response, most charges are false (they end without contact when the bear veers away, sometimes just a few feet away).

If a bear charges and is about to make contact, at the last possible second drop to the ground and "play dead." Don't do this until the bear actually touches you or is just about to. Leave your pack on, put your hands over the back of your neck, and make no noise. This may defuse a bear's aggression. Try to wait literally 2 to 3 minutes after you last see or hear the bear before moving. If it sees you move, it may renew its attack.

On rare occasions, a bear (most likely a black bear) may perceive a person as food. If a bear bites repeatedly, and the attack is prolonged, it may be a predatory attack. In this case, the Alaska Department of Fish and Game recommends fighting back vigorously.

Remaining alert and taking precautions are the most important things to do in bear country. Carrying a gun often leads to a false sense of security. However, many Alaskans routinely carry guns. If you choose to do so, learn to handle it responsibly and to shoot accurately. A wounded bear may actually make the situation worse. Carry your gun where you can get to it to use it. The Alaska Department of Fish and Game recommends that a .300 Magnum rifle or a shotgun with rifled slugs is the most effective weapon if you know how to use it and can shoot accurately with it. Handguns may be inadequate.

If you prefer not to carry a gun or are unable to shoot, carry something else to discourage an inquisitive bear. Many Alaskans carry defensive aerosol sprays that contain capsicum (red pepper extract) and are available at sporting goods stores. These sprays may be effective at a range of 15 to 20 feet if there is no wind or the wind is from your back. Buy an extra spray can to try out before leaving on your trip, but be sure the wind will not blow the spray back on you. Carry a fully charged can in the field. Carry the spray can in a resealable plastic bag in a vehicle. (Most airplanes prohibit carrying these.) The pepper spray is better than nothing; it is sometimes, but not always, effective. Some people also carry noisemakers (e.g., firecrackers, shriek alarms); the common highway flare used by motorists has also discouraged bears. In tents, campgrounds, cabins, and other restricted or populated situations where use of firearms would be dangerous, plan to use one of these alternatives.

Many experienced Alaskans recommend against taking an unleashed dog into the wilds; the dog may run after a moose or bear and end up being chased back to its master. On the other hand, a well-behaved dog that can be controlled by voice can provide an early warning that a bear is nearby. Small, yappy dogs may irritate a bear. Pet food can attract bears.

For more information, pick up a copy of "Bear Facts: The Essentials for Traveling in Bear Country," a leaflet jointly prepared by the Alaska Department of Fish and Game and eight other resource agencies. It is available at the Alaska Public Lands Information Center in Anchorage (see Appendix) and at wildlife management agencies.

MOUNTAIN BIKING

Not many of these *55 Ways* are well suited to mountain biking. Because mountain biking is popular, we address the issue, especially in the summary tables on pages 42-51. Of the trips in this book, we judge nine to be good for mountain biking. The biking for six of these nine is on the unmaintained access roads to the main trails and not the trails themselves. Six more of the 55 may make good rides, but we do not recommend them wholeheartedly because of strong potential for conflict with hikers. The rest of the trails are simply not good rides for most cyclists, or are closed to cyclists.

Those of us who ride mountain bikes tread a fine line. Cyclists are quiet, like hikers, but fast, and this can lead to safety and aesthetic conflicts with walkers. In the Lower 48, the conflicts are extreme. It is incumbent upon those of us who value riding in the woods and mountains to ride responsibly and build goodwill to prevent that kind of conflict here. To this end, mountain bikers should do the following:

- Avoid riding trails that are closed or not recommended by the land manager for bikes.
- Avoid wet trails, and try not to spin or skid.
- Never ride off a trail.
- Walk bikes over water bars to avoid destroying them and to indicate your respect for the work that goes into keeping water off the trail.
- Yield to walkers as they pass head on. Mount a pleasant bike bell on your bars, and use it as you overtake walkers and as you approach corners to let people and wildlife know you are coming.
- Keep trail speeds down.

When you take a trip by bike, for your own safety, carry tools and know how to use them. Regroup often with companions in case there is a breakdown or a spill in the back. Wear a helmet. Be careful not to overextend your trip and get so far off the road system that you would be overcome by darkness or exhaustion if you should have to walk back. Before going on overnight rides, load your bike and test its handling on a trail near home.

CANOEING

Two of the trips in this book describe canoeing through a chain of lakes. Both present you with the option of combining the lakes with a river section. Lakes present few obvious dangers, but their safe appearance can lead to complacency. Even on small, apparently calm lakes, wind can kick up white caps in a hurry. The rivers described here are not difficult but should not be attempted without experience and training.

Alaska waters are very cold, and that includes the lakes and rivers described in this book for canoeing. A plunge into such cold water can lead to hypothermia. Know how to treat it and how to give cardiopulmonary resuscitation (CPR).

There are a few basic guidelines that should always be followed. Know how to swim. Always wear a life jacket. Never stand up in a canoe. Keep your weight low and hold on to the gunwales as you move. Move one person at a time. Leave the dog at home. On lakes, paddle close to shore. If a strong wind comes up, get off the lake.

Be sure your boat will float even when full of water, and lash all gear securely. If you capsize, stay with the boat and work it to shore to ensure that your survival equipment is not lost. Have plenty of dry warm clothes handy in a waterproof bag.

The lake trips in this book involve some portaging. Lashing a stout stick or two-by-four across the top of a large backpack as a canoe rest can make portaging easier. Portaging areas can be high-impact areas, with eroded trails and evidence of canoers' bathroom breaks. Be especially careful in these areas to take litter with you and bury feces more than 200 feet from water.

STREAM CROSSINGS

A few hikes described in this book include potentially hazardous stream crossings. When confronted with such a crossing, take the following precautions:

1. Cross at the widest part of the stream where the water will be the shallowest and least swift.
2. Wear boots to ensure good footing; fast streams regularly roll large rocks down their beds. If you remove your socks and keep them dry until reaching the other side, walking in wet boots will not be too uncomfortable. Some people carry old running shoes for crossings, but the foot protection is not as good. A thin pair of wet-suit socks inside boots will make the icy cold water feel less painful.
3. Undo the waist strap of your pack for ease in getting it off, should you fall. Put your camera inside the pack in a waterproof sack. Having the strap around your shoulders may make it impossible to remove your pack quickly.
4. Consider using a rope belay from shore for each person when crossing very swift water.
5. Use aids to enhance stability. If you are by yourself, use a stick or ice ax. With companions, link arms for stability in groups of two to four, and walk in a line parallel with the current so that only one person feels the full force of the river. This technique works best if the group members all grab hold of a stick held horizontally in front of them at waist level. When crossing with others, make sure only one person moves at a time.
6. Avoid high-water periods. If a trip will take you across glacial streams, plan the trip in early summer, or cross in early morning when water levels are likely to be lower. Adding rocks to your pack for weight, especially if you are small, will provide you with more secure footing.
7. Expect to be wet and cold, and take the crossing slowly. You are more likely to lose your balance by hurrying, especially in murky glacial waters where the bottom is invisible.

You will be able to cross large braided streams more easily if you take advantage of the stream's natural flow pattern. Scout the river and find an area with many channels. Cross from the upstream end of one gravel island to the upstream end of the next, where the water is shallower and slower due to gravel deposition. The downstream end of a gravel island where channels converge may hide a deep turbulent hole or soft sand. Try to avoid crossing toward a vertically cut bank; the water is deepest and swiftest along such banks.

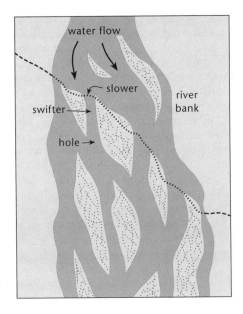

Crossing an icy river in thigh-deep water quickly saps body heat on the best of days. If it is rainy or windy, or if you are fatigued, the crossing could bring on hypothermia (see the next section). Before crossing any stream where there is danger of falling, mentally plan to avoid hypothermia. Are warm, dry clothes and sleeping bags packed in truly waterproof bags? Is there a place on each bank to set up a hasty camp should sleeping bags and hot drinks be needed? A little forethought can go a long way in making a trip safe.

HYPOTHERMIA

Cold weather is never far away in Alaska, even in midsummer. Excessive loss of body core heat can result in hypothermia—often called "exposure"—in which the metabolic and physiological processes of the body are slowed. Death can result if body heat continues to be lost. Prevention is necessary, because you may not be able to treat a victim of severe hypothermia successfully in the field. Hikers, bikers, boaters, and skiers should always travel with extra warm clothing and high-calorie snack foods. They should monitor their bodies for exhaustion and dehydration (factors contributing to exposure) as well as temperature, and they should keep an eye on the weather. Never overextend a trip to the point that all the body's fuel stores are used up.

Cool weather, rain or perspiration, wind, lack of food, fatigue, or poor conditioning can impose a stress on the cardiovascular system. Whenever the rate of cooling exceeds the body's energy supply and ability to produce heat, hypothermia begins. Falling into cold water or wearing a sweaty shirt in windy conditions at 50°F can easily bring on hypothermia.

Watch for the symptoms of hypothermia: uncontrollable, continued fits of shivering; vague, slow, slurred speech; memory lapses; incoherence; fumbling hands; frequent stumbling; drowsiness; and apparent exhaustion.

The victim often refuses to admit anything is wrong, so companions must insist that treatment begin immediately. To avoid further heat loss, help the victim change into dry clothing and warm layers. Find shelter from the wind. Body heat can be restored in mild cases by exercising, drinking warm liquids, and eating high-calorie foods.

When the body temperature drops below 90°F, symptoms of severe hypothermia appear. This is a medical emergency overcome only by rewarming the body core with external sources of heat, because the victim is no longer able to generate his or her own heat. Shivering stops; the victim becomes unable to walk alone and shows poor judgment, leaving a parka unzipped or forgetting hat and mittens. Eventually, the victim may lose consciousness.

Field treatment of severe hypothermia must be attempted if help is far away. Place the victim in a sleeping bag that has been prewarmed by somebody else. Place bottles of warm water along the victim's body core in the warm bag. The addition of one or preferably two other warm bodies in the bag is even better. Depending on the sexes of those involved, this may be awkward, but other bodies are the most readily available source of heat, and skin-to-skin contact speeds transfer of heat. Just placing a victim in a sleeping bag will not warm the body core, because the victim's body is unable even to warm the bag.

The extremities of a severely hypothermic person must not be rewarmed before the internal organs are warmed. If circulation of blood in the extremities is stimulated through massage or application of heat, that blood (which is still colder than blood in the body core) can cause ventricular fibrillation, an abnormal heart rhythm that can lead quickly to death. Moving or jarring a severely hypothermic person can also trigger ventricular fibrillation, so treat the victim carefully, but don't let these cautions lead to inaction. Get medical help even if recovery seems complete; in severe cases, pneumonia or heart problems can occur later.

Before making a trip to a remote area, read about hypothermia in *Medicine for Mountaineering and Other Wilderness Activities,* fifth edition, James A. Wilkerson, M.D., editor (Seattle: The Mountaineers Books, 2001). The book notes that a victim of severe hypothermia may not have a detectable heartbeat yet may still be alive. Always rewarm a hypothermia victim before assuming death has occurred.

FROSTBITE

At temperatures below freezing, particularly on windy days, be alert for frostbite, or freezing of body tissues. Fingers, toes, the face, and ears are normally the first to show the characteristic white patches that indicate frostbite is beginning. Windchill speeds freezing, as does direct contact with metal. Be careful filling camp stoves, because the very cold and highly volatile gas can freeze flesh instantly. When dexterity is important—for handling cameras, ski bindings, tent poles, and the like—wear thin gloves.

Backcountry partners should make a habit of checking each other's faces and ears. Monitor changing sensation in your own hands and feet. If feeling disappears, especially after a period of pain from the cold, immediately check for frostbite. A severely frostbitten extremity may freeze hard to the touch like meat in a freezer, but permanent damage results from more subtle frostbite as well.

Treatment is complicated. To avoid permanent damage to tissues or joints, learn prevention and first aid for frostbite before making trips at low temperatures. Find further information in wilderness medicine books such as Wilkerson's, mentioned above under "Hypothermia."

Frost nip, the first stage of frostbite in which the surface of the skin shows white waxy patches but the underlying tissue still feels normally soft, should be treated immediately. Hold a warm hand over a frost-nipped nose, ear, or cheek to return the flesh to a healthy pink. For fingers and toes, remove tight mittens or boots. Warm nipped fingers in your armpits, between your legs, or on your stomach. Nipped toes may be warmed on a brave companion's stomach. Never rub frost-nipped or frostbitten tissues.

A person with frostbite may also be hypothermic (see the previous section); treat hypothermia first. Do not rewarm a severely frostbitten appendage in the field if there is a chance of it refreezing or if you must walk on it. If evacuation to a hospital is not possible, frozen fingers or toes may be thawed in water at 104°F to 110°F until color, pain, and pliability return. Maintain any blisters intact, if possible, and seek medical help as soon as possible.

AVALANCHES

Hans van der Laan, to whom this book is dedicated, completed the maps for the first edition of 55 Ways but died in an avalanche near Eklutna Glacier (Trip 39) before it was published. If you travel through snow-covered mountains, even if only by automobile, know about avalanches. Snow slides kill people every year in southcentral Alaska, but such accidents are avoidable with proper knowledge.

Avoiding Avalanches

Take an avalanche awareness course through the Alaska Avalanche School (see Appendix). Current training emphasizes not only the mechanics of snow but also the judgment of outdoor enthusiasts. Skiers not only must be constantly alert for clues to avalanche potential but must pay equal attention to their thought processes to ensure that route decisions are based solely on these clues and not on a desire to ski an untracked slope or reach a summit, not on "gut feelings," and not on the impulsive actions of others. Travelers can take their clues from three things: the snowpack, the terrain, and the weather.

A classic avalanche starting zone, track, and run-out zone readily visible in forested terrain. Avalanche tracks may be invisible above tree line. (John Wolfe Jr.)

Snowpack. The snowpack is an accumulation of layers of snow from different storms, layers of ice from thaws, and layers of crystals formed within the layers of snow and ice. The snowpack adapts to changes slowly. When weight is added rapidly and becomes too much for a weakness in the snowpack, snow slides. Humans get in trouble when their own weight is the proverbial straw that breaks the camel's back. You may detect instability by observing natural slides on similar slopes, hearing ominous "whumping" noises as weak layers collapse, hearing hollow sounds, or seeing cracks shoot through the snow from your skis. Continually test the snow by pushing a ski pole in deep and feeling for different densities.

Terrain. Avalanches happen on terrain with slopes of 25 to 65 degrees. The lower angles are those on which intermediate skiers love to carve their turns, and even novice skiers will traverse them. Prime avalanche angles are 35 to 45 degrees. Slope orientation, or *aspect,* is critically important: if natural avalanches are apparent on slopes facing a certain direction—say, north—or if wind is obviously depositing snow on these hypothetical north-facing slopes, beware of the north-facing slope you want to ascend. Also, a skier on flat terrain can trigger a snow failure that brings down snow from a slope above. People often overlook steep spots in otherwise gentle terrain, but more than 50 percent of avalanche accidents are on slopes less than 300 feet high. Human-triggered avalanches have caught more than ninety people on a short foothill to Flattop Mountain, where the Flattop summer trail takes off from the Blueberry Knoll loop (Trip 28). A boy in Homer was killed when he triggered the collapse of a slope only 65 feet high.

Weather. When wind moves snow, it adds weight on the lee slope where the snow is deposited and can create instability in minutes. New snow and rain also quickly add weight to the snowpack. Warming trends can weaken a snowpack. Even long periods of very cold weather can create unstable conditions by altering the crystal structure in the snowpack, or they can allow existing instabilities to persist.

Plan for Being Caught

A group plan is the key to survival if something goes wrong. Equipment and training are the first part of any plan. Each member of a party venturing out in winter must wear an avalanche-victim locator beacon and be trained in its use. These battery-operated radio transceivers emit a signal picked up by other transceivers. Each person also must carry a shovel and avalanche probe, which are readily available at outdoor shops. Because each person may be the savior of the others, each should care deeply about the equipment others are carrying.

Spread out so that your party is not caught together. If you get caught, yell to attract your companions' attention. Try to stay on top of the snow. As the snow slows, make an extra effort to reach the surface, and thrust an arm upward. Rescuers will find you much faster if even a finger shows above the snow. If you cannot dig yourself free, try to relax to conserve oxygen.

Plan for a Search

If an avalanche buries your companion, you are his or her only hope. First, watch your companion in the slide, noting his path and the spot where he was last seen. Then spend your energy searching. Going for help is asking for a body search. The first 15 minutes are critical. Chances of survival after 30 minutes are less than 50 percent. Few avalanche victims are found alive after 2 hours. Most survivors are rescued by people who were on site when the avalanche occurred. All available hands should assist in the search.

Initial and Beacon Search. Immediately turn all avalanche transceivers to "receive" to avoid false signals. Mark the area the victim was last seen. Make a quick but thorough visual search, listening to your transceiver as you go but initially paying most attention to what you see. Leave any discarded equipment or clothing where it was found to help mark the path. Check anything found to see if it is attached to the victim, and follow the strength of the beacon signal. If the visual search turns up nothing, use the beacon for a systematic search, carefully but quickly narrowing the possibilities to the area of strongest signal (get training for this). Digging is exhausting. Ensure that shovel efforts count by assessing all clues first.

Probe Search. Should you be without beacons, or if no signal is audible, the last resort is systematic probing. Use whatever you have to probe the snow (ski poles, skis, branches), but know that probing hard snow is not easy even with probes designed for the purpose. Organize your party (again, get training). Check particularly areas where the snow has accumulated—above trees or rocks, at the foot of the slide, on benches or areas where the slope decreases, and on the outsides of turns.

Don't endanger your own life by making yourself susceptible to hypothermia, exhaustion, or additional avalanche hazard, but search as long as humanly possible. A rare few have been found alive after being buried well over 4 hours. If you find your companion, administer CPR if necessary, and treat for hypothermia.

More thorough explanations are available in avalanche books and through workshops. One such book is *Snow Sense: A Guide to Evaluating Avalanche Hazard*, by Jill Fredston and Doug Fesler (Anchorage: Alaska Mountain Safety Center, 1999), a book written in Alaska that is used internationally.

Don't let the fear of avalanches deter you. Winter is a time when rivers and swamps cease to be barriers and become highways to exciting new country inaccessible in summer. Just be aware, and ensure a safe trip.

A NOTE ABOUT SAFETY

Safety is an important concern in all outdoor activities. No guide-book can alert you to every hazard or anticipate the limitations of every reader. Therefore, the descriptions of roads, trails, routes, and natural features in this book are not representations that a particular place or excursion will be safe for your party. When you follow any of the routes described in this book, you assume responsibility for your own safety. Under normal conditions, such excursions require the usual attention to traffic, road and trail conditions, weather, terrain, the capabilities of your party, and other factors. Keeping informed on current conditions and exercising common sense are the keys to a safe, enjoyable outing.

—*The Mountaineers Books*

ABOUT THIS BOOK

This section explains how we compiled trip information, and it presents two Trip Summary Tables as an aid to choosing the right trip for your available time, the season, and your goals (pages are denoted with darkened edges for reference). We hope you enjoy using this book as much as we have enjoyed preparing it. Exploring this magnificent land and compiling the information for you has brought to us a deep appreciation for all that Alaska represents. We ask that you treat the land with respect and help others to see the value of respecting it too. Alaska has an unequalled wilderness heritage. Consider supporting the efforts of park, recreation, and conservation groups dedicated to maintaining these lands (see Appendix). Such groups exist in nearly every Alaska community, and they are perpetually in need of volunteers.

ORGANIZATION

The trips are listed in geographic order, starting with a "Kenai Peninsula" section and progressing north and east with the highway system. The "Portage to Potter" section covers trips along Turnagain Arm southeast of Anchorage including the southern part of Chugach State Park. The "Anchorage Bowl" section guides readers to the western part of Chugach State Park visible from downtown Anchorage. The "North of Anchorage" section covers the northern part of Chugach State Park and extends from Eagle River to Denali State Park, just south of Denali (Mount McKinley). The last section, "Chickaloon–Nabesna–Valdez," explores the vast area accessible via the eastern end of the Glenn Highway and southern end of the Richardson Highway.

Trip Headings

For each trip, before the description, route statistics appear, including distance, hiking time, high point, elevation gain, season, map information, and managing agency.

Distances are given to the nearest 0.1 mile when we have that kind of accuracy. Fractions (e.g., ½) indicate less precise estimates that are accurate to within about a quarter of a mile. The hiking times often indicate a range. This reflects the range for non-athlete adults for steady yet leisurely foot travel. Times assume stops to enjoy the view, have a snack, and take a few pictures. Couch potatoes, children, or competitive runners may have times outside the times shown.

The high point indicates the highest elevation reached, even if it is not the end point. The "total elevation gain" shown is cumulative, accounting for multiple ascents and descents where applicable, and, together with trip length, indicates difficulty. Depending on the map you use, elevations given may not exactly match your map. See "Maps," below, for further explanation.

Picking the time of year when each trip is "best" or snow-free enough for use is difficult. The disappearance of the snowpack varies from year to year, but we've chosen representative dates. After a winter of heavy snowfall, expect trails to open later than indicated. May is a tricky month: at low elevations, summer has arrived, but above 3,000 feet winter weather dominates. If heading into the mountains, take winter equipment. An easy climb in summer may call for a rope under winter conditions. Hiking is usually good through September everywhere in southcentral Alaska; below 3,000 feet, trails may be snow-free well into October. Trips near sea level often offer hiking throughout the winter.

Driving Directions

Often, getting to the trailhead is an interesting excursion in itself. Outside of Anchorage, Alaska's highway system is mostly two-lane roads, most of which are paved and all of which pass through wonderful scenery. A few of the access roads are not maintained or marked. Each trip description gives specific information where "driving directions" are highlighted.

Highways and primary side roads have mileposts every mile (more or less). These are often used for reference. We used car odometers to measure from mileposts and on side roads. Because odometer readings vary with the car, the tire size, and reference points, our distances may vary slightly from yours, but you will be close to the trailhead and should find it with ease.

Alaska's highways are known by their names, not numbers. It may be helpful to understand the milepost system for each. Glenn Highway (Alaska Route 1) and Parks Highway (Route 3) mileposts begin in Anchorage. Richardson Highway (Route 4) mileposts begin in Valdez. Seward Highway (Routes 1 and 9) and Sterling Highway (Route 1) mileposts start in Seward. Edgerton Highway (Route 10) mileposts begin at the Richardson Highway. Straightening highways has created inconsistencies in the milepost system, with some pairs of posts closer than 1 mile and others well over a mile apart. Our figures are generally derived from the nearest standing milepost.

When a road does not receive public maintenance, its condition varies greatly from year to year, with no guarantee it will be drivable. We note which roads might present problems. If you have doubts about whether your car can make it, don't try. Getting a tow truck may take hours and be very expensive. Furthermore, driving on a soft, muddy road tears it up, which is unfair to residents who may maintain it themselves.

Maps

The maps in this book are made as overlays of published topographic maps, usually U.S. Geological Survey (USGS) maps. Although it was often

Ground squirrel investigates topographic map (Trip 47) (John Wolfe Jr.)

necessary to change the scale of the maps to make them fit in the book, relationships between features are to the scale indicated on each map. These are not just "sketch maps," but this does not mean they show enough detail for travel. These maps are to be used with topographic maps. There are several different publishers of maps that may be useful:

- U.S. Geological Survey (USGS)
- Imus Geographics: "Chugach State Park"

- National Geographic Trails Illustrated: a series that covers Kachemak Bay State Park, the Kenai Peninsula, the Wrangell Mountains, and Prince William Sound
- Todd Communications Road and Recreation Maps: a series that covers the Kenai Peninsula, Anchorage, and Palmer-Wasilla areas

Each trip heading lists the map we recommend. Typically, we recommend the map with the best scale and coverage for the trip. If the single Chugach State Park map, for example, covers a well-marked trail that requires three USGS maps, we recommend the park map. If the trip has no trail and requires careful map reading, we may recommend multiple USGS maps at a better scale. Be aware that there are likely other maps available than the ones we recommend and that USGS publishes maps for every trip, as shown in Trip Summary Table II on pages 48–51.

USGS publishes southcentral Alaska maps at 1:63,360 scale (1 inch equals 1 mile), with titles like "Anchorage A7" and "Seward D8." USGS also publishes maps with greater detail. These 1:25,000-scale maps divide the 1:63,360 maps into four sections (labeled northwest, northeast, southwest, and southeast) and blow them up. The 1:25,000 maps show the most up-to-date road systems, and the better scale offers greater detail. But these maps can be cumbersome: the sheet sizes are larger, it often takes more sheets to cover one trip, they are in metric, and they are only available for the most settled areas. Note that if this book indicates "Anchorage A7 NW," you can purchase "Anchorage A7" at 1:63,360 or the "Anchorage A7 NW" map at 1:25,000.

Elevations for the same point on different maps may not match exactly. This is, in part, because advances in technology have allowed the USGS to refine its elevations on newer maps. The newer maps are the ones published in meters. The Imus "Chugach State Park" map converts these to English (standard, non-metric) units. We list elevations in feet as found on the older USGS 1:63,360 maps. An exception is in our Chugach State Park description, where our elevation numbers are taken from the Imus map.

Whichever publisher you choose, never travel off the beaten path without a good map. Note that true north differs substantially in Alaska from magnetic north, to which a compass needle points. Learn how to correct for the difference. Contact information for the USGS and outdoor shops that carry maps is listed in the appendix. Symbols used on maps in this book are defined in the legend following the Contents.

TRIP SUMMARY TABLES

The following pages provide trip information at a glance that would otherwise take much page flipping to extract from the text. The tables are designed to help you select trips to fit your constraints and desires at any given time. They also suggest portions of longer trips that make good short outings and other ways of looking at trips that may not be in the main text.

Trip Summary Table I: Length of Trip, Time of Year, and Suitability for Children

Trip	Time of Year[1]				
	April	May	June	July	Winter
KENAI PENINSULA					
1. Grewingk Glacier		glacier (late May) and lake	Alpine Ridge		
2. Homer Beach Walk	Homer end	Diamond Gulch			✔
3. Swan Lake and Swanson River		late May			✔
4. Skilak Wildlife Recreation Area		✔			✔
5. Fuller Lake and Skyline Traverse			✔		
6. Russian Lakes–Resurrection River Trail System		Russian River end	Cooper Lake end		Cooper Lake end
7. Crescent Lake			✔		Carter
8. Caines Head		✔			
9. Mount Marathon, Race Point		✔			
10. Exit Glacier and Harding Ice Field			✔		access road
11. Lost Lake Traverse			late June		✔
12. Ptarmigan Lake		✔			
13. Johnson Pass			✔		either end
14. Resurrection Pass Trail System		low-elevation cabins	entire system		Resurrection Pass Trail
15. Palmer Creek Lakes				✔	
16. Hope Point		✔			
17. Gull Rock		✔			✔
18. Turnagain Pass Ski Tour				✔	✔
PORTAGE TO POTTER					
19. Byron Glacier View			✔		
20. Portage Pass				✔	✔
21. Winner Creek Gorge– Girdwood Iditarod Loop		late May			✔
22. Crow Pass and Eagle River Traverse			mid-June		north end
23. Bird Ridge	✔				
24. Indian Valley		✔			traverse

[1]"Time of Year" trips are noted by the month in which the route usually becomes snow-free enough for hiking, and whether the route is generally good for skiing, snowshoeing, or winter hiking.

[2]"Length of Trip" is noted by destination. Trips marked with an asterisk * are more difficult or longer. Day trips with a "tent"^ make good overnight trips. The "Number

| Length of Trip[2] | | Number of nights | Trips for Children[3] |
Short day	Full day		
lake from trailhead^	lake from Homer; glacier/alpine from trailhead^	1–3 nights	Glacier Lake day or overnight
either end	traverse		any portion
1–2 lakes^	2–3 lakes^	either lake system (1+ night)	day or overnight
1 trail	2+ trails	(use nearby campgrounds)	any one trail
lower lake	upper lake^, traverse*	lakes (1 night)	lakes (overnight)
Lower Russian Lake^	lower lake and falls^	upper lake or Cooper traverse (1–2); Resurrection River traverse (2–3);	lower lake (cabin)
Carter Lake^; Crescent: first bridge	Crescent Lake^	either end (1 night); traverse (2 nights)	overnight (cabin)
Tonsina Creek^		North Beach (1); South Beach (2)	overnight (cabin)
runners' trail	hikers' trail		hikers' trail
toe of glacier	Harding Ice Field		lower trail
	to tree line^	to lake and back (1 night); traverse (1–2 nights)	overnight (cabin)
west end of lake	east end of lake*^	east end of lake (1)	overnight
Bench Creek		traverse (1–2 nights)	either end
Juneau Falls	Caribou or Trout Cabins*^; entire trail by bike*^	Summit Creek/Devils Pass Trail (1); entire Resurrection Pass Trail (2–5 nights)	cabins*
any trail or route	2+ trails^		lakes
first mile+	summit		first mile
	Gull Rock	overnight not recommended	partial
lower trails^	upper trails		lower trails*
glacier			snowfield
pass	lake (summer); winter traverse*		pass
gorge; up Winner Creek until brush gets thick	Girdwood Iditarod Loop; Upper Winner Cr. bushwhacking		all or part of loop
pass	Raven Glacier^	traverse (2 nights)	pass (overnight; cabin)
lower	higher		any portion*
	Indian Pass; winter traverse*^	winter traverse (1 night);	

of nights" column indicates destinations that most hikers are likely to enjoy most as overnights rather than day hikes.

[3]The "Trips for Children" column is for children 5 to 10 years old. Trips marked * are more suitable for experienced children; other trails should be suitable for most children. The shortest, easiest trails are suitable for children as young as 3. See also "Hiking with Children" in the Introduction.

Trip	Time of Year[1]				
	April	May	June	July	Winter
25. Falls Creek			✔		
26. McHugh and Rabbit Lakes	Table Rock	Overlook and McHugh Peak	lakes		
27. Turnagain Arm Trail	✔				✔
ANCHORAGE BOWL					
28. Flattop			✔		hike
29. The Ramp			✔		to pass
30. Williwaw Lakes			✔		✔
31. Wolverine Peak			✔		hillside loop trails
32. Near Point and Tikishla Peak		Near Point	Tikishla Peak		hillside loop trails
33. Rendezvous Peak		✔			pass
NORTH OF ANCHORAGE					
34. South Fork of Eagle River			✔		✔
35. The Perch		✔			✔
36. Round Top and Black Tail Rocks			✔		✔
37. Thunder Bird Falls	late				✔
38. East Twin Pass			to brushline	pass	
39. Bold Peak Valley		Lakeside Trail	Bold Peak valley (late)		Lakeside Trail
40. Pioneer Ridge			✔		
41. Bodenburg Butte	late				
42. Lazy Mountain and Matanuska Peak Trail		Lazy Mtn.		Matanuska Peak	Lazy Mtn.
43. Reed Lakes				✔	lower portions
44. Craigie Creek				✔	✔
45. Nancy Lake Canoe Trails		late May			✔
46. Peters Hills				✔	
47. Kesugi Ridge (Curry Ridge)			late June		

[1]"Time of Year" trips are noted by the month in which the route usually becomes snow-free enough for hiking, and whether the route is generally good for skiing, snowshoeing, or winter hiking.

[2]"Length of Trip" is noted by destination. Trips marked with an asterisk * are more difficult or longer. Day trips with a "tent"^ make good overnight trips. The "Number

Short day	Length of Trip[2] Full day	Number of nights	Trips for Children[3]
	Falls Lake; Ridge/South Suicide Peak*		
Table Rock; overlook	McHugh Lake^; McHugh Peak	Rabbit Lake (1 night)	Table Rock or overlook
any segment one way	longer segments round trip; whole trail one way		any portion
Flattop	Peaks 2, 3; Flaketop*		summit*
Powerline Pass by bike	Ramp, pass, or Wedge^	traverse to Indian (1+ night)	valley below pass (overnight)
	first lake via Glen Alps^	upper lakes (1); loop (2)	lakes overnight; trailhead loops
brushline	summit		
	Near Point, Tikishla Peak*^	Tikishla (1 night)	
summit	traverse to #34		summit
bridge	Symphony^ or Eagle Lakes; Eagle River Overlook^; Hanging Valley Lake^	North Fork Ship Creek (1–2 nights)	Symphony Lake (overnight)
Echo Bend; trailhead loops	The Perch^	traverse to #22 (1–2 nights)	portion; Perch (overnight, cabin)
brushline	summits		Baldy*
falls			falls
to brushline; Idlu Bena Trail	pass or peaks		
Yuditnu Creek	Bold Valley^; Serenity Falls (bike)^	Eklutna Glacier (1+ night); East Fork Eklutna River (1+)	Lakeside Trail, on foot or bike (cabin)
first picnic table	ridge or summit*		
summit		overnight not recommended	summit
	Lazy Mtn.; Matanuska Peak Trail^; or summit*		Lazy Mtn.*
lowest pools; Snowbird Mine	falls and upper lake^; Snowbird Glacier		lower lake (overnight)
Dogsled Pass	Purches Creek*^	Peters Creek* (2)	Dogsled Pass
1–2 lakes	Lynx Lake Loop^	Lynx Lake Loop (1+ night)	day or overnight (cabins)
	point 3600	(1–2 nights)	partial*
Byers Lake Loop	Little Coal, Ermine, or Cascade Trail to ridge crest	traverse (2–4 nights)	Byers Lake Loop; Little Coal; Ermine

of nights" column indicates destinations that most hikers are likely to enjoy most as overnights rather than day hikes.

[3]The "Trips for Children" column is for children 5 to 10 years old. Trips marked * are more suitable for experienced children; other trails should be suitable for most children. The shortest, easiest trails are suitable for children as young as 3. See also "Hiking with Children" in the Introduction.

Trip	Time of Year[1]				
	April	May	June	July	Winter
CHICKALOON-NABESNA-VALDEZ					
48. Hicks Creek–Chitna Pass			✔		
49. Syncline Mountain			✔		
50. Mentasta Mountains			✔		
51. Dixie Pass			✔		
52. Kennecott Mines			✔		
53. Worthington Glacier Overlook			late June		
54. Historic Valdez Trail		mid-May			
55. Shoup Bay			✔		

[1]"Time of Year" trips are noted by the month in which the route usually becomes snow-free enough for hiking, and whether the route is generally good for skiing, snowshoeing, or winter hiking.

[2]"Length of Trip" is noted by destination. Trips marked with an asterisk * are more difficult or longer. Day trips with a "tent"^ make good overnight trips. The "Number of nights" column indicates destinations that most hikers are likely to enjoy most as overnights rather than day hikes.

| | Length of Trip[2] | | | Trips for Children[3] |
Short day	Full day	Number of nights		
		traverse (4–5); Boulder Creek from Purinton trailhead (1)		
	Belanger Pass round trip	circuit or traverse (2–4)		
		loop (2 nights)		
	Nugget Creek or Kotsina mtn. bike*^	Dixie Pass (2–4) Nugget or Kotsina hike		
McCarthy and Kennecott	Mines from Kennecott			Kennecott; Erie Mine
knob overlook				first half mile
any segment	whole trail			any segment
beach	Gold Creek	Shoup Bay (1+ nights)		beach; Gold Creek

[3]The "Trips for Children" column is for children 5 to 10 years old. Trips marked * are more suitable for experienced children; other trails should be suitable for most children. The shortest, easiest trails are suitable for children as young as 3. See also "Hiking with Children" in the Introduction.

Trip Summary Table II: Maps, Peaks, Mountain Biking, and Public Transportation

Trip	USGS Maps[1]	Peaks[2]	Mountain Bike[3]	Public Transportation[4]
KENAI PENINSULA				
1. Grewingk Glacier	Seldovia C3, C4 NE, SE	Alpine Ridge (point 4050)	closed	bus, air, or ferry to Homer + water taxi
2. Homer Beach	Seldovia C5 NE, NW		↔	bus, ferry, air + 1–2 miles
3. Swan Lake and Swanson River Canoe Routes	Kenai C2 NW, NE, SE, SW; C3 NE, NW, SE; D1 SW; D2 SE, SW; D3 SW		closed	bus + shuttle by canoe rental service
4. Skilak Wildlife Recreation Area	Kenai B1 NE, NW		closed	bus + 0.7 mile–5.4 miles
5. Fuller Lakes and Skyline Traverse	Kenai B1 NE, C1 SE	Mystery Hills 3,520'	closed	bus
6. Russian Lakes–Resurrection River Trail System	Sew A7 NW, A8, B8; Kenai B1 NE		lower lake↑; upper lake ↔; Resurrection River↓	bus + 1 mile (Russian Lake end)
7. Crescent Lake	Sew B7, B8, C7, C8		Crescent Creek↔; otherwise closed	Carter: bus; Crescent: bus + 3.3 miles
8. Caines Head	Sew A7 SE, SW; Blying Sound D7	Callisto Peak* 3,657'	closed	bus + 2.3 miles; rail + 3.8 miles; air + 4.3 miles
9. Mount Marathon, Race Point	Sew A7 SW	Race Point 3,022'; Mount Marathon * 4,063'	↓*	bus; air + 2 miles; rail + 1.5 miles
10. Exit Glacier and Harding Ice Field	Sew A7 NW, A8		closed	
11. Lost Lake Traverse	Sew A7 NE, B7 SE	Mount Ascension* 5,710'	↔	bus + 0.7 mile (south end) or 1 mile (north end)
12. Ptarmigan Lake	Sew B6, B7 NE		Falls Creek ↓; Ptarmigan Creek ↓*	bus
13. Johnson Pass	Sew C6, C7		↔	bus
14. Resurrection Pass Trail System	Sew B8, C7, C8, D8		↔	Seward/Sterling Hwy trailheads: bus; Bean Creek: bus + 0.9 mile

Trail	Peaks	Mountain Bike access road↑; lakes↓*	Public Transportation	USGS map
15. Palmer Creek Lakes	point 4851			Sew D7
16. Hope Point	Hope Point 3,708'	closed		Sew D8 NE
17. Gull Rock		↔		Sew D8
18. Turnagain Pass Ski Tour	Tincan Ridge* (point 3900)	closed	bus	Sew D6
PORTAGE TO POTTER				
19. Byron Glacier View	Byron Peak* 4,700'	→		Sew D5 SW
20. Portage Pass		→	rail or ferry to Whittier + 1.5 miles	Sew D5 SW
21. Winner Creek Gorge–Girdwood Iditarod Loop		unpaved trails ↓*	bus + 2.5–4 miles	Sew D6 NW, NE
22. Crow Pass and Eagle River Traverse		closed	bus + 7.5 miles	Anc A6, A7
23. Bird Ridge	Bird Ridge (point 3505)	closed	bus	Sew D7 NW; Anc A7
24. Indian Valley		powerline↓; Indian tr. closed	bus + 1 mile	Sew D7 NW; Anc A7
25. Falls Creek	South Suicide Peak* 5,005'	closed	bus	Anc A7; Sew D7 NW
26. McHugh and Rabbit Lakes	Ptarmigan Peak* 4,880'; McHugh Peak 4,311'; Suicide Peaks* 5,065' and 5,005'	closed	bus	Anc A7, A8 SE
27. Turnagain Arm Trail	Rainbow Peak 3,543'	closed	bus	Anc A8 SE; Sew D7 NW, D8

[1]USGS map abbreviations: Anc=Anchorage; Sew=Seward. Other maps may be best for any given trip; see text. See also "Maps" in "About this Book."

[2]The "Peaks" column lists peaks accessible via a trip. Most are mentioned in main text. An asterisk (*) here means the peak is difficult and may require special training and equipment.

[3]The "Mountain Bike" column lists trails open or closed to mountain bikes. An ↑ arrow indicates the route has good terrain for average mountain bikers. A ↓ arrow indicates the trail is open but steep or rocky such that only advanced cyclists are likely to enjoy it. Those indicated ↓* are not good/require carrying the bike. A ↔ symbol indicates a trail that may have reasonable cycling terrain but cannot be recommended because of high potential for biker-hiker conflict.

[4]See Public Transportation in the Appendix. An entry followed by "+ x mile(s)" indicates additional walking to the trailhead.

49

Trip	USCS Maps[1]	Peaks[2]	Mountain Bike[3]	Public Transportation[4]
ANCHORAGE BOWL				
28. Flattop	Anc A8 SE	Flattop Mountain 3,510'	closed	city bus + 3.7 miles
29. The Ramp	Anc A7, A8 SE	Ramp 5,240'; Wedge 4,660'	powerline↑; Ramp closed	city bus + 3.7 miles
30. Williwaw Lakes	Anc A7 (A7 NW), A8 NE, SE	NW Williwaw Mount* 5,445'	closed	city bus + 1.6 miles
31. Wolverine Peak	Anc A7 NW, A8 NE	Wolverine Peak 4,491'	old road portion↑; otherwise closed	city bus + 1.6 miles
32. Near Point and Tikishla Peak	Anc A7 NW, A8 NE	Near Point 3,051'; Tikishla Peak* 5,229'; Knoya Peak 4,668'	old road portion↑; otherwise closed	city bus + 1.6 miles
33. Rendezvous Peak	Anc A7 NW, B7 SW	Rendezvous Peak 4,101'; Mount Gordon Lyon 4,134'	closed	
NORTH OF ANCHORAGE				
34. South Fork of Eagle River	Anc A7 NE, NW	Cantata* 6,391'; Calliope* 6,820'; Eagle* 6,909'	closed	
35. The Perch	Anc A6, A7 NE		closed	
36. Round Top and Black Tail Rocks	Anc B7 SW, SE, NW	Round Top 4,786'; Black Tail Rocks 4,446'; Vista Peak 5,000'	closed	Ptarmigan Valley: city bus + 0.6 mile; Meadow Creek: city bus + 2.4 miles
37. Thunder Bird Falls	Anc B7 NE		closed	bus
38. East Twin Pass	Anc B6 NW	East Twin Peak* 5,873'; Pepper Peak 5,450'	closed	
39. Bold Peak Valley	Anc B6	Bold Peak* 7,522'	Lakeside Trail↑; otherwise closed	
40. Pioneer Ridge	Anc B6, C6 SE	Pioneer Peak* 6,398'	↓*	
41. Bodenburg Butte	Anc C6 SE		↓*	
42. Lazy Mountain and Matanuska Peak Trail	Anc C6 NE, SE	Lazy Mountain 3,720'; Matanuska Peak* 6,119'	↓*	bus + 4 miles

50

#	Maps	Peaks	Mountain Bike[3]	Public Transportation[4]
43. Reed Lakes	Anc D6	Lynx Peak* 6,536'	access road↑; trail↓*	
44. Craigie Creek	Anc D7		access road↑; routes↓*	
45. Nancy Lake Canoe Trails	Tyonek C1; Anc C8		closed	bus + 4.7 miles
46. Peters Hills	Talkeetna C2		access road↑	
47. Kesugi Ridge (Curry Ridge)	Talkeetna C1; Talkeetna Mountains C6, D6		closed	bus
CHICKALOON–NABESNA–VALDEZ				
48. Hicks Creek–Chitna Pass	Anc D2, D3, D4	Monarch Peak 7,108'	both ends↓; pass↓*	bus
49. Syncline Mountain	Anc D1, D2	Syncline Mountain 5,471'; Gunsight Mountain 6,441'	Squaw Creek Road (if dry)↑; remainder↓	bus
50. Mentasta Mountains	Nabesna C5	Noyes Mountain 8,147'	access road↑; remainder↓*	
51. Dixie Pass	Valdez C1; McCarthy C8	point 5770	Nugget Creek and Kotsina ATV trails↑	bus + 3.9 miles
52. Kennecott Mines	McCarthy B5, B6, C5, C6		access road↑	air to McCarthy; or bus
53. Worthington Glacier Overlook	Valdez A5		closed	bus + 0.4 mile
54. Historic Valdez Trail	Valdez A5, A6 SE		↓*	bus; or ferry to Valdez and bus
55. Shoup Bay ▸	Valdez A7		closed	ferry or bus to Valdez + 1 mile

[1] USGS map abbreviations: Anc=Anchorage; Sew=Seward. Other maps may be best for any given trip▸see text. See also "Maps" in the Introduction.

[2] The "Peaks" column lists peaks accessible via a trip. Most are mentioned in main text. An asterisk (*) here means the peak is difficult and may require special training and equipment.

[3] The "Mountain Bike" column lists trails open or closed to mountain bikes. An ↑ arrow indicates the route has good terrain for average mountain bikers. A ↓ arrow indicates the trail is open but steep or rocky such that only advanced cyclists are likely to enjoy it. Those indicated ↓* are not good/require carrying the bike. A ↔ symbol indicates a trail that may have reasonable cycling terrain but cannot be recommended because of high potential for biker-hiker conflict.

[4] See Public Transportation in the Appendix. An entry followed by "+ x mile(s)" indicates additional walking to the trailhead.

KENAI PENINSULA

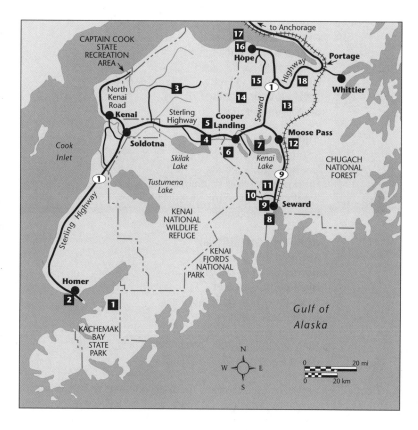

The Kenai Peninsula is a vast area of mountains, ice fields, beaches, and forests that lies between Prince William Sound, the Gulf of Alaska, and Cook Inlet. The peninsula, which includes Chugach National Forest, Kenai Fjords National Park, the Kenai National Wildlife Refuge, and Kachemak Bay State Park, offers some of the best hiking trails in the state. Many of the trails were constructed long ago and are well established and well maintained. The drive along the Seward and Sterling Highways is beautiful, the topography gentler than other areas in southcentral Alaska, the mountains green. Trips near Homer and Seward combine mountains and ocean. Heavier summer rainfall in the Seward area and mountains on the eastern side of the Peninsula give way to a somewhat drier climate and flatter land on the western side of the peninsula. South of Homer lie more mountains across Kachemak Bay.

Opposite: *Gull Rock in Kachemak Bay, July* (Helen Nienhueser)

1 GREWINGK GLACIER

Glacier Lake Trail
Round trip: 6.5 miles
Hiking time: 3–5 hours
High point: 158 feet
Total elevation gain: 158 feet
Best: May–October

Alpine Ridge
Round trip: 5 miles or more
Hiking time: 4.5 hours–2 days
High point: 2,000–4,050 feet
Total elevation gain: 2,000–4,050 feet
Best: June–September

Grewingk Glacier Trail
Round trip: 13 miles
Hiking time: 6–10 hours
High point: 550 feet
Total elevation gain: 550 feet
Best: late May–October

Map: Trails Illustrated "Kachemak Bay State Park"
Agency: Kachemak Bay State Park

Kachemak Bay State Park offers hikes for everyone—from families with infants to experienced backpackers—and even the easiest comes complete with a glacier lake, icebergs, towering peaks, and a spectacular coast. This book covers some of the most accessible trails. One leads to a large, iceberg-dotted lake at the foot of Grewingk Glacier; one to a high ridge overlooking the lake, the ice, and the ocean; and one to Grewingk Glacier itself.

The park, across Kachemak Bay from the city of Homer, requires boat or airplane access. Water taxis and air taxis are available in Homer. Experienced ocean kayakers can cross the bay but only on the calmest days. Water taxis can carry kayaks on other days.

Driving directions. Homer is at the end of the Sterling Highway, 226 miles south of Anchorage. Follow the main highway and signs for Homer Spit, a narrow 4-mile peninsula that juts into the bay. The small boat harbor and water taxis are near the end of the spit. Look for signs advertising State Park or Kachemak Bay water taxis.

The Grewingk Glacier trail system starts from Halibut Cove (the actual

Grewingk Glacier and Grewingk Glacier Lake, July (Gayle Nienhueser)

cove, not the community), 8 miles across the water from Homer Spit. Beach-front trailheads are designated by orange markers.

Glacier Lake Trail

The easy 3.2-mile trail to Grewingk Glacier Lake begins at the Glacier Spit trailhead. Glacier Spit is a 2-mile tongue of gravel north of Halibut Cove. The trail actually begins well south of this long landmark spit and just north of a shorter spit enclosing Rusty's Lagoon. Just behind the beach the trail passes an outhouse. Initially the trail wanders through cottonwood and spruce forest, then emerges on a glacial outwash plain covered with low vegetation. At 1.4 miles a left fork in the trail leads to a tram across Grewingk Creek and to the Grewingk *Glacier* Trail. Stay on the main trail (right fork). At mile 2.7 the main trail intersects the Saddle Trail. Here the trail to the lake turns east, reaching the lake in about ½ mile. This last part of the route is marked with cairns, but these rock piles may be difficult to pick out at first against the background of glacial cobbles. The lake's broad beach invites picnicking, camping, or just sitting and watching the light and the clouds play on the mountains and the big glacier across the lake.

This is a popular day hike from Homer. You can be dropped off at Glacier Spit by water taxi and picked up later at the Saddle trailhead. From the junction of Saddle Trail with Glacier Lake Trail, it is a mile over the 400-foot-high saddle to the Saddle trailhead in Halibut Cove. Total distance between trailheads, with a side trip to the lake, is 4.7 miles. Downed trees may block the trail; check conditions with State Parks.

If camping near the lake, pick a site away from the water to avoid tying up the beach so others do not have access to it as well as for safety. Landslides falling into the water could generate large waves. Drinking water is an issue for camping. The lake is glacial; the silty water is drinkable (with treatment) but not appealing. Let it settle as much as possible and skim off the clearer water for boiling before consumption. (The silt will quickly clog a water filter.) A better bet is to melt icebergs for water. Take an ice ax or other chipping tool to break ice into pot-sized chunks, and be prepared to take a step or two into the icy water to reach a grounded berg. There is a small stream about 200 yards up the Saddle Trail. You cannot see the stream, but you can hear it in a small gully to the right of the trail as you go uphill. Several small footpaths lead from the main trail to the stream.

This area could easily be ruined by insensitive use. Find and use the outhouse provided near the Glacier Spit trailhead and near the lake.

Another camping option is to use the park's established hike-in campsite located on Rusty's Lagoon, less than a mile from the Glacier Spit trailhead. From there, the lake is an easy day hike. Camping is also possible near the Glacier Spit trailhead.

Alpine Ridge

The quickest access to the Alpine Ridge Trail is from the Saddle Trail beachhead. Saddle Trail also provides a steep 3-mile route (round trip) to Grewingk Glacier Lake. Known by local hikers as the stairway to heaven, the climb up Alpine Ridge Trail allows access through the forest and brush to spectacular alpine country. The ridge crest, which parallels Grewingk Glacier for more than 7 miles, consists of rolling tundra knobs interspersed with tiny ponds. It provides views across the mile-wide glacier and the much larger ice field that feeds it.

From the beginning of Saddle Trail on the east side of Halibut Cove, climb steeply about 400 vertical feet to a trail intersection at a saddle in the ridge. The saddle may also be attained from Glacier Lake Trail, as already described. At the saddle, a sign points the way to the Alpine Ridge and Lagoon Trails. Follow this fork a short way to another fork. Go left to reach the ridge. The large Sitka spruce (many killed by spruce bark beetles) and the thick green understory create a different forest than is found along most trails in southcentral Alaska. In May and early June, before the trail crews

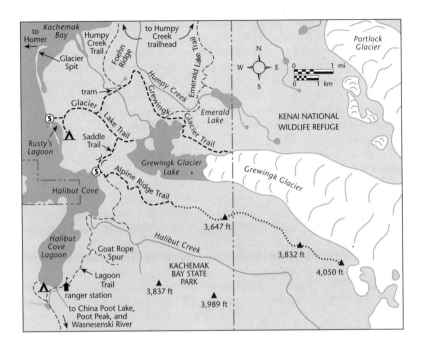

do their work, hikers may find some of these big trees across the trail. By midsummer the lower parts of the Alpine Ridge Trail may be badly overgrown and, after rainy weather, the grass and bushes may be very wet. The trail has few flat spots, and, because the forest is thick, few vistas are available until the trail breaks into meadow and brush about 1¼ miles from the saddle at about 1,400 feet. Conveniently, the trail levels briefly in this area and invites a rest.

Continuing upward, the trail enters the alpine zone, where the ridge again levels off, this time at a series of knobs and pocket-sized valleys. Camping is possible here, although water may be scarce after the last snow patches melt in mid- to late June. Pond water should be purified by boiling, filtering, or treating. Continuing up the ridge toward point 3647, which is 3.5 miles from the saddle, the well-worn path eventually peters out, but the ridge may be walked to at least point 4050. The views increase with elevation.

Grewingk Glacier Trail

To reach Grewingk Glacier itself, follow the directions above for the Glacier Lake Trail. Then, at the intersection described previously, take the Grewingk Glacier Trail (the trail to the tram) northeast out of the woods and across an inviting dryas-covered bench. The trail passes through a forest of young spruce and cottonwood to the tram across Grewingk Creek (a mile from the intersection). The tram requires a certain amount of upper body strength to operate but is quite manageable for two people with one in the cable car and one on the platform, both pulling. Take gloves.

Across the stream, the Humpy Creek Trail goes left and the Grewingk Glacier Trail goes right. Follow the Grewingk Glacier Trail upstream briefly, and then into thick woods of alder and beetle-killed spruce. This part of the trail is not as well used as the trail to the tram, and it may be overgrown or blocked by deadfall in spots. The trail climbs steeply up 400-foot Foehn Ridge, reaching a great view of the glacier, lake, and route of the hike in about 20 minutes. This viewpoint makes a good destination for those with limited time.

The trail climbs over Foehn Ridge and then descends in switchbacks to the valley floor and across this outwash plain though alder, fireweed, grasses, and young cottonwoods to an intersection, 2.6 miles from the tram. The trail to the left leads uphill a couple of miles to Emerald Lake. The Grewingk Glacier Trail goes straight, and a short side trail to the right leads to Grewingk Glacier Lake, perfect for a lunch stop. A kittiwake rookery across the lake provides a raucous musical accompaniment to lunch.

From the lake, retrace your steps to the intersection, turn right, and follow the Grewingk Glacier Trail another 1.5 miles to the glacier, paralleling the lakeshore. After crossing a fireweed-studded meadow, the trail enters a classic U-shaped glacial valley. Camping in the meadow is possible. Water is 5 minutes away in a stream in the U-shaped valley. Shortly after entering this valley the trail crosses an old streambed, follows it for about 10 feet, and exits on the right side at a rock cairn. Watch carefully, as it is easy to miss this exit. Just past a glacial tarn the route descends a steep gravel slope to the relatively flat alluvial fan. From here there are good views of the blue icefalls. The ambitious can walk up the relatively level gravel floor to the lateral moraine of the glacier. From the top of these gravel mounds there is a close-up view of the glacier, but be prepared for a foreground of gravel-coated ice rather than pristine blue-and-white ice.

There are several possible campsites near the tram. For water, follow the Humpy Creek Trail, on the north side of the tram, a few hundred yards to a small clear-water lake. Near the far end of this lake is a dryas-covered bench along the trail that offers good camping. Camp as far off the trail as possible. Bears frequent the Grewingk Creek area, especially when the salmon are running, so take appropriate precautions (see "Moose and Bears," in the Introduction).

Other Trails

Emerald Lake and Humpy Creek Trails can be done as a 13½-mile loop from the tram. Call the Division of Parks in Homer for information on other trails and trail conditions and call either the Division of Parks or the Homer Chamber of Commerce for information about transportation across the bay (see Appendix for telephone numbers).

2 | HOMER BEACH WALK

From Homer
Round trip: 4 miles or more
Hiking time: 3–8 hours
High point: sea level
Total elevation gain: none
Best: low tide anytime

Diamond Gulch to Homer
One way: 7 miles
Hiking time: 4–8 hours
High point: 450 feet
Total elevation gain: none
Best: May–October

Map: Trails Illustrated "Kachemak Bay State Park"
Agencies: Kachemak Bay State Critical Habitat Area (Alaska
 Department of Fish and Game) and Alaska Division of
 Parks and Outdoor Recreation

A delightfully different Alaska experience in summer or winter, a walk along the Homer beach takes you away from the bustle of the town. Kachemak Bay, with its mountain backdrop, is one of Alaska's loveliest areas. Overlook Park, located halfway between two access points, is a special treat in the spring.

On the beach at low tide, look for sea stars (starfish), many kinds of clam shells, mussels, whelk (neptune) shells, rocks covered with barnacles, sea urchins, snails, crabs, small shorebirds, gulls, scoters, loons, Harlequin ducks, and kittiwakes. Coal and sometimes fossils can be found below the cliffs that border the beach. Bald eagles often soar along the steep, eroding shoreline bluffs. Waterfalls cascade to the beach; driftwood logs thrown up by storm waves provide ready benches and tables for picnics. Walkers of all ages will enjoy a walk in the brisk salt air.

At low tide a broad sandy beach extends seaward and provides easy walking. High tides cover the sand, forcing the hiker onto gravel and rocks near the cliffs, making walking more difficult. Consult tide tables, available from banks and sporting goods shops, before setting out. Pick a day with a reasonably low tide, and schedule the walk to leave before low tide, returning at least 2 to 3 hours before high tide. The highest tides come in all the way to the cliffs and in some places the cliffs cannot be climbed. The highest tides could trap the unwary. However, watch the hour and you'll have no problems. Wear rubber boots or well-greased hiking boots; many

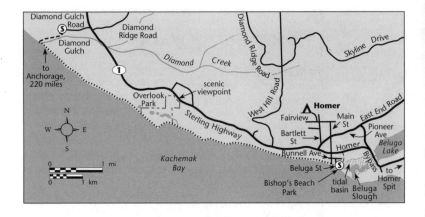

little inlets left behind by the retreating water must be crossed. Don't be caught as the tide pours back into these inlets, turning peninsulas into islands.

Two public access points to the beach make several variations of this walk possible. Hike from either direction and return to your car or walk the beach for about 7 miles between the two access points. One access is from Bishop's Beach Park in Homer; the other access is from Diamond Gulch Road about 6 miles northwest of Homer. Diamond Gulch provides access to a wilder, more remote part of the beach, and hikers are less likely to share the beach with off-road vehicles. If hiking between the two access points, the view is better starting at the Diamond Gulch end because you are walking toward the mountains. In deciding which way to walk, pay attention to the wind; walking with the wind to your back is strongly recommended on windy days because of blowing sand.

Driving directions, Homer access. Homer is a charming seaside community at the end of the Sterling Highway, 226 miles south of Anchorage. To reach the beach, drive to the bottom of the Sterling Highway hill as it enters Homer. From the intersection with Pioneer Avenue, which leads to the business district, proceed straight on the Homer Bypass. In 0.2 mile, turn right on Main Street. Take the first left, Bunnell Avenue, and then the next right, Beluga Street (follow signs for "Beach Access"). This street ends in a parking area for Bishop's Beach Park (outhouses and picnic shelter but no camping).

Wander the beach to the west as far as time permits. A good destination, an hour's walk away, is the rocky spit about 2 miles from the parking area. Extending far out into the water at low tide, this spit offers excellent beachcombing. Shortly after low tide, this spit is covered by water, so plan your walk accordingly, allowing more time if you beach-comb en route.

Driving directions, Diamond Gulch Road. Drive to mile 167.1 of the Sterling Highway, about 6 miles northwest of Homer. Turn west (toward the ocean) on an unmarked road (Diamond Gulch Road) that is diagonally across the Sterling Highway from Diamond Ridge Road. Drive past an open gate and continue for 0.8 mile to a small parking lot (elevation 450 feet).

From the parking lot, walk the Diamond Gulch trail toward the ocean through a forest of beetle-killed spruce. At a fork, go left down into the green gully of Diamond Gulch where tall grasses and myriad wildflowers mingle. In places steep parts of this trail are slippery when wet. You will reach the beach in about 20 minutes.

From this end of the beach the best tide pooling is at a rocky point about 2½ miles to the southeast (toward Homer), below Overlook Park. If walking to Homer, start at least 2 to 3 hours *before* low tide; allow 4 hours to walk the beach plus time for tide pooling. Watch the time carefully as there are several places where high tides reach the cliffs.

Overlook Park

The state has acquired 137 acres behind the beach and just below the viewpoint on the Sterling Highway hill above Homer. Hence the name Overlook Park. The Alaska Legislature agreed to the addition to the state park system if no money was spent on its operation. The Kachemak Bay Conservation Society therefore agreed to manage Overlook Park. The best access is from the beach. Part of the park sits on a small shelf just above the beach and harbors several small ponds. The park offers a microclimate where spring comes early, making this a delightful, early-season excursion. It is a mecca for birds such as common mallard, Barrow's Goldeneye, American widgeon, green-winged teal, northern pintail, and greater yellowlegs. At the time of this writing there were no trails in the park, but the access should be marked. In spring, when the grass is low, visitors can follow moose trails. Visiting the park in late summer before trails are developed is not recommended because grasses tower over your head and even the moose trails are difficult to find.

Overlook Park is located about halfway between the two beach access points. It is easy to recognize because it is where the lower part of the bluff flattens out into a shelf. The northwestern and eastern parts of the shelf are private land. If coming from Diamond Gulch, go past the first prominent grove of cottonwoods and find a route up. The eastern boundary of the park is several hundred feet west of a small stream located in Section 22 (see Trails Illustrated map). Contact Alaska Division of Parks, Homer Ranger Station (see Appendix for telephone number) for current information on access and trails. Snow lingers on the Diamond Gulch Road and Trail longer than it does in Overlook Park, so in early spring the best access is from Homer.

Beluga Slough Trail

Bishop's Beach Park is also the trailhead for Beluga Slough Trail, a short trail that is mostly a boardwalk and gives access to good bird-watching, particularly for shorebirds such as spotted and western sandpipers. As you

Beach at Homer, May (Helen Nienhueser)

face Kachemak Bay, the trail goes left and skirts Beluga Slough. Made of recycled plastic milk jugs and designed so that parts of the boardwalk float at high tide, the trail is best walked when the tide is in and there is water in the slough. The walk takes about 10 minutes and comes out on the Homer Bypass. There is currently no parking at this end of the trail.

Camping is available for a fee in the city campground on the hill above town (access from Bartlett Street) and on the Homer Spit.

3 | SWAN LAKE AND SWANSON RIVER CANOE ROUTES

Up to 60 miles (Swan Lake) or 80 miles (Swanson River)
Allow: 2 days–1 week
Gradient (both rivers): 4 feet/mile
Best: late May–early October
Map: Trails Illustrated "Kenai National Wildlife Refuge"
Agency: Kenai National Wildlife Refuge

A long chain of lakes, streams, and rivers in the wooded northwestern Kenai Peninsula offers outstanding canoeing. Take a day or a week—many route variations are possible. More time means more fun exploring and fishing. Portages are marked and cleared, and most are short. The lakes come in a variety of sizes and shapes, the smaller ones usually protected from wind and rough water, the larger ones offering bays for exploring and views of the Kenai Mountains. A rich variety of waterbirds inhabit these waters, including many species of ducks and shorebirds, loons, snipes, and swans. Anglers will find rainbow trout, Dolly Varden, steelhead trout, and landlocked salmon. Watch for moose, beavers, muskrats, and bears. In early winter the lakes can offer good ice skating, and after the snow pack is in place, the ski touring potential is endless.

Driving directions. The Swan Lake and Swanson River canoe routes are two separate systems. Both are reached from mile 83.2 of the Sterling Highway, 1.4 miles west of the Moose River bridge (136 miles from Anchorage and on the western edge of Sterling). Note that the river takeout for the Swan Lake route is at the Izaak Walton State Recreation Site adjacent to the Sterling Highway bridge over the Moose River.

At mile 83.2, turn north onto Swanson River Road. Expect no automobile fuel beyond here. About 17 miles from the Sterling Highway is a junction with Swan Lake Road. Swanson River Road continues north 0.4 mile to the Swanson River Landing, a parking area with two picnic tables and an outhouse. This is an access point for the Swanson River canoe route.

To reach the other canoe route entrances, turn east (right) onto Swan Lake Road. The Swan Lake canoe route lies south of the road; the Swanson River canoe route lies north of it.

The Swan Lake system has two entrances, the west entrance at Canoe Lake, about mile 4 of Swan Lake Road, and the east entrance at Portage Lakes, mile 9.8. For the Paddle Lake entrance to the Swanson River system, drive to mile 12.2 and take a left fork (marked). Another 0.5 mile brings you to a parking area above Paddle Lake.

Swan Lake System

There are many ways to link the lakes. Paddling from one entrance to the other makes a good 2- to 3-day trip. Strong paddlers can expect to reach Gavia Lake late the first day from either entrance (it is closer to the west entrance), but many will be happier to take it more slowly. From either entrance, the canoeist can reach Moose River and float it to the Sterling Highway bridge (near the beginning of Swanson River Road). Most people can do this trip in 3 days; strong, seasoned canoeists may complete it in 2 long, hard days, but more time is recommended. From the east entrance (Portage Lakes), expect to reach Swan Lake the first day. Plan to take at least 6 to 8 hours to paddle the Moose River to Sterling. Camping along the Moose River is reasonable below the confluence with the East Fork of the Moose River but is poor above this. Strong winds can create whitecaps and difficult to dangerous canoeing on Swan Lake and other larger lakes.

Swanson River

The Swanson River canoe route entrance is at Paddle Lake. From there, explore various routes through the lakes or take a 2- to 3-day trip through

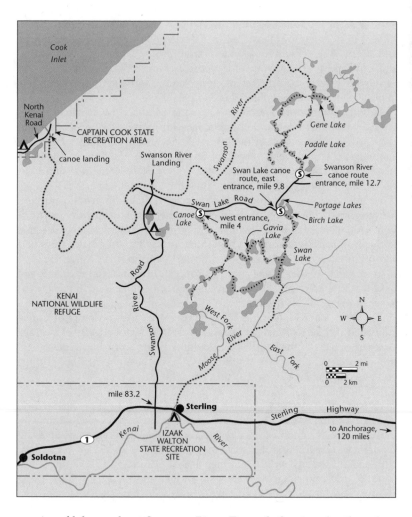

a series of lakes and out Swanson River. To reach the river, head north to Gene Lake (1 long day) and then down Swanson River for 12 to 14 hours to Swanson River Landing.

Another exit, about 12 hours farther, is near the mouth of the Swanson River at Captain Cook State Recreation Area. Highway access is from the city of Kenai. Drive to mile 38.5 of North Kenai Road, and follow a side road south to reach the canoe landing.

Before setting out, check the Swanson River water level with the Kenai National Wildlife Refuge office (see Appendix for contact information). Low water can make the first several miles of the river nearly impassable as it flows sluggishly through muskeg and dense masses of lily pads. The

Trailhead at Portage Lake, May (John Wolfe, Jr.)

small stream connecting Gene Lake and Swanson River is difficult; it requires lining the boats and includes two portages. There is a campsite at the end of the second portage. Most campsites along the river are some distance from the riverbank through muskeg and marsh.

Good primitive campsites are available at most lakes in both systems. A camping stove is generally best in this popular area. If you do build fires, do so only in existing fire pits, not on moss or peat. Do not enlarge fire pits, and be sure to pour a lot of water on the fire and surrounding earth when you are finished. Campfires may be restricted in dry years. Cutting of dead and down wood only is allowed. Wear rubber boots because lakeshores and portages are often wet and boggy. Use of islands is discouraged, because of impact to wildlife.

A brochure with maps showing the canoe routes is available from the refuge manager and usually at the trailhead and at the refuge visitor center at mile 58 of the Sterling Highway. These maps are extremely helpful in locating connecting channels and portages, both of which are marked with small, unobtrusive brown signs that are difficult to see from a distance.

Canoes can be rented in Anchorage, Soldotna, and Sterling (see Appendix for addresses). Guided trips are available. The Swan Lake and Swanson River canoe routes are part of the National Trail and National Wilderness systems. No wheeled or motorized vehicles are permitted within the canoe route areas; this includes powerboats, snowmobiles, aircraft, off-road vehicles, mountain bikes, and wheeled canoe carriers. Group sizes are limited to fifteen.

4 | # SKILAK WILDLIFE RECREATION AREA

Hideout Trail
Round trip: 3 miles
Hiking time: 2 hours
High point: 1,535 feet
Total elevation gain: 850 feet

Hidden Creek Trail
Round trip: 3 miles
Hiking time: 2 hours
High point: 500 feet
Total elevation gain: 0 feet in, 300 feet out

Skilak Lookout
Round trip: 5 miles
Hiking time: 3–4 hours
High point: 1,450 feet
Total elevation gain: 750 feet

Best: May–October
Map: Trails Illustrated "Kenai National Wildlife Refuge"
Agency: Kenai National Wildlife Refuge

The Skilak Wildlife Recreation Area offers a number of trails that start from the Skilak Lake Road. Several of the most interesting are highlighted here. All offer views of the mountain wilderness south of Skilak Lake and the Kenai River. Hunting is restricted to promote wildlife-viewing opportunities. Watch for spruce grouse, moose, and an occasional bear.

Hideout Trail

This short, uphill trail offers great rewards for the effort expended. It switchbacks up a bump near the east end of Skilak Lake Road, through an old burn, and provides fabulous views of Skilak Lake, the blue-green Kenai River winding through the forest below, and the snow-streaked mountains beyond.

Driving directions. At mile 58 of the Sterling Highway (111 miles south of Anchorage), immediately west of the Skilak Wildlife Recreation Area Visitor Center and a sign for the Kenai National Wildlife Refuge, turn south onto the eastern end of unpaved Skilak Lake Road. Drive 1.9 miles to the trailhead, on the north or right hand side of the road. The trailhead (elevation about 785 feet) is marked.

The trail snakes its way uphill in some seventeen switchbacks, past silvery ghost trees and abundant wildflowers. Because of the switchbacks, the grade

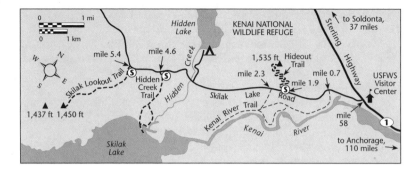

is not terribly steep. The views expand with the elevation. The rocky outcrops at the top are like a rock garden. Bear Mountain, Russian Mountain, and the valley of Surprise Creek beckon across the Kenai River. To the west loom the distant, snow-covered peaks of the Redoubt and Illiamna volcanoes.

Because the trail faces south, and because the area receives less snow than other parts of the Kenai Peninsula, this trail opens earlier than most. It is likely to be muddy and slippery when wet.

Hidden Creek Trail

A pleasant, easy trip for the whole family, Hidden Creek Trail winds to the shore of Skilak Lake near the mouth of Hidden Creek. Look for salmon at the mouth of Hidden Creek. At the lake, fish for rainbow trout, lake trout, Dolly Varden, and silver and red salmon. (Check regulations regarding seasons, fishing methods, and bag limits.)

Driving directions. See the directions above for Skilak Lake Road. Drive 4.6 miles from the east entrance; the trailhead, on the south or left side of the road, is marked. Park in the area provided across the road.

Hidden Creek Trail starts at an elevation of 500 feet and descends through pleasant woods to Skilak Lake, at 195 feet elevation. The trail quickly drops into wet meadows and a forest recovering from an early 1990s fire. Logs have been laid across the trail to make walking drier, but there are still wet sections. The trail forks about halfway in. Both trails end at Skilak Lake, offering the option of a loop trip. The right hand fork is more direct. Continue through a forest of evergreens and birch trees protecting a forest-floor covering of moss, cranberry, crowberry, and Labrador tea. The world opens up at the lake, where an endless supply of driftwood invites log hopping and taking photographs, and the scenery invites you to stop for a picnic. A short walk to the east along the shore leads to the mouth of Hidden Creek. Lovely mountain vistas grace the horizon. Campers should prepare for possible strong winds near the lake. (Be careful with campfires during these conditions. Dismantle any windbreaks you build before leaving.)

To return via the loop, retrace your steps to a fork in the trail in the woods, a few feet back from the lakeshore (marked Hidden Creek). Follow the path to the right (east), through the woods, to the bank of Hidden Creek. Head upstream a short distance until a well-defined trail heads left into the woods. This path meanders though the forest and into the burn where it rejoins the original trail. Most of the wet spots have boards across them.

Skilak Lookout Trail

The trip to Skilak Lookout offers a mostly easy trail through pleasant spruce and cottonwood forest with a lovely view at the end. This is a moderate trip that is good for children who can walk 5 or so miles.

Driving directions. From the east end of Skilak Lake Road (see driving directions for Hideout Trail, above), drive 5.4 miles to the trailhead (marked; elevation 700 feet). Parking is across the road from the trailhead.

Skilak Lookout Trail leaves the south side of the road and rambles gently through pleasant woods. A 1996 burn resulted in fine views of Skilak Lake from the trail. It is interesting to see differences in vegetation types between areas that burned and those that did not. A few spots on the trail may be wet, and it may be necessary to go around or over a few fallen trees. In August raspberries line the trail and might attract bears as well as hikers. Make plenty of noise during berry season!

Near the end, the trail climbs a couple of short, steep grades to a knob (elevation 1,450 feet) and is slippery when wet. From the knob, the view of Skilak Lake, the 2-mile-wide braided Skilak River, and the Kenai Mountains is outstanding. In fact, there are 360-degree views, framed by the bent trunks of scattered windblown trees. From rocky islands below, listen for sounds of bird rookeries. Mount Redoubt volcano lies to the west, and Mount Spurr and Mount Gerdine to the northwest. The view is worth the trip, even in misty weather.

Other Trails

The Kenai River Trail (marked) leaves Skilak Lake Road 0.7 mile from its east junction with the Sterling Highway. The trail heads down an old dirt road 0.2 mile to a fork just before the river; turn right, uphill, for about

Skilak Lake near Hidden Creek, May (Helen Nienhueser)

10 minutes to a good viewpoint overlooking the Kenai River canyon. The trail continues downriver but is neither maintained nor particularly rewarding. Another access to the trail is at mile 2.3 of the Skilak Lake Road. From here, hike to the river and downstream for about a mile until the trail disappears, a total round trip of about 4 miles and 2 hours. Along the river the trail is easy, though the descent to the river (200 feet) is steep in places. In salmon season watch for half-eaten fish left by bears.

A new trail starts in the Upper Skilak Lake Campground. The trail departs from the vehicle camping loop, across from the restrooms by Skilak Lake. The trail climbs steadily uphill for about two miles and offers incredible views.

There are seven public campgrounds located along Skilak Lake Road, and the road leads to several other trails. All trails are closed to off-road vehicles, including snowmobiles and mountain bikes, all year. Pick up information at the Skilak Wildlife Recreation Area Visitor Center on the Sterling Highway.

5 | FULLER LAKES AND SKYLINE TRAVERSE

Fuller Lake
Round trip: 6 miles
Hiking time: 4–7 hours
High point: 1,725 feet
Total elevation gain: 1,425 feet in, 35 feet out
Best: June–October

Traverse
One way: 12 miles
Hiking time: 10 hours–2 days
High point: 3,520 feet
Total elevation gain: about 5,500 feet westbound, 5,300 feet eastbound
Best: June–September

Maps: USGS Kenai B1 NE, C1 SE
Agency: Kenai National Wildlife Refuge

Fuller Lake, a tempting jewel, lies at tree line surrounded by scattered hemlock, spruce, willow scrub, and grassy meadows. Lower Fuller Lake, smaller and nestled just below tree line, is a good destination for families. Hikers can make Fuller Lake their goal or continue up the ridge to the west for a panoramic view. A point-to-point route for really energetic hikers connects these lakes and the Skyline Trail, farther west, via the ridge of the Mystery Hills.

Fuller Lakes

Driving directions, Fuller Lakes Trail. To reach the lakes, drive to mile 57.2 of the Sterling Highway (110 miles south of Anchorage), and park in a parking area on the north side of the highway (elevation 300 feet). The trail begins up a set of steps from the parking lot.

Climb the steps, and follow the Fuller Lakes Trail north as it ascends through forest and meadows. Look back frequently for views of Skilak Lake and the mountains to the southeast. This is a moderately steep hike, but the footing is not difficult. Most of the elevation gain is between the trailhead and Lower Fuller Lake. Exposed tree roots and occasional fallen trees may cross the trail along the way.

At Lower Fuller Lake cross the outlet stream on a bridge, and continue along the left side of the lake and over a low pass to Fuller Lake, an ideal overnight spot. The lakes are in different drainages; Fuller Lake drains north into Mystery Creek, and Lower Fuller Lake drains south into the Kenai River. The wood supply at Fuller Lake is limited; use a backpacking stove rather than a fire.

Ridges and knobs beckon from Fuller Lake; explorers can mostly avoid brush. The trail continues around the east side of the lake and then branches. One branch heads north and leads toward upper Mystery Creek, eventually disappearing. A left branch crosses the Fuller Lake outlet stream. This footpath traverses gradually away from the outlet stream and up and across the side of a long ridge that extends north off the 3,520-foot summit of the Mystery Hills. When the trail has risen to near the elevation

Lower Fuller Lake, August (Helen Nienhueser)

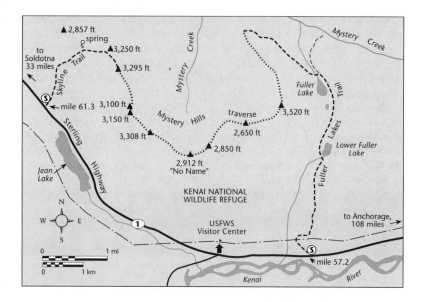

of the ridge top and it is clear there are no more brush patches or rock outcrops between the path and the ridge crest, head off the trail and more directly uphill. On the ridge crest, double back and follow the ridge to the summit, a fine destination for those camped at the lake. The ridge beyond is the traverse.

Skyline Traverse

The ridge of the Mystery Hills is the last of the Kenai Mountains for drivers heading west, and the first for those heading east from the flats of western Kenai Peninsula. The sides of the ridge are quite steep. The ridge top is rolling but mostly easy. The rolling crests go on and on, however, over eight summits without water, and the route is easy to underestimate. A couple of the ascents of these rolling summits are long and steep. A 1-day traverse is best done in mid-June or July when there is plenty of light. People have been caught by darkness. A high meadow and spring at the western end offer a possible campsite, but otherwise snowbanks provide the only water. A small intermittent path is worn in over much of the route, but not all of it, and there are no route markers. For those adequately prepared for a long day, the ridge presents fine views, and its variety is rewarding.

The route may best be done from Fuller Lake westward, mostly because of potential confusion finding the route coming off the ridge in the opposite direction. To reach the ridge from Fuller Lake, see the Fuller Lakes description above. Follow the ridge crest to the notch north of point 3295, and then drop off the crest on the west side. A path cuts across the slope below the last summit and then continues down into the forest to the Skyline trailhead. Use a good map to keep yourself oriented. For those following the ridge *toward* Fuller Lake, walk north of the high point (point 3520), descending along the ridge crest. Hike nearly to the end of the ridge, past all rock outcrops and brush that might thwart descent to the east. Just before a last gentle rise in the ridge, look below to the right for hints of a trail and a bare gravel patch. A rock cairn may be visible. Descend, and find a small footpath heading south, toward Fuller Lake.

Driving directions, Skyline Trail. To reach the Skyline trailhead, drive to mile 61.3 of the Sterling Highway, and park on the west side of the highway (elevation 450 feet). The trail begins on the east side of the highway, diagonally north from the parking area and beyond the guardrail. The Skyline Trail itself is short, about 1¾ miles from the highway to point 3295 on the ridge. It is maintained but climbs very steeply, and can be slippery.

All trails and routes described here are included in the National Wilderness System. Off-road vehicles (including mountain bikes) are not permitted during snow-free months, and snowmobiles are prohibited above tree line in winter.

6 RUSSIAN LAKES–RESURRECTION RIVER TRAIL SYSTEM

Lower Russian Lake
Round trip: 6 miles
Hiking time: 3 hours
High point: 800 feet
Total elevation gain: 300 feet in, 250 feet out

Upper Russian Lake
Round trip: 24 miles
Allow: 2 days
High point: 850 feet
Total elevation gain: 800 feet in, 800 feet out

Cooper Lake to Russian River trailhead
One way: 21.5 miles
Allow: 2 days
High point: 1,450 feet
Total elevation gain: 1,600 feet

Resurrection River–Russian Lakes
One way: 32 miles
Allow: 3–5 days
High point: 1,200 feet
Total elevation gain: 1,500 feet

Best: May–October (Russian Lakes); June–October (other trails)
Maps: Trails Illustrated "Kenai Fjords National Park and Surrounding Area" (for Resurrection River, add USGS Seward B8)
Agency: Chugach National Forest

The trails linking Russian River, Cooper Lake, and the length of the Resurrection River traverse broad valleys linked by flat passes and make possible anything from an afternoon jaunt to a serious multiday backpacking trip. These routes offer big forests breaking to alpine meadows, cascading clear and glacial streams, fine lakes, brilliant wildflowers and berries in season, moose, and bears. Glaciated mountains are visible through the trees. Fishing can be excellent in the Russian River; check fishing regulations before casting.

The trail to Lower Russian Lake or the Barber Cabin (6 or 7 miles round trip) is a nice 1-day or overnight trip for families and a pleasant mountain bike trip. Another fine overnight hike is the 21.5-mile trip from Cooper Lake to the Russian River trailhead. This route is used by mountain bikers but has potential for conflict with hikers. A more strenuous, adventuresome hike, unsuitable for mountain bikes, is from the Resurrection River trailhead near Seward to either the Russian River trailhead (32 miles) or the Cooper Lake trailhead (21.5 miles). Combining Resurrection River Trail with the Resurrection Pass Trail (Trip 14) can create a backpacking trip of 10 days and 70 miles.

Russian Lakes

Driving directions. Reach the Russian River Campground trailhead from mile 52.5 of the Sterling Highway (106 miles south of Anchorage). At this point, turn south onto a paved side road marked "Chugach National Forest Campground, Russian River" (do not confuse it with the Kenai National Wildlife Refuge's Kenai–Russian River Campground at mile 55). Follow the side road to a stop sign and gatehouse. During salmon runs from mid-June through mid-August, the area is crowded with anglers, and the Forest Service charges fees for parking, camping, and fishing. Beyond the gatehouse, go left, and follow the road 0.8 mile to the Russian Lakes trailhead (marked) at an elevation of 500 feet. There is a public pay phone near the gatehouse.

The trail to Lower Russian Lake is maintained to difficult wheelchair-accessible standards. About 1½ miles from the trailhead, just before a bridge over Rendezvous Creek, a trail takes off to the right. This is a short spur to Russian River Falls and a viewing deck. To reach Lower Russian Lake and the Barber Cabin (about 3½ miles in, elevation 550 feet), cross the Rendezvous Creek bridge, and turn right at a second fork. To reach Upper Russian Lake (12 miles in, elevation 690 feet) and a cabin there, go left at

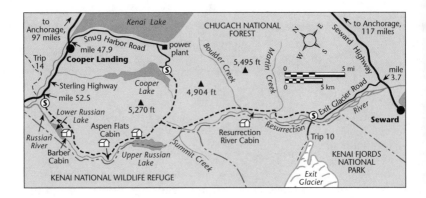

this second fork. The route to Upper Russian Lake is well used but much narrower and sometimes rocky. The Aspen Flats Cabin is between the lakes along a short side trail (marked, about 9 miles from the trailhead). In addition, there are two established tent sites on short spurs along Lower Russian Lake and another site 40 yards off-trail about halfway to Aspen Flats Cabin. Make cabin reservations through the Forest Service nationwide reservations system (see Appendix). Lake cabin rentals include the use of a rowboat.

In winter, take the spur trail toward Russian River Falls, but bear left and upstream along the Russian River on a winter-only trail to Barber Cabin. The main trail beyond Rendezvous Creek is not recommended in the winter because of avalanche runout zones along Lower Russian Lake. The access road to the trailhead is not plowed.

Cooper Lake–Russian Lakes Trail

Driving directions. Reach the Cooper Lake trailhead from mile 47.9 of the Sterling Highway (101 miles from Anchorage). Turn southeast on Snug Harbor Road, and follow it 11.5 miles to a parking area marked by a sign for Russian Lakes Trail. The 9-mile trail to Upper Russian Lake is a scenic walk through wooded mountain valleys. The 12 miles from there to the Russian River trailhead are described above. Check with the Forest Service before setting out, especially on spring trips, to be sure trees blown down across the trail during winter have been cleared.

The trail from Cooper Lake to Upper Russian Lake trail makes a good ski trip in winter. It is also used by snowmobiles. Snug Harbor Road is plowed in winter 8.7 miles to a power plant on Kenai Lake.

Resurrection River Trail

Driving directions. To reach the Seward end of Resurrection River Trail by road, drive to mile 3.7 of the Seward Highway. Turn onto Exit Glacier Road (marked). Follow this paved road about 7 miles to a parking area on

View from Resurrection River Trail, August (Helen Nienhueser)

the right (elevation 400 feet), just east of the Resurrection River. The trail begins at the river and parallels it.

Resurrection River Trail joins the Russian Lakes Trail about 5½ miles from the Cooper Lake trailhead and 16 miles from the Russian River trailhead. Ideal campsites are scarce. Occasional meadows offer possible tent sites in dry weather. The Forest Service Resurrection River Cabin, about a mile south of Boulder Creek on a short spur trail (marked), can be reserved. Eight miles of trail, from the Resurrection River Cabin to the Russian Lakes Trail junction, is managed as "primitive." This means it is low priority for clearing blown-down trees. The Forest Service may not clear it for two to three years at a stretch, which can mean more than 100 trees to climb over or skirt around if the crew has not been there.

Several stream fords are required. Martin Creek, 5 miles from the trail's south end, Boulder Creek (8½ miles), and Resurrection Creek (15 miles) can be easy to wade at lower flows, but difficult or impossible at high flows. The Boulder Creek crossing is poorly marked. The trail goes somewhat upstream to the crossing and somewhat downstream on the other side. Resurrection River at the ford runs north–south and is smaller than Summit Creek, which flows in from the west. Floods have washed out portions of the trail. A short distance above the confluence, cross the smaller stream. Do not cross or follow Summit Creek. Finding the trail may require bushwhacking and patience. Autumn rains can cause dangerous floods at all three crossings, and other parts of the route are subject to flooding as well. Also, the Kenai Peninsula's largest concentration of grizzlies feeds upstream of the trail crossings of Boulder and Martin Creeks. For many, these challenges may thwart a trip, but for those seeking a good long adventure in the heart of a beautiful wilderness, this is a classic—especially when combined with the Resurrection Pass Trail. Just call to check trail conditions before going.

To link from this trail system to the Resurrection Pass Trail, walk about 0.9 mile along the access road for the Russian River trailhead and 0.6 mile west along the Sterling Highway to the southern end of Trip 14 (mile 53.1).

All these trails are closed to off-road vehicles from May 1 through November 30 and to horses from April 1 through June 30. Mountain bikers should observe the horse prohibition to avoid eroding soft trails. Exit Glacier Road, beginning at about mile 2, is not plowed November 1 to May 1 but is used by snowmobilers, skiers, and dog mushers. However, much of Resurrection River Trail is poor for skiing.

7 CRESCENT LAKE

Crescent Creek Trail
Round trip: 12.8 miles
Hiking time: 5–8 hours
Total elevation gain: 960 feet in, 100 feet out

Carter Lake Trail
Round trip: 6.6 miles
Hiking time: 3–5 hours
Total elevation gain: 1,050 feet in, 100 feet out

Traverse: 18.5 miles
High point: 1,550 feet
Best: June–October
Map: Trails Illustrated "Kenai National Wildlife Refuge and Adjacent Chugach National Forest"
Agency: Chugach National Forest

Hidden in a cluster of mountains north of Kenai Lake and south of the Y where the Sterling and Seward Highways split is smile-shaped Crescent Lake. Trails lead to it from each of the highways. Both the Crescent Creek Trail and Carter Lake Trail take hikers to high country right at tree line where open forests and patches of stunted evergreens give way to areas of tundra and grassland.

The Crescent Creek Trail leads to the west end of Crescent Lake and is longer, gentler, and drier than the Carter Lake Trail. With more deciduous trees, it makes a glorious September hike through the golds and reds of autumn. The Carter Lake Trail climbs through rocky switchbacks for

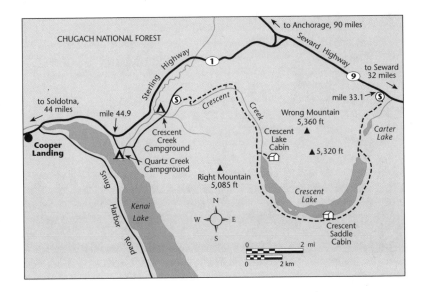

quicker access to tree line at Carter Lake and a beautiful, sometimes muddy trek across high wildflower meadows to the east end of Crescent Lake. The Crescent Creek Trail is especially good for families with children if they have reservations for overnight use of the U.S. Forest Service cabin at the west end of Crescent Lake. A rowboat goes with the cabin, and fishing for grayling is good. Nine miles of primitive trail connect the two ends of Crescent Lake along the lake's south side.

Camping is good near both ends of the lake, although the Forest Service has sometimes disallowed camping in overworn spots at the western end to allow vegetation to grow back. Please be aware of your impact and try to avoid further damage. Moose and bears may be spotted in summer, wolverine occasionally in winter. More detail follows.

Crescent Creek Trail

Driving directions. To reach the Crescent Creek trailhead, drive to about mile 44.9 of the Sterling Highway (construction may change the mileage slightly), 98 miles south of Anchorage and about 8 miles west of the junction of the Seward and Sterling Highways. Quartz Creek Road begins immediately west of the Sunrise Inn. Follow this road 3.3 miles to the start of Crescent Creek Trail (marked), 0.5 mile beyond Crescent Creek Campground.

Crescent Creek Trail starts directly across the road from the parking area (elevation 590 feet). The path winds through birch and aspen along a tiny stream, climbs over a low ridge, and descends into the Crescent Creek valley. Follow the trail upstream, crossing the creek on bridges twice. The

Carter Lake, July (John Wolfe Jr.)

second crossing is in a broad, open meadow dotted with trees near the lake outlet (elevation 1,454 feet). The cabin is a short distance beyond the bridge. Make cabin reservations through the Forest Service nationwide reservations system (see Appendix).

Avalanche terrain makes the Crescent Creek Trail hazardous in winter (see "Avalanches," in the Introduction), and even in spring, the deep, dense snow in avalanche paths melts last, making for slippery footing on this route that is otherwise known for its fine trail. The route as far as the Crescent Lake Cabin is good for mountain bikes but presents potential conflict with hikers.

Carter Lake Trail

Driving directions. To reach Crescent Lake via Carter Lake, drive to mile 33.1 of the Seward Highway (94 miles south of Anchorage). The trail leaves from a parking area on the west side of the highway (elevation 500 feet).

Cross a footbridge at the trailhead, and climb the switchbacks of this pleasant but steep 2.3-mile trail to Carter Lake (elevation 1,486 feet). Another mile brings you to Crescent Lake. The trail forks about a ⅓ mile before Crescent Lake. The left fork, marked by a rock cairn and sign, leads around Crescent Lake. In winter, Carter Lake Trail makes an excellent snowshoe or ski tour, although climbing skins may be desirable for the initial ascent on skis. Once past the switchback area, skiers can continue across the flats and across Crescent Lake to the cabins. The Carter Lake Trail is too rocky and steep at the beginning and often too muddy beyond to be pleasant for most mountain bikers.

The Traverse

The trail that connects the Crescent Creek and Carter Lake Trails is the Crescent Lake Trail, a Forest Service "primitive trail." This means that clipping back brush is low priority. The Crescent Saddle Cabin lies about halfway along this connector trail below a low point in the ridge. Check with the Forest Service regarding current conditions. The grass can be quite thick in late summer and the trail not always obvious. Some cautions: a stream near the western end of Crescent Lake can be difficult to cross at high water. Toward the east end of the lake, there is an avalanche chute that holds snow late. It is steep, can be icy, and a slip could end in the lake. The only area good for camping on the traverse is in the middle, partway between a creek coming from Crescent Saddle and islands in the lake. Water is available but must be treated. Take a cooking stove.

Both the Carter Lake and Crescent Creek Trails are closed to snowmobiles May 1 to November 30. They are closed to horses from April 1 through June 30 because of soft trail conditions. Mountain bikers should observe the horse prohibitions to prevent trail erosion. The trail around Crescent Lake is proposed to be closed to bikes and horses.

8 CAINES HEAD

Round trip: North Beach 9 miles, Caines Head 13 miles
Hiking/kayaking time: allow 2 days
High point: 650 feet (Caines Head)
Total elevation gain: 950 feet
Best: late May–September
Map: Trails Illustrated "Kenai Fjords National Park and Surrounding Area"
Agency: Caines Head State Recreation Area

Caines Head, with an abandoned World War II army fort and exquisite bay views framed by coastal rainforest, offers a blend of historical curiosity and natural wonder. The area has great beaches, rock outcrops, and soaring coastal cliffs. The main access trail is not a trail at all but a beach walk that appears only at low tide. A fantastic side trail leads to alpine country. Look for a variety of seabirds, shorebirds, and songbirds en route, along with bald eagles, black bears, and spawning salmon. If the tides are wrong the only time you can go, consider launching a sea kayak and exploring this area from the water.

Driving directions. Follow the Seward Highway into Seward (it becomes 3rd Avenue), and proceed until the road ends at an intersection with Railway Avenue. Turn right, and follow Railway Avenue as it parallels the coastline, becomes the gravel Lowell Point Road, and ultimately bends left

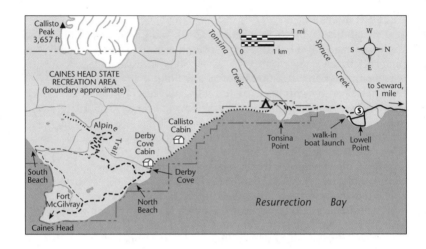

toward Lowell Point. Here, about 2.2 miles from 3rd Avenue, turn right on Martins Road and almost immediately right again at a sign for Lowell Point State Recreation Site. The trailhead is up a short driveway. Martins Road forms a small loop with Beach Drive, which parallels the coast. Kayak rentals and a water taxi may be arranged along Beach Drive. Where Martins Road and Beach Drive join, there is a walk-in boat launch ramp for kayaks. Cliffs prevent walking the beach from here; use the trail.

From the trailhead, the route joins a private road, which becomes a footpath and then suddenly drops down a series of switchbacks to Tonsina Creek. At the first big bridge, look for spawning salmon in clear water. The second long bridge crosses a siltier stream and leads to run-down but serviceable campsites with picnic tables, fire pits, a picnic shelter, and outhouse. Beyond a screen of tall grass is a fine, broad beach that kids and romantics will love. A trek to a Tonsina campsite (1¾ miles) makes a good half-day hike or first overnight backpacking trip for young children. The coastal route is from this point to Derby Cove, another 2½ miles farther.

Water closes the route between Tonsina Point and Derby Cove except for a couple of hours before and after low tide. Cliffs plunge right to the water. There is no reasonable way around; a man fell and died making an attempt. Luckily, the ocean pulls back twice a day and, on most days, leaves a continuous thread of walkable beach for those paying attention to their tidebooks (available at sporting goods stores and banks).

This route is recommended only at low tides of +3 feet or lower (+2 or -1, for example). Tides fluctuate day to day around a theoretical "sea level." When weather is stormy and gray, the barometric pressure is lower and the ocean can come up a bit higher because there is less air pushing down on it. Low pressure coupled with wind-driven waves that are common in stormy weather mean that hikers are more likely to get wet. A +3-foot low tide is marginal for this route in good weather. Minus tides are best in windy, rainy weather.

A couple of small but difficult rocky headlands are at the heart of this otherwise simple beach walk. People who don't hit this stretch at the lowest part of the tide cycle or who go on a day with a low tide that was too high find themselves scrambling over these low headlands. The highest is perhaps 15 feet above water and is slippery with seaweed. People have skidded into the water. Those uncomfortable with scrambling over the slippery headland should plan their trip for zero or minus tides. Leave plenty of time to get from the trailhead to this area by the lowest part of the tide cycle. It's about 2 miles; allow an hour or more.

Upon reaching Derby Cove, all fretting about tides is left behind. There are public-use cabins just inland from the Callisto beach and Derby Cove beach. Reserve them through State Parks (see Appendix). These are among the state's most popular; make summer reservations five to six months ahead. Where the Derby Cove beach pinches out, the trail (marked) climbs into the woods and goes less than ½ mile to North Beach.

North Beach is the site of a former military dock and the beginning of an old road up to Fort McGilvray. There are two picnic pavilions, outhouses, and a ranger cabin at North Beach, and it is the best camping option. It is about 2 miles up the winding road to the concrete fortress buried in the ground at the top of Caines Head (elevation 650 feet). Two concrete circles, where guns were mounted to protect the Port of Seward during World War II, flank the fort. The concrete passageways are fun to explore (take a flashlight), and the command room with its slit windows overlooking

Resurrection Bay from Fort McGilvray, May (John Wolfe Jr.)

Resurrection Bay stokes the imagination. The trail to the fort passes old concrete ammunition bunkers. Poke your head in and yodel; the acoustics ring! From North Beach to South Beach it is about 2.5 miles via a fork to the right. Behind South Beach is a large collection of collapsed buildings that once housed hundreds of soldiers who built and operated the place.

Alpine Trail

At the crest between Derby Cove and North Beach is a trail junction (marked) for the Alpine Trail. It climbs steadily but never too steeply out of the forest to the tundra zone and peters out at about 1,600 feet. The trail snakes in and out of dense forest, open meadow, and wrinkles in the topography, framing the view differently at every turn. The walking is easy below Callisto Peak (3,657 feet) after the trail runs out.

About halfway to the end of the trail, near elevation 800 feet and just as the main trail begins the first in a series of switchbacks, there is another faint trail that takes off downhill to the south. The trail to the south, at this writing, was hard to follow and appeared unmaintained. But it is worth mentioning for the hardy because it comes out at South Beach and can be used to make a grand loop of about 5½ miles. The Alaska Division of Parks plans to mark it better. Without maintenance, this route requires keen observational skills and a willingness to climb back up if you lose the route. The thick forest, patches of devil's club, and convoluted topography make the prospect of navigating in this area without the route daunting; if you attempt it, don't lose the trail.

Resurrection Bay is often breezy. Drizzle is common. The snowpack can stay in the shady forest until late May near sea level, and well into June on the Alpine Trail. Portions of the Alpine Trail are lined with head-high grass that holds moisture; take raingear. Some streams dry up, but drinking water should be possible to locate.

9 | MOUNT MARATHON, RACE POINT

Round trip: 3–4 miles
Hiking time: 43 minutes–7 hours
High point: 3,022 feet
Total elevation gain: 2,800 feet
Best: May–October
Map: USGS Seward A7 SW
Agencies: City of Seward and Alaska Division of Mining, Land, & Water

In 1915, a bet in Seward started a race up Mount Marathon that is still repeated every Fourth of July. Back then, there was no Seward Highway,

Resurrection Bay from hikers' trail, August (John Wolfe Jr.)

no city of Anchorage, and railroad construction was just beginning, but there was a Mount Marathon race. The runners in this mountain marathon start from the town center near sea level, climb to Race Point (elevation 3,022 feet on the southeast ridge of Marathon Mountain), and return. The record is 43 minutes, 11 seconds, set in 1981 by Bill Spencer. Independence Day is the most exciting time to make the climb, whether you are in the race or not, but it is a good hike anytime during the summer.

A hikers' trail and the runners' trail climb toward Race Point, although the hikers' trail has easier destinations as well. The hikers' trail is steep, the runners' trail steeper. Fortunately, both provide spectacular views of Resurrection Bay, giving a ready excuse to pause. You may choose to go up the hikers' trail and down the runners' trail; the two lower ends are within easy walking distance.

Runners' Trail

Driving directions. To reach the runners' trail, find Jefferson Street in Seward and drive on it toward the base of Mount Marathon. At First Avenue, Jefferson becomes Lowell Canyon Road, which soon ends at the

Lowell Creek Picnic Area and a gate. Park here (elevation 200 feet). A gravel service road beyond the gate and a footpath that begins behind picnic tables both lead shortly to an inclined fan of gravel deposited at the base of a gully and rock outcrop. This is where things get interesting.

This paragraph describes the typical race route up the first short section of the mountain. The next paragraph describes an easier route for those not impaired by competitive adrenalin. Historically, most runners have headed into the woods on a narrow but prominent trail just before the gravel fan and ascended a forested cliff to the right of the gully. The route requires the use of handholds. Those wishing to try this most authentic of routes should test holds before depending on them, and be careful not to knock debris on other hikers below. Competitors have scrambled over a broad area; you should pick the route that looks best, but do stay in the trees and avoid the rock outcrops and gully farther to the left. The first stretch is brief and ends at comparatively level ground where the several routes coalesce to one steep trail.

A less intimidating hike crosses the lower part of the gravel fan and picks up a steep switchback trail to the left of the gully. Once above the rock outcrops, this trail leads directly into the gully. At this point, cross the gully and find a nearly level trail that traverses to the right. This leads to the top of the cliff area described in the previous paragraph and joins the usual race route.

After these initial options, the route is clear. The runners' trail has separate up and down routes that form a figure eight. A single upward track follows a ridge crest above and to the right of the gully. Emerging from the trees, the ascent route continues up the ridge and is crossed by the down

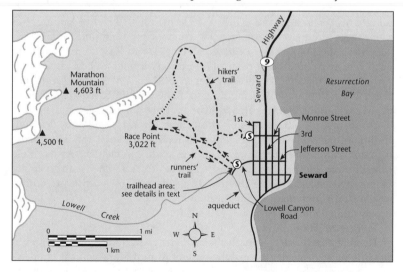

route, which enters from the right and descends into the gully on the left. Unless you are a runner, sit a while to enjoy the glacier-streaked mountain view. Look for ptarmigan, ground squirrels, marmots, mountain goats, Dall sheep, and a variety of wildflowers.

The trail to the "summit" of Race Point at 3,022 feet becomes poorly defined on the rocky ridge; just continue toward the skyline. Race Point is the nearly level ridge top that appears suddenly. The descent route starts down the east face of the mountain. Snow patches on the east side remain near the top well into July. Although runners slide on the snow for a quick descent, note that this is where many runners injure themselves. The snow is steep and fast and ends in rock. It is easy enough to avoid the snow, and below, descending with long strides in loose gravel (scree) is fun.

Descending the gully in early summer often involves snow. The gully ends in the rock outcrop cliffs. Although many runners descend the outcrop, most hikers will want to exit the gully to the right and return to the switchback route they came up.

The Hikers' Trail

Driving directions. Reach the hikers' trail (sometimes called "Jeep Road") by following First Avenue along the mountain base to its intersection with Monroe Street. Between houses, a yellow gate blocks vehicle access to an old track up the hillside. Park on the road shoulder (elevation 150 feet), and start immediately uphill.

Beyond the gate, round two switchbacks. Go left at a fork; the right fork dead-ends. Within 5 minutes, go right at another fork. Within a few more minutes, the wide main trail passes a large hemlock with an arrow spray-painted on its bark. Follow the narrow trail to the left to join the runners' trail (be sure to note where the hikers' trail intersects the runners' trail as the intersection could be hard to find on the way down). Stay on the wider main trail for a different adventure.

The main trail appears to end a short time later at a small, fenced reservoir near tree line. Walk along the fence uphill of the reservoir, and find a well-defined but much narrower footpath, sometimes called "Bench Trail," that parallels a creek. Part of the creek may be a hand-dug channel carved out in the early 1900s to bring drinking water to Seward. The mostly gentle grade leads to a ridge that drops to the northeast off Race Point. Round this ridge, and step into Marathon Bowl, a beautiful alpine cirque beneath the true summit of Marathon Mountain.

The northeast ridge is a longer, less-steep route to Race Point, but reaching the cirque will satisfy most hikers venturing this way. As you enter the cirque, listen for a waterfall, and make your way north to see it. Snow can obscure the upper end of this trail well into the summer.

To climb the true summit of Marathon Mountain (elevation 4,603 feet) by any route requires experience and mountaineering gear.

10 EXIT GLACIER AND HARDING ICE FIELD

Round trip: up to 7.5 miles
Hiking time: 4–8 hours
High point: 3,400 feet
Total elevation gain: 3,000 feet
Best: June–September
Maps: USGS Seward A7 NW, A8
Agency: Kenai Fjords National Park

While valley glaciers nestle between high peaks, ice fields bury mountains entirely or leave just their tops—called *nunataks*—jutting out of the ice. The Harding Ice Field Trail may be the only established trail in the country that leads to an ice field overlook. Getting there is a stiff uphill walk, but the trail parallels the frozen blue-white waterfall that is Exit Glacier all the way. Views of the glacier contrast sharply with the deep green of thick summer foliage and the magenta of fireweed blooms to create a memorable walk even for those who tire before reaching the highest point. Keep an eye out for mountain goats on the rocks above the trail and for black bears in the green lower meadows.

Driving directions. To reach the trailhead near the toe of Exit Glacier, drive to mile 3.7 of the Seward Highway, on the edge of the city of Seward, and turn west on Exit Glacier Road (marked). Proceed about 8.6 miles on this paved road to a parking area (elevation 400 feet) a short distance from a National Park Service nature center. Expect to pay a park entrance fee.

A paved, wheelchair-accessible path (bikes and pets not allowed) leads toward the nature center and the obvious hunk of ice spilling off the mountainsides. After ¼ mile, the paved trail ends near an information kiosk. A short distance farther, a "Harding Ice Field Trail" sign directs hikers to the right. The less ambitious will enjoy a network of short trails around the toe of the glacier, including close-up views (stay on trails to avoid falling ice) and a nature trail loop back to the ranger station.

On the Harding Ice Field Trail, hikers will appreciate the work of the Student Conservation Association. High school students have worked for many summers to carve a beautiful trail, with relatively easy grades, from the steep hillside. The view of the glacier through the trees and from frequent overlooks steadily improves.

Eventually, well above tree line, the trail becomes less distinct. Early in the season, steps in leftover snow will usually guide hikers. Later in the summer, if the trail seems to peter out as you crest a rise and get your first view of the ice field, look for an intermittent path that leads to the right of a black-rock cliff that faces Exit Glacier. Before reaching the cliff, the route

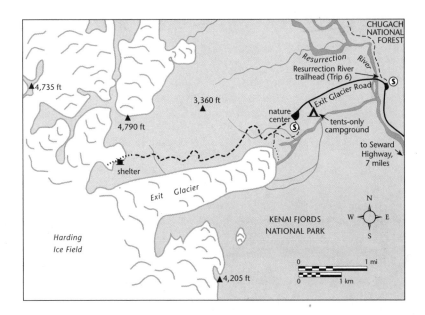

bears right and up the right-hand side of a creek to a saddle, crossing the creek just below the saddle crest. From there, the route is relatively straightforward. It is little more than half an hour from that spot to the high point overlooking the ice field and its many nunataks.

Hikers should prepare at any time of year for ice-cold winds that often blow off the Harding Ice Field, even on sunny days. Bad weather can roll in quickly in this area, too, and because of this, the Park Service has established an emergency mountain shelter near the ice field. It is on a hill of gravel and rock on the route, but it does not overlook the ice field. It cannot be reserved but may be used by anybody in bad weather. Limited camping is possible in this area. Wherever this route is above tree line, hikers should stay on the main trail and observe any park signs about trail use. Old scars evident on the tundra should be ample reminder that even walkers can impact the land. Those camping should set up only at the top end of the trail on bare rock and gravel or on snow to avoid damaging the fragile alpine plants that may take more than a century to regenerate.

Only experienced mountaineers with crevasse rescue training and proper equipment should venture onto the ice field. Park rangers lead summer naturalist walks on area trails, including treks to the ice field. Some other notes: (1) a small tents-only campground near the trailhead parking lot offers the only free camping in the Seward area; (2) Exit Glacier Road is not maintained in winter, from November 1 to May 1, but the road is used by skiers (and dog mushers and snowmobilers) when snow conditions are

Harding Ice Field spilling into Exit Glacier, with lupine, August
(John Wolfe Jr.)

good, and a Park Service cabin is available near the Exit Glacier trailhead for public use in the winter; and (3) the park's headquarters, which can provide more information, is in Seward, just south of the harbormaster's building and adjacent to the small boat harbor.

11 | LOST LAKE TRAVERSE

Traverse: 15 miles
Hiking time: 7–10 hours, or 2 days
High point: 2,150 feet
Total elevation gain: 2,350 feet northbound; 2,150 feet
    southbound
Best: July–September
Map: Trails Illustrated "Kenai Fjords National Park and
    Surrounding Area"
Agency: Chugach National Forest

In July this is perhaps the most beautiful trail the Kenai Peninsula has to offer. Climbing through a hemlock and spruce forest, the trail emerges above tree line on tundra and flowered meadows. The area was at one time heavily glaciated. Now brilliant blue and green lakes fill every depression, reflecting the snow-covered summits of surrounding mountains. Lost Lake, the largest, is forced into a strange shape by the topography. Parts of the alpine portion of trail are accented by stands of weathered, gnarled hemlocks. The area invites camping and exploring. Water is plentiful. A few small fish populate Lost Lake, and marmots abound in the nearby rock slides. The trail is good for family outings and ski or snowshoe trips.

Approach to Lost Lake from Primrose Campground, August (Dave Wolfe)

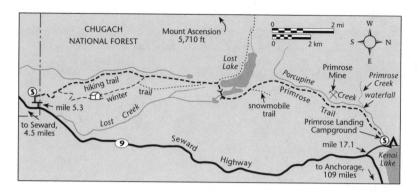

There are two trailheads. The northern trailhead is in Primrose Landing Campground on Kenai Lake, and the southern trailhead is in a housing subdivision outside Seward. Lost Lake is halfway between these points. The following pages describe a traverse from north to south, as the views are best looking south, but hikes out and back from either end are grand as well.

Driving directions. To reach the Primrose trailhead (north end), turn off the Seward Highway at mile 17.1 at a sign for Primrose Landing Campground (110 miles south of Anchorage). Drive about a mile to the end of the access road, and park in the boat ramp area at the entrance to the campground. The trailhead (elevation 450 feet) is about 1,000 feet back from the lake at the end of the campground road and is marked. To reach the southern trailhead, drive to mile 5.3 of the Seward Highway (5 miles north of Seward, 120 miles south of Anchorage). Turn west on Scott Way, and follow the road uphill 0.2 mile to a T intersection. Turn left on Heather Lee Lane. In 0.2 mile, just past a large building, turn right on Hayden Berlin Road. Drive 0.3 mile to the end of the road and the trailhead (elevation 250 feet).

Beginning at the Primrose end, the trail climbs gradually for about 5 miles through forest to tree line and then crosses about 2 miles of meadows and ridge tops to reach Lost Lake (elevation 1,913 feet). En route, take time for a short side trip on an unmarked route through the woods to a pretty waterfall a little more than 2 miles from the campground. If the clouds close in above tree line, follow wooden four-by-four markers to the lake. In some years snow may persist into July, making the trail above tree line hard to follow. If snow or fog obscures the way, note where the trail emerges onto the ridge so that you can find it if you return this way.

In the alpine areas, walking well off the trail to camp is easy. The mountain views are fantastic. Climbing to the summit of Mount Ascension (elevation 5,710 feet), the prominent peak west of Lost Lake, is a goal best left to mountaineers, who will need ice axes and crampons. However, scrambling part way up the steep lower slopes for a sweeping view is definitely recommended. A side trip, with easy walking over firm tundra, around the southwest edge of the lake and up the valley to the west brings a splendid

Lost Lake high country, August (Dave Wolfe)

view of the steep north side of Mount Ascension. Look for mountain goats and bears. An off-trail cross-country hike from here into miles of broad, high-country drainages is possible, with overlooks to Kenai and Cooper Lakes.

The trail skirts Lost Lake to the east, crossing Lost Creek on a bridge at about mile 7½. The bridge is generally snow-free from mid- to late June into September. Beyond the lake, the route climbs a bit, crossing a glacier-scarred bedrock bench before beginning a gradual descent. On a good day, the views across meadows, low bent hemlock, and the tops of the big trees on hills below to Resurrection Bay and surrounding peaks makes this as fine a walk as there is anywhere. Finally, the trail drops into the forest proper for the last 3 to 4 miles to the trailhead. Almost within shouting distance of the trailhead, the path crosses a creek bed. Most of the summer this is dry or a trickle, but it can leave hikers with wet feet well into June.

About 4 miles above the southern trailhead and 11 miles from Primrose Campground, there is a fork to the east. Look for ripe salmonberries in this area in August. The fork (marked) leads to the Dale Clemens Memorial Cabin. This picturesque spur reaches the cabin in about 1½ miles. The cabin, with views to Resurrection Bay, Seward, and the nearby Resurrection Peaks, can be reserved through the Forest Service nationwide reservations system (see Appendix). In summer, it is best to backtrack from the cabin to the main trail to descend to the southern trailhead. In winter, there is a trail that continues below the cabin, and it is the main access route to the high country after the snow gets deep. The winter trail below the cabin is not maintained for summer use; it is overgrown and wet, and may be hard to follow.

For those starting at the southern trailhead, there are minor forks in the first mile that might be puzzling. The first right-hand fork is a short alternate route, less steep than the main trail. The second junction is where the trails rejoin. A third intersection is the winter trail branching off to the right.

The winter trail is popular with snowmobilers. Lower elevations of the winter trail can be icy, fairly steep, and marginal for skiing, although there can be excellent springtime skiing in the vicinity of the cabin. Skiers may want to walk the first part of the trail.

The entire area is open to mining. There are active claims off the Primrose end of the trail. At least one miner has a permit to use an all-terrain vehicle on this portion of the trail to reach his claim.

The trail is closed to horses from April 1 through June 30. Mountain bikers should observe these dates to minimize trail erosion. Snowmobile closure dates may vary. Call the Forest Service for updated information (see Appendix).

12 | PTARMIGAN LAKE

Round trip: 7–15 miles
Hiking time: 3–8 hours
High point: 1,000 feet
Total elevation gain: 550 feet in, 250 feet out
Best: May–October
Maps: USGS Seward B6, B7 NE
Agency: Chugach National Forest

A turquoise beauty, Ptarmigan Lake reflects the mountains that surround it. Two trails lead from the highway to magnificent views across forested mountain slopes and join shortly before the lake. A 4-mile extension of the trail, with views of hanging glaciers across the water, continues around the lake to its east end.

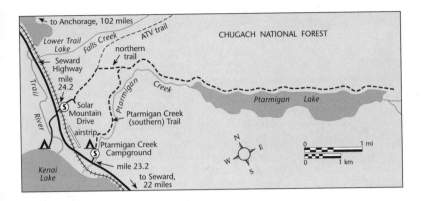

The trailheads are a mile apart, making a car shuttle easy for those who wish to use both access trails to make a loop, as described below. The Seward Highway is scheduled to be reconstructed in the next few years. When shoulders or a parallel path are added, it will be easier to walk the distance between trailheads. High grasses may obscure the turnoff to the northern trail when you return from Ptarmigan Lake, so the loop is best hiked beginning at the northern trailhead. Anglers will find grayling, salmon, Dolly Varden, and rainbow trout in Ptarmigan Creek and grayling in Ptarmigan Lake.

Driving directions. To reach the northern trailhead, drive to mile 24.2 of the Seward Highway (103 miles south of Anchorage). Just north of the Trail River Campground entrance, and on the opposite side of the highway, turn onto Solar Mountain Drive. Proceed east across railroad tracks, and park near the tracks (elevation 450 feet). The southern trailhead, for Ptarmigan Creek Trail, leaves from Ptarmigan Creek Campground (elevation 450 feet) at mile 23.2 of the Seward Highway. Use the campground driveway, and then find the trailhead parking lot (marked) on the right.

On foot from the northern trailhead, continue east a short distance. The road passes a house and an old log cabin. Respect private property. Near the old cabin, the main road turns right to another house. Instead of turning right, pass around a Forest Service gate straight ahead, and start up the trail. A sign may mark the trailhead: "Falls Creek 3; Ptarmigan Lake Access 1." Ptarmigan Lake is about 3 miles away. The first mile follows an old mining road.

Just up a hill, beyond a creek crossing and an old clearing, a marked fork to the right leaves the old road. The trail ascends a low timbered ridge and then contours along the mountainside at about 900 feet elevation, well above the valley floor. Look for glimpses of Ptarmigan and Kenai Lakes. As the views improve, this trail leads to an intersection with Ptarmigan Creek Trail, which originates at Ptarmigan Creek Campground.

The Ptarmigan Creek Trail, 3 miles long, begins at the campground and

Ptarmigan Lake, July (Gayle Nienhueser)

follows the tumbling clear creek upstream. Eventually, it turns away from the creek to climb through a quiet conifer forest to meet the northern trail on a steep grassy meadow high above the creek.

From the junction of the two trails, the trail descends slightly to Ptarmigan Lake (elevation 755 feet). This can be destination enough for a picnic or overnight camping, or continue around the north shore of the lake about 4 miles to the eastern end, which also offers good campsites. The route is reported to have once continued beyond Ptarmigan Lake into Paradise Valley. There is no continuing trail today, and the walking and routefinding are tough, but those with an exploring bent might want to bushwhack into this wild country.

Avalanche hazard precludes winter use of either trail beyond the first 1½ miles. Ptarmigan Creek Trail is closed to horses from April 1 through June 30 and to motorized vehicles May 1 through November 30. The routes to Ptarmigan Lake are not suitable for bicycles. Mountain bikers may use the northern trailhead and follow the mining road 3 miles to Falls Creek, although the route is difficult. Four-wheelers use the old road.

13 | JOHNSON PASS

Traverse: 23 miles
Allow: 2 days
High point: 1,450 feet
Total elevation gain: 900 feet southbound, 1,100 feet
  northbound
Best: June–September
Maps: USGS Seward C6, C7
Agency: Chugach National Forest

Between 1908 and 1910, the Alaska Road Commission constructed a trail for packhorses and dog teams through Johnson Pass en route to the gold fields of the Iditarod area. The first shipment of gold, more than a half million dollars worth, left Iditarod in December 1911 and took 54 days to reach Seward. This popular point-to-point trail follows portions of that route, now designated the Iditarod National Historic Trail. The country is a beautiful mix of forest and alpine terrain, placid lakes, and rowdy streams. The terrain is good for mountain biking, although the trail can be muddy, and there is potential for conflict with hikers.

Driving directions. To reach the Granite Creek (northern) trailhead just south of Turnagain Pass, drive to mile 63.8 of the Seward Highway (63 miles south of Anchorage). A 0.4-mile side road, marked Johnson Pass Trail, leads south to a parking area (elevation 700 feet). The southern trailhead (elevation 500 feet) is at mile 32.7 of the Seward Highway, near Upper Trail Lake and its fish hatchery.

From the Granite Creek trailhead, the route winds through open meadows and forest, crossing Center Creek (mile 2.2) and Bench Creek (mile 3.8) on bridges. Walking only as far as either bridge makes a pleasant day's

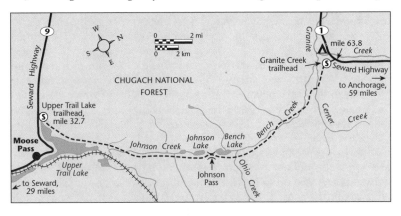

Waterfall overlook along Bench Creek, August (John Wolfe Jr.)

outing. Beyond the second bridge, the trail enters V-shaped Bench Creek valley and follows the creek to Ohio Creek and Bench Lake. There are a couple of short, steep, gravelly stretches. At the top of a long hill is a short, informal side path to an airy overlook of a waterfall. In this area, and through the pass, the grass grows tall and dense, as does cow parsnip (see "Plants," in the Introduction). The wildflowers hold their own. Note that the Trails Illustrated map (1996) incorrectly shows the trail remaining on the west side of Bench Creek; it actually crosses to the east side just before the steep climb.

After crossing Ohio Creek at mile 8.9, the trail follows the eastern shore of Bench Lake and climbs imperceptibly to Johnson Pass (mile 10; elevation 1,450 feet). South of Johnson Lake, the trail parallels Johnson Creek but is above the creek in the woods. About 9 miles south of the pass, after dipping through several creek drainages, the trail emerges on the shore of Upper Trail Lake and roughly parallels the shore to the southern trailhead.

Good campsites can be found at Johnson Pass above tree line and at the south end of Johnson Lake (mile 11). This trail is popular and gets enough traffic that there is on-going risk of aesthetic damage from carelessness. See "Leave No Trace," in the Introduction.

The Center Creek valley and the first 7 miles of trail from the southern trailhead make good ski trips, but stay well away from slopes that could avalanche (see "Avalanches," in the Introduction). Winter travel through the pass between the Bench Creek bridge and mile 12, which is 2 miles south of Johnson Lake, is not recommended due to severe avalanche hazard.

The trail from the Bench Creek bridge to the northern trailhead and all of the Center Creek drainage are closed to motorized vehicles year round; other parts of the trail are closed to them from May 1 through November 30. Bikers should observe the horse prohibition dates to avoid causing trail erosion.

14 | RESURRECTION PASS TRAIL SYSTEM

Traverse: up to 38.5 miles
Allow: 3–6 days
High point: 2,600 feet
Total elevation gain: 2,400 feet either direction
Best: June–September
Map: Trails Illustrated "Kenai National Wildlife Refuge and Adjacent Chugach National Forest"
Agency: Chugach National Forest

Hikers looking for a long trip, a good trail, mountain scenery, cabins, and fishing all at once will find them along the Resurrection Pass Trail. The most popular route, 38.5 miles between the Hope trailhead and the Sterling Highway, normally takes 3 days for strong hikers in good condition and 5 or more for families. It is one of few single track trails that makes a 2- or 3-day mountain-bike ride, but the trail is very popular with hikers and there is potential for conflict. This route was traveled in the late 1890s by gold seekers coming from Resurrection Bay to the gold fields near Hope. Today it is a designated National Recreation Trail. Several access options create a variety of possible trips, and the trip can be linked to the Russian Lakes and Resurrection River trail system for a more adventurous hike of up to 70 miles (see Trip 6).

The main trail from Hope follows the wooded Resurrection Creek valley and quickly narrows to a well-maintained path that occasionally

Juneau Lake Cabin, September (John Wolfe Jr.)

climbs in and out of side drainages. Above tree line, the trail is a narrow ribbon buried deep in wildflowers. Watch for moose, Dall sheep, marmots, and grizzly (brown) bears. Resurrection Pass itself is covered in low alpine tundra. The trail descends Juneau Creek valley through forests and beside mountain lakes to the Sterling Highway.

While the cabins are well spaced for a 5-day hike, it is not possible to reserve sequential cabins with a single reservation, and many people reserve only one. Therefore, if you wish to use a different cabin every night in summer, secure reservations as soon as they come available six months ahead (see Appendix for contact information). Because the cabins are popular, summer reservations for even a single cabin are hard to get. The lake cabins have boats for cabin renters, and there are several species of fish in the lakes, including Dolly Varden, rainbow trout, lake trout, and sockeye salmon. Campsites are easy to find.

Three other trails connect with this main route to make an intriguing trail system: Devils Pass Trail and Summit Creek Trail to the Seward Highway and Bean Creek Trail to Bean Creek Road off the Sterling Highway. A hike from the Hope trailhead to either of the Seward Highway trailheads is about 31 miles. From either of the Seward Highway trailheads to the south end of the Resurrection Pass Trail is about 27 miles. From one Seward Highway trailhead to the other is about 20 miles. The Bean Creek Trail is the least maintained and serves best as an alternate southern access that reduces the distance by up to 2½ miles, depending on where you park.

The following table lists points of interest along the main route, keyed to the map.

Number on Map	Point of Interest	Mileage	
Hope trailhead (northern end)		**0**	**38½**
1	Caribou Creek Cabin	7¼	31¼
2	Fox Creek Cabin	12¼ ·	26¼
3	East Creek Cabin	14¾	23¾
4	Resurrection Pass, elevation 2,600 feet	20	18½
5	Summit Creek Trail access at the pass	20	18½
6	Devils Pass Cabin and trail junction	21¾	16¾
7	Swan Lake Cabin	25¼	13
8	Juneau Lake Cabin	29¼	9¼
9	Romig Cabin on Juneau Lake	29¾	8¾
10	Trout Lake Cabin via a ½-mile side trail	31¼	7¼
11	Bean Creek Trail Junction	34	4½
12	Juneau Creek Falls	34½	4
Sterling Highway trailhead (southern end)		**38½**	**0**

Driving directions, Resurrection Pass Trail (Hope). To reach the northern trailhead, drive to mile 56.4 of the Seward Highway (70 miles south of Anchorage). Turn north onto Hope Highway, drive to mile 16.1, and then turn left onto the gravel Palmer Creek Road. After about 0.7 mile, follow the more-traveled route as it takes a sharp bend to the right onto Resurrection Creek Road (marked). Drive a total of 4 miles from Hope Highway to the trailhead (elevation 400 feet) at Resurrection Creek. The trail begins by crossing the creek on a bridge.

Driving directions, Resurrection Pass Trail (Sterling Highway). The trail (marked) begins in a parking lot just off the Sterling Highway at mile 53.1 (elevation 400 feet), just west of the Kenai River near Schooner Bend.

Driving directions, Bean Creek Trail. Drive to mile 48.6 of the Sterling Highway and, just east of the Kenai River, take Bean Creek Road to the north. Drive 0.9 mile, and turn right on Slaughter Ridge Road, which may not be marked except by a yellow "gate ahead" sign. It goes uphill through a bulldozed draw that looks forbidding. In dry conditions, two-wheel-drive cars may be able to make it 1.8 miles to a somewhat open gravelly area suitable for parking (elevation approximately 750 feet). Road conditions change, and soils get muddy and slippery when wet; it may not be prudent or even possible to go all the way in a two-wheel-drive car. Winter parking is generally in the pullout along Bean Creek Road (elevation approximately 475 feet).

Driving directions, Devils Pass Trail. Devils Pass Trail begins at mile 39.5 of the Seward Highway (elevation 1,000 feet). The trailhead is marked.

Driving directions, Summit Creek Trail. Turn west off the Seward Highway at mile 43.9, just south of Upper Summit Lake. Hidden behind trees is a

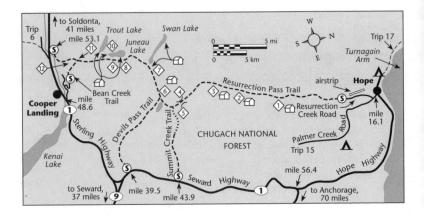

parking area and a trailhead bulletin board (elevation 1,350 feet). There is no sign on the highway.

Devils Pass Trail climbs from its trailhead to 2,400-foot Devils Pass. It joins Resurrection Pass Trail at about the same elevation. This is an easy (but freqently muddy) trail with a gradual elevation gain. The Summit Creek Trail climbs uphill, traversing the slope above and north of Summit Creek. Parts of the trail were originally a mining access route. Other old mining tracks are visible across the valley. The route crosses two passes (elevations 3,450 and 3,350 feet) and descends to Resurrection Pass. Finding Summit Creek Trail from Resurrection Pass Trail can be difficult.

Bean Creek Trail begins by following the Slaughter Ridge Road. About ¼ mile beyond the upper parking area noted in the driving directions, there is a fork. Go left, descending briefly, and cross a wet area on logs. There may be orange diamond-shaped markers. The route bends to the right and winds its way about 2 miles gradually uphill, crossing occasional mucky spots, to the Resurrection Pass Trail.

The trail from Hope to either the Sterling Highway or Bean Creek trailheads makes a fine ski or snowshoe tour in winter, but prepare for blizzards and cold winds above tree line. The Devils Pass Cabin has an oil heater, requiring users to haul diesel/stove oil. Devils Pass and Summit Creek Trails are not recommended for winter use due to avalanche hazard.

At this writing, the Forest Service had scheduled work on the Devils Pass Trail and the northern 21 miles of Resurrection Pass Trail by small bulldozer and by hand over several summers. The Forest Service was also intending to more strictly enforce a rule that use of the area within 300 feet of cabins is limited to those with reservations only.

Resurrection Pass and Devils Pass Trails are closed to vehicles, including snowmobiles, from February 16 through November 30 and closed to horses from April 1 through June 30 because of soft spring trail conditions. Mountain bikers should observe the horse prohibition to help prevent trail erosion.

15 | PALMER CREEK LAKES

Round trip: 3 miles (with options for more)
Hiking time: 1½–4 hours
High point: 2,950 feet or more
Total elevation gain: 850 feet
Best: July–September
Map: USGS Seward D7
Agency: Chugach National Forest

High in the hills above the old mining community of Hope is the scenic valley of Palmer Creek. Here, waterfalls and weathered hemlocks punctuate the rolling tundra. Higher yet, a hanging valley cradles two alpine lakes. This is a delightful day trip for children and agile grandparents alike. The only sobering note is the last 5 miles of road—high, narrow, winding, and slow, but normally drivable in dry weather by passenger cars. The road is unsafe for large campers and trailers but is good for mountain bikes.

Gold was first discovered along Palmer Creek by George Palmer in 1894. A rush to the Turnagain goldfields took place in 1896. Two towns, Hope and Sunrise, grew out of the rush, and as many as 5,000 people were reported living in the area in 1898. Palmer Creek was the site of early placer mining and, later, lode mining, beginning in 1911 with the Lucky Strike vein. The Lucky Strike and Hirshey Mines figure in the hikes offered here. Active mining continued into the 1930s, and some people still have claims in the area today.

Driving directions. At mile 56.4 of the Seward Highway (70 miles south of Anchorage), turn north on the Hope Highway, drive to mile 16.1, and then turn left onto the gravel Palmer Creek Road. In 0.7 mile, when the wider main road bends to the right (Resurrection Creek Road), continue straight on Palmer Creek Road. Seven miles from this intersection, at Coeur

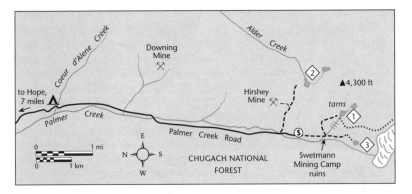

d'Alene Campground, the road maintenance becomes less consistent and the road smaller. There are two stream crossings with bridges and a couple of fords. The fords usually are minor, but beavers have been known to increase the water depth. About 4.4 miles from the campground, park at a rusted gate marked "Lucky Strike Mine" (elevation about 2,100 feet). The road beyond the gate is closed to motor vehicles year round. This track becomes narrower and steeper, there is a larger creek to ford, and turn-around opportunities are poor, so even if the gate is open, park at the gate.

On foot, follow the road beyond the gate less than ½ mile to a stream flowing from the east. This is the area marked as "Swetmann Camp" on topographic maps. The trail begins about 30 feet before the stream (elevation 2,250 feet). It climbs the hillside to the east and leads to a pretty hanging valley (marked 1 on the map) with tarns (alpine lakes). It passes a waterfall. Although steep, the grade is consistent, the footing is generally excellent, and the trail to the first lake is less than a mile long. The tarns, nestled at 2,950 feet below steep mountain walls, are fine picnic spots.

Salvaging porcupine quills, September (John Wolfe Jr.)

Hikers who enjoy rock scrambling will find many inviting ridges and small peaks in the area. A ridge particularly fine to climb is southwest of the tarns, between the tarns and the main Palmer Creek valley. It is an easy hour's walk up this ridge to a view of the small glacier at the head of Palmer Creek valley. This glacier, not shown on the topographic map, is the remnant of the glacier that carved the valley. Snow lingers on the ridges well into July.

Camp at Coeur d'Alene Campground or well away from the trails and lakes to minimize impact on the fragile tundra. Children will enjoy fishing for golden fin trout in the beaver ponds along Palmer Creek.

Mining relics may be private property and should be left alone. Elevation and northern exposure often keep the road in this valley closed until July. Avalanche danger makes this area hazardous in winter and spring.

Other Options

Another set of lakes (marked 2 on the map) lies at about 3,000 feet elevation at the head of Alder Creek, just over the ridge above the Hirshey Mine. Use the old vehicle track to the Hirshey Mine to reach these lakes; it turns off the main road just beyond the second bridge. Some of the Kenai Peninsula's elusive caribou may be spotted on upper Alder Creek. For another option, try following Palmer Creek Road up the valley to its end and beyond, where there is a small knob with a fine view. A tiny gemlike tarn (marked 3 on the map) lies hidden behind the knob.

16 | HOPE POINT

Round trip: 5 miles
Hiking time: 4–8 hours
High point: 3,708 feet
Total elevation gain: 3,600 feet
Best: May–October
Map: Imus Geographics "Chugach State Park"
Agency: Chugach National Forest

Spectacular, though very steep for a while, the route to Hope Point offers impressive views of Turnagain Arm from a different angle than is usually available. The vista north across Turnagain Arm puts into perspective familiar Chugach Mountains southeast of Anchorage. Check the Chugach State Park map to help locate favorite spots.

Driving directions. To reach the trailhead, drive to mile 56.4 of the Seward Highway (70 miles south of Anchorage). Turn north onto the Hope Highway (marked), and drive about 18 miles to the road's end, a mile beyond Hope, at Porcupine Campground. Park in a pullout at the campground sign

Grasshopper (John Wolfe Jr.)

(elevation 100 feet) or in the campground at the parking lot for the Gull Rock trailhead (Trip 17).

At Porcupine Creek, just beyond the campground entrance, a marked but minimally maintained foot trail follows the right-hand side of the stream. Although portions of the trail are very steep, the hike begins as a lovely creek-side walk beside water tumbling gently over mossy rocks. This meandering trail under a forest canopy lasts about a third of a mile.

The trail then climbs a slope to the right and continues steeply upward through forest. Soon the trees thin, and hikers enter an inclined meadow parkland studded with evergreens. Climb at least to the beginning of this area at the first rocky outcropping (elevation 800 feet), far enough to get a view up the Resurrection Creek valley. The valley is particularly pretty in autumn when the birch and aspen forest is a brilliant gold. Plan on taking about fifteen minutes to stroll along the stream and another half hour to reach the outcropping. To this point the trip is

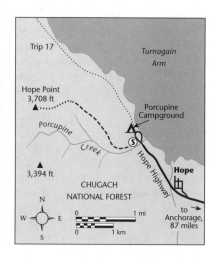

Overlooking Turnagain Arm, September (John Wolfe Jr.)

suitable for children with some experience, and they may be lured farther onward with the promise of seeing grasshoppers once you break out of the trees. At the outcropping you are nearly at tree line. The trail continues upward very steeply for perhaps another half hour. Then the angle eases, and the route all the way to Hope Point (elevation 3,708 feet) is laid out ahead along the broad crest of a ridge. Follow this ridge and then head left and up steeply again toward the top of Hope Point.

En route are sweeping views of Turnagain Arm, the mountains rimming it, Cook Inlet, and Fire Island. Watch for a bore tide, the well-defined leading wave of an incoming tide. Grass and moss with scrub hemlock and a few alder patches, crowberries, bearberries, caribou lichen, and ground cedar cover the slopes. Moose and bear droppings are abundant, so watch for the animals themselves. For those staying in the campground late in the season, the route is a particularly fine evening hike, because the sun stays up far longer on the ridge than at the campsite.

On the steepest stretches, trail erosion is becoming a problem. Hikers should try to stay on the trail and not contribute to making the eroded section wider by trampling the fragile tundra plants alongside.

From the top of Hope Point, the ridge to the south beckons for miles. Lack of water is the most limiting factor (expect no water after Porcupine Creek), although in early summer snow patches should be available for melting. Plan to spend as much time as possible in this alpine wonderland.

The trail is closed to off-road motorized vehicles May 1 through November 30 but is not practical for them in winter. The route is not highly recommended in winter because of the potential for avalanches.

17 | GULL ROCK

Round trip: 10.2 miles
Hiking time: 4–7 hours
High point: 620 feet
Total elevation gain: 520 feet in, 480 feet out
Best: May–October
Map: USGS Seward D8
Agencies: Chugach National Forest and Kenai National Wildlife Refuge

To enjoy an easy trail with intermittent views of the ocean, take this woodsy path to Gull Rock along the southwest side of Turnagain Arm. Watch for moose on land, beluga whales in the water, and bald eagles in the air. The views of the Arm and the mountains beyond are especially nice in spring and fall when the trees bordering the trail are free of leaves. Hikers of any age will appreciate this gentle trail.

The trail, an old wagon road built in the late 1920s, leaves the Hope area and parallels Turnagain Arm west for 5.1 miles. Although today's trail ends at Gull Rock, the wagon road—no longer maintained or free of brush—once connected with the broad flat area west of the Kenai Mountains, where a tractor trail now follows a natural gas pipeline from the Swanson River oil field to a crossing of Turnagain Arm. The reminders of earlier days are fascinating: the remains of a cabin and stable on Johnson Creek near the end of the trail, a mossy old bridge that once crossed the creek, and the ruins of a sawmill.

Driving directions. To reach the trailhead, drive to mile 56.4 of the Seward Highway (70 miles south of Anchorage). Turn north onto the Hope Highway (marked), and drive about 18 miles to the road's end, a mile beyond Hope, at Porcupine Campground. The trailhead (elevation 100 feet) is at the far end of the campground loop.

The trail begins as a wide path through alder, ferns, and devil's club,

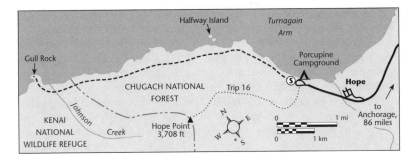

then enters spruce forest, some killed by spruce bark beetles. Blowdowns may cross the trail although the Forest Service generally has the trail cleared by early to mid-June. A nice destination for a short trip is an overlook about a mile and half down the trail and right above Halfway Island. A 15-foot side trail (just before two boulders) leads through thick spruce forest to the cliff top, great views, and some nice sitting rocks.

Winding along the shoreline well above tidewater, the trail reaches an elevation of 620 feet at one point before it drops back down to Gull Rock. The way is never steep, and walking is pleasant, although along with a lot of bumpy roots there may be a few slippery spots. Breaks in the trees afford views of the Arm and shoreline. The vegetation along the trail varies from pleasant birch and aspen woods to alder-choked gullies, from stately hemlock forests carpeted by deep moss to a tundra-like area with tiny spruce, mosses, lichens, lingonberries, and saxifrages. At one point the trail crosses a steep, straight avalanche gully that ends in Turnagain Arm. (Snow lingers here into early June; use caution in crossing it.)

Gull Rock, late May (Helen Nienhueser)

Near Johnson Creek the trail enters the Kenai National Wildlife Refuge. Beyond Johnson Creek, continue on the trail to the rocky promontory of Gull Rock (elevation 140 feet). At the trail's end, sit and listen to the turbulent water swirl around the rocks below as the tides flow in and out. On the other side of Turnagain Arm, a tiny stream of cars flows by on the Seward Highway near McHugh Creek Picnic Area.

Water can be found along the trail, but the only reasonable tent sites are at Gull Rock, where fresh water is not immediately at hand and where, unfortunately, some campers have impacted the area for all. Some trees have been denuded for firewood, and there are multiple old fire pits. This is best treated as a day hike, but those who do camp should bring a gas stove and avoid building a fire. The best camping is at Porcupine Campground.

The trail is open to mountain bikes as far as the boundary with the Kenai National Wildlife Refuge, although the proliferation of exposed tree roots will discourage all but hard-core riders. The trail is closed to motorized vehicles from May 1 through November 30 and to horses from April 1 through June 30. Mountain bikers should observe the horse prohibition to avoid causing trail erosion when the trail is soft. Also, cyclists should recognize that the route is popular with walkers of all ages and should not take the trail's easy grades as invitation to ride so fast as to surprise them.

18 | TURNAGAIN PASS SKI TOUR

Round trip: 3–6 miles
Skiing time: 3–5 hours
High point: 2,200 feet
Total elevation gain: 1,200 feet
Best: November–April
Map: USGS Seward D6
Agency: Chugach National Forest

For a delightful ski or snowshoe tour, try Turnagain Pass, which generally is buried in deep snow during winter and is one of the few places with separate areas designated for skiers and snowmobilers. Winter was meant to be like this—snow crystals glinting in the sunlight or huge flakes falling softly among thick hemlock trees, with a backdrop of towering snowy peaks. The Forest Service has designated the west side of the highway for snowmobiles and the east side for nonmotorized winter sports. At this writing, the Forest Service was planning a summer route to Center Ridge, promising year-round access to this scenic alpine hilltop.

Driving directions. To reach the trailhead (elevation 1,000 feet), drive to mile 68 of the Seward Highway and the Turnagain Pass winter sports area,

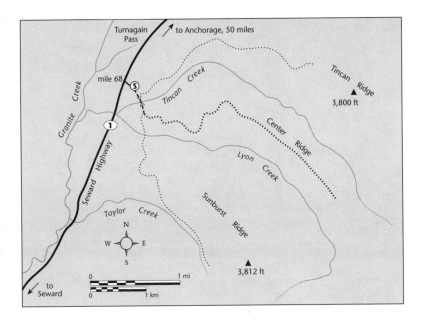

about 50 miles south of Anchorage. Access to the parking area for skiers and snowshoers, on the east side of the highway, is 0.2 mile south of the snowmobilers' pullout, which is west of the highway.

On skis, there are several options. This description focuses on a tour up Center Ridge, the low hump that divides Tincan and Lyon Creeks, but telemark skiers have made the higher mountains on either side of Center Ridge some of their favorite destinations.

Depending on previous ski traffic, the main trail may appear to head to the left, as you face away from the highway. This is the telemarkers' Tincan Ridge route. To access the easier Center Ridge route, head slightly to the right and away from the highway, descending gently to a bridge over the small gorge of Tincan Creek (in summer, there is an easy winding path to the bridge). Cross the gorge, and proceed straight ahead, angling up a broad slope and beneath powerlines. The route bends to the left and heads into the conifer forest, following small natural meadows. It bends back to the right, then left again before leveling somewhat and following the base of Center Ridge, which now lies to your left. Snow hangs heavily on the trees, creating myriad imaginary giants and monsters. Look for intermittent markers on tree trunks, imperfectly indicating the trail for the first mile.

After about a mile, the route swings left and mounts the base of Center Ridge, climbing through a treeless area to a low spot on the ridge crest. Check snow stability before climbing the open slope to the ridge. Do not continue into the narrow Lyon Creek valley along the base of the ridge; the slopes on either side of Lyon Creek could avalanche.

Hilltops of Center Ridge, March (Gretchen Nelson)

Even a short trip winding through these snow-laden trees is an excursion into the best that Alaska's winters have to offer. Tree line, at about elevation 2,000 feet and 1½ miles from the parking area, makes a good destination for a short day. If time allows, continue on the crest of this rolling ridge, traversing along the north side of the higher knobs, until the route begins to climb toward a mountain peak. In midwinter the sun seldom reaches Center Ridge, so dress warmly. Fortunately, wind is unusual there. Jagged white mountain ridges rise all around, making this an unforgettable experience.

The summer route, still taking shape as this edition went to press, crosses the bridge and roughly parallels the winter route, but is not exactly the same. At this writing, a trail was flagged, partly brushed, difficult to follow, and subject to changing plans. Check with the U.S. Forest Service Glacier Ranger District (see Appendix) for current trail conditions. Once the new route is cut through and well established, it may become the favored winter route as well.

North of Center Ridge is the much higher Tincan Ridge. The Tincan Ridge Trail is popular with telemark skiers and backcountry snowboarders. The route, which veers left shortly after leaving the parking area, often splits into several trails, but they converge to one before the route becomes truly steep. On the opposite side of Center Ridge, to the right and beyond the point where the Center Ridge route enters the forest, is a less-used route into Taylor Creek or up what is known as Sunburst Ridge. If there is no previous track, pick your way from meadow to meadow up the hill and into this higher valley to the south. Either of these would require bushwhacking for summer access. The first pullouts on the east side of the highway both north and south of Turnagain Pass provide alternate access, respectively, to Tincan Ridge and Sunburst Ridge.

Most skiers on both of these alternate routes use climbing skins on the bottoms of their skis for extra grip while ascending, and any existing tracks are likely to be too steep and frustrating for skiers without skins (this could be the case on Center Ridge, as well, so be prepared to break your own trail on the few steeper parts, even if there is a good trail leaving the parking area). All these routes, and especially the alternate routes to the higher ridges, should be undertaken only by those trained in avalanche avoidance and rescue. Experienced backcountry skiers have died in avalanches on the high mountain slopes. Before venturing out in the snowy Alaska mountains, take one of many interesting avalanche seminars offered to the public each winter (see "Avalanches," in the Introduction).

The east side of the Seward Highway from Bench Creek to Ingram Creek, including the Turnagain Pass area, is closed to motorized vehicles year round.

PORTAGE TO POTTER

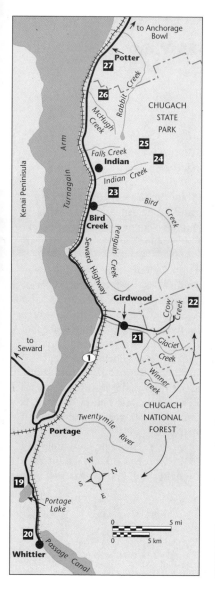

Portage is an old townsite at the head of the Turnagain Arm, and Potter, at the edge of urban Anchorage, is now the headquarters for Chugach State Park. The area from Portage to Potter, stretching between the Kenai Peninsula and Anchorage, offers a spectacular drive along fjordlike Turnagain Arm, with a lot of hikes along the way. Portage Valley in Chugach National Forest, at the southern end of this section, is the state's most-visited tourist destination. Girdwood hosts the state's major ski resort. North of Girdwood, the Seward Highway runs through Chugach State Park with numerous pullouts, waysides, and trailheads.

Above: *Red fox* (Dave Wolfe)

Opposite: *Turnagain Arm from Table Rock (Trips 26 and 27), September* (Gayle Nienhueser)

19 | BYRON GLACIER VIEW

Round trip: 1.6 miles
Hiking time: 1 hour
High point: 300 feet
Total elevation gain: 100 feet
Best: June–October
Map: USGS Seward D5 SW
Agency: Chugach National Forest

This wide gravel trail is a delightful walk for families with small children, for Aunt Minnie, and for spry great-grandfather. An easy hike with no climbing, the trip is exciting for those who have never seen rugged mountain and glacier terrain up close. Bring a picnic lunch and relax in the heart of snow-and-ice country.

Driving directions. From Portage, at mile 78.9 of the Seward Highway (48 miles south of Anchorage), drive 5.1 miles east on the Portage Glacier Highway. At a sign for the Begich Boggs Visitor Center take the right-hand fork. Go another 1.1 miles from this fork, taking a second right-hand turn away from the visitor center, and find the Byron Glacier trailhead parking area on the right (elevation 200 feet). The continuing road leads another mile to the departure point for summer boat tours of Portage Lake.

On foot, follow the trail south to a fine view of Byron Glacier and snow-capped Byron Peak. The alders along the pathway make wonderful horses for young children to ride. Byron Creek, along the last half of the trail, is handy for throwing stones into; the vast quantities of stream-washed stones build into tottering towers and fortresses.

About a mile from the parking area, a large, permanent, snowfield is a remnant of avalanches that swept across the valley in previous winters; it is great for summer snow fights. This snowfield should be approached with

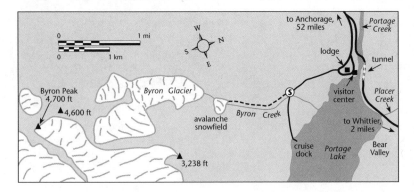

Leftover snow near Byron Glacier, August (Gretchen Nelson)

caution. There could be crevasses, and unwary hikers could fall into the ice cave beneath the snowfield and into Byron Creek. The snowfield is beyond the end of the maintained trail; the route to reach it is rocky with several small streams to step across.

Look on the snowfield for ice worms—black, less than an inch long, and slender as a thread. Yes, they really do exist! They look like tiny pieces of black hair. In the evening and on cool, cloudy days, these tiny annelids, relatives of the earthworm, emerge onto the surface of the snow where they eat pollen and algae. Because they can live only near the freezing point of water, ice worms must escape from the heat of the sun or the subfreezing cold of winter. They do this by sliding into the snow or ice between crystal faces, an amazing niche in the ecosystem. The search for ice worms turns a cloudy late afternoon into an adventure. A spoon is useful for turning over or scraping away snow in the search. But don't touch them—the heat of your hand would, most likely, kill them. For reasons not understood, ice worms are not found on all glaciers, but they are often found on the snow and ice of Byron Valley.

Traveling onto the glacier itself is for experienced and properly equipped mountaineers only. Do not venture into ice caves or near towering ice faces, any of which can collapse.

Although summer temperatures are cooler than in Anchorage, the Byron Valley is protected from the icy winds that blow across Portage Lake. Here the sun is warm. For camping, use one of the Forest Service campgrounds along the entrance road. Considerable avalanche danger makes Byron Valley unsafe during winter and spring (see "Avalanches," in the Introduction).

View across Portage Lake to Byron Valley, March (John Wolfe Jr.)

Ask at the visitor center for information on the two short nature trails in the Portage Valley and the Trail of Blue Ice. Late in the summer of 2000, construction began on the Trail of Blue Ice, leading from the Williwaw Salmon Viewing area, about mile 4.2 on the Portage Glacier Highway, toward the Begich Boggs Visitor Center. When completed, this trail will be handicapped accessible, good for bicycles, and will run much of the length of the valley, connecting various points of interest along the way.

For winter trips in this area see Trip 20, Portage Pass. Byron Valley, Portage Lake, and Bear Valley are closed to off-road vehicles year round and to horses from April 1 through June 30.

20 | PORTAGE PASS

Round trip: 2 miles to viewpoint, 4 miles to Portage Lake
Hiking time: 2–5 hours
High point: 750 feet
Total elevation gain: 700 feet to viewpoint (600 feet additional upon return from Portage Lake)
Best: July–September
Map: USGS Seward D5 SW
Agency: Chugach National Forest

On a good day, the first part of this hike offers the greatest reward for effort expended of any hike in this book. In less than a mile, after a relatively easy climb that gains about 700 feet of elevation, the trail reaches a breathtaking view of Portage Glacier and the black, glacier-laden peaks that rise above it. With somewhat more effort you can reach the shore of Portage Lake, some 600 feet below, and enjoy what is most likely a private view of this fast disappearing glacier.

The strategic location of Portage Pass, between Turnagain Arm and ice-free Passage Canal, gave it an historic role. Hundreds of years ago Alaska Natives and Russians used it as a trading route, crossing the pass on Portage Glacier. Following the discovery of gold in the Turnagain Arm area in the early 1890s, Alaska's first gold rush began. When Cook Inlet was clogged with ice flows, ships dropped prospectors at Passage Canal. The approach to the glacier was so steep that ropes and pulleys were required

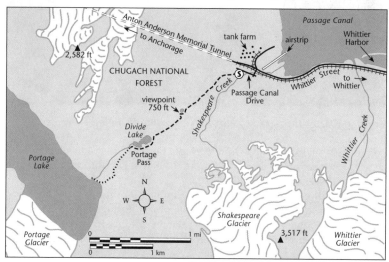

Portage Glacier from trail to Portage Pass, August (Helen Nienhueser)

to pull heavily loaded sleds up the grade. Portage Pass is also a major flyway for migrating birds, including arctic terns, sandhill cranes, swans, ducks, and geese.

Driving directions. From Portage at mile 78.9 of the Seward Highway (48 miles south of Anchorage), drive the paved Portage Glacier Highway east toward Portage Lake. At mile 5.1 take the left fork toward the Whittier tunnel. Drive through the first tunnel into Bear Valley, and, at mile 6.7, queue up for the next opening of the second tunnel. This 2-mile tunnel, the longest in North America, is shared by cars and trains and operates in one direction at a time. Cars are allowed through for a short period every hour or two from early morning until late evening in summer. There is a not-insignificant toll. Check the Alaska Department of Transportation website, listed in the appendix, for the current schedule and cost.

On the Whittier side of the tunnel, take the first right, cross the railroad tracks and Shakespeare Creek, then turn right at a cinder block building onto Passage Canal Drive (likely not marked). Proceed about 1,000 feet, recrossing Shakespeare Creek, to near the end of this road. Eventually, the Forest Service intends to construct a trailhead here. Park on the edge of the road and find a grassy old road heading toward the pass. The old road, lined by alder and salmonberry bushes, climbs to Portage Pass. The first part of it currently crosses private land; please stay on the trail. Look behind occasionally for great views of Passage Canal. At the top, the road disappears into a tiny pond. Pause to enjoy the spectacular view of Portage Glacier or climb the rocky escarpments on either side and sit awhile amidst mountain splendor.

Beyond the pond the trail narrows. In a few feet take a narrow footpath to the left, downhill, and pick up the continuing old road toward the glacier and Divide Lake. Head left around the lake to its outlet, which drains toward Portage Lake. Start downhill along the outlet for 75 to 100 yards until you see a large boulder with rocks piled on top. This marks an informal path through the brush.

At the time of this writing the descent to Portage Lake was a challenging exercise in routefinding, alder bashing, and rock hopping. Alders cover most of the slope, interspersed with occasional open patches. Follow the path as best you can, roughly paralleling the outlet stream. Eventually the path reaches an overgrown dry streambed that can be followed to the lakeshore (the outlet stream is to the right of the dry stream as you go downhill). At the lakeshore the stream is normally easy to cross, and a 30-foot high moraine on the opposite side of the stream offers fine views of the lake and Portage Glacier. Watch and listen for blocks of ice calving into the lake. Wave to the tourists if the tour boat goes by.

Portage Glacier is retreating rapidly. When the first edition of this book was published in 1972, Portage Glacier extended beyond Portage Pass toward the lake outlet and was visible from the Begich Boggs Visitor Center. Those who hiked downhill from Divide Lake could touch the glacier. Elevation loss was reported to be about 200 feet, rather than 600.

The first few hundred feet of the trail is expected to be moved closer to the mountain to avoid private land. Check with the Chugach National Forest Glacier District Office for current information (see Appendix for contact information). Train service to Whittier from Anchorage is available, and bus service through the tunnel to Whittier may be available. Check with the Anchorage Convention and Visitors Bureau regarding bus service (see Appendix).

Portage Glacier from Portage Lake below Portage Pass (Helen Nienhueser)

Watch the weather in Portage Pass, and go prepared. The pass can be a wind funnel, and Whittier has one of the highest levels of rainfall in the state.

Winter Trips

The Forest Service advises against winter use of this trail due to potential avalanche danger. However, those with proper avalanche training and equipment may make the trip on skis when they determine conditions are right. Park at the Begich Boggs Visitor Center, and ski across the lake when the ice is at least 4 inches thick. Give icebergs frozen into the lake a wide berth, because they sometimes roll, splitting the ice around them. The route from the lake to the pass is relatively gentle and may make a good ski even if conditions are not good for a traverse. The route down toward Passage Canal is narrow and is reportedly treacherous when icy. Follow the best terrain and not the summer trail.

Skiing on Portage Lake is tempting though potentially dangerous. Avoid thin ice near the lake's outlet into Portage Creek and at the mouth of Placer Creek. If pressure ridges are present, watch for open water. Do not travel near the ice cliffs of Portage Glacier; in winter the glacier may calve from the bottom, sending waves that break up the lake ice near the glacier.

A good ski or snowshoe trip is Bear Valley, in between the two Whittier access tunnels. Limited parking is available in the staging area for the second tunnel. Stay away from the mountainsides to avoid avalanche danger. Portage Lake and Bear Valley are closed to off-road vehicles year-round and to horses from April 1 to June 30.

21 | WINNER CREEK GORGE– GIRDWOOD IDITAROD LOOP

Winner Creek Gorge
Round trip: 5.5 miles
Hiking time: 2–4 hours
Total elevation gain: 260 feet in, 200 feet out

Winner Creek–Iditarod Loop
Loop trip: 7.7 miles
Hiking time: 4–6 hours
Total elevation gain: 500 feet

High point: 600 feet
Best: late May–October
Map: USGS Seward D6 NW
Agencies: Chugach National Forest and Municipality
of Anchorage

A pleasant trail through tall spruce and hemlock trees at the base of Mount Alyeska leads to the plunging waters of Winner Creek gorge and is a popular half day hike for Girdwood visitors and residents. A bridge over Winner Creek and a hand-pulled tram over Glacier Creek make it possible to connect with a portion of the restored Iditarod National Historic Trail and walk a loop trip. Watch for moose and bears.

Winner Creek Gorge
Driving directions. At mile 90 of the Seward Highway (37 miles south of Anchorage), turn north onto Alyeska Highway and drive 3 miles to its end at a T intersection with Arlberg Avenue in the ski-resort town of Girdwood. Turn left, and follow Arlberg 1.1 miles to its end at the posh Alyeska Prince Hotel. Park in the hotel lot (elevation 350 feet), and make your way on the hotel's trail network around either side of the hotel toward the mountain. To find the Winner Creek Trail, look for the tram cable exiting the hotel and disappearing up Mount Alyeska. A Winner Creek Trail sign, on the edge of the woods about 50 yards uphill from the tram terminal, marks the route. At this point, cross under the cable and follow the trail into the forest.

Under the trail's tall conifers, ferns, blueberry bushes, and mosses carpet the forest floor. The trail crosses pleasant creeks and short sections of muskeg on bridges and boardwalks.

About 1¾ miles from the hotel, the hiking trail comes to a T intersection above Winner Creek. Go left to Winner Creek gorge. The right branch goes

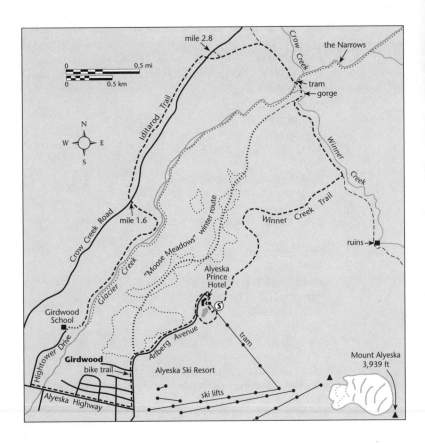

toward the headwaters of Winner Creek, with bushwhacking access to Twentymile River and other intriguing areas.

The gorge (elevation 400 feet) is less than a mile away to the left and well worth the walk. Go past the wide snowcat bridge to the narrow hiker's bridge over the gorge, a spray-in-your-face viewing platform over roiling water. A side route cut through the trees (apparent as you approach the bridge) is a winter ski route but is too wet for summer walking.

The route to upper Winner Creek is narrow but reasonably good for more than a mile from the intersection. It passes a collapsed historic cabin. After the trail leaves the hemlock forest, the brush begins to close in. There is reasonable camping before the brush gets thick. Bushwhacking and possibly some stream walking are required beyond. (Take USGS map Seward D6 NE with you for this trip.) Except for the upper reaches of Winner Creek, the trails are gentle with no severe ups or downs.

Winner Creek Trail is closed to horses and off-road vehicles, including snowmobiles, year round. The trail is not appropriate for mountain bikes due to hazards, such as narrow boardwalks and short sight distances, and root and vegetation damage. The trail is managed by the U.S. Forest Service on an easement through state-owned land. Upper Winner Creek is in the National Forest.

Winner Creek–Girdwood Iditarod Loop

Girdwood volunteers have reopened the Girdwood section of the historic Iditarod Trail that went from Seward over Cross Pass and north to the gold fields of the Interior. Construction of a tram over Glacier Creek in 2000 links the Winner Creek Trail with the Girdwood Iditarod Trail and makes possible a 7.7-mile loop. About 2½ miles of the loop are on paved bike trails through the community of Girdwood between the Alyeska Prince Hotel and the Girdwood School. You can walk the whole loop, you can bike this section, or you can leave a second car at the hotel or the school and do a 5½-mile walk.

Driving directions. To leave a car at the hotel, see directions for Winner Creek gorge. To leave a car at the school, drive the Alyeska Highway 2.2 miles from the Seward Highway to Hightower Drive, just before the bridge over Glacier Creek. Turn left and continue north to the Girdwood School at the end of the road. Leave the car in the school parking lot (elevation 150 feet).

Winner Creek gorge, August (Helen Nienhueser)

Glacier Creek tram nearly complete in June 2000 (John Wolfe Jr.)

The following description assumes that you start at the hotel. From the hotel parking lot, find the bike trail that parallels Arlberg Avenue and follow it through tall evergreen trees back to Alyeska Highway, where you turn right on another bike trail that parallels the highway. Follow this to Hightower Drive, just past the bridge over Glacier Creek. Turn right, and follow Hightower to its end at the school. Bikes can be locked to the fence here. To find the trail, face Glacier Creek and walk to the far left corner of the playing field that lies between the school and the creek. There find a gravel trail that parallels Glacier Creek, heading upstream through hemlock and white spruce with some nice views of the creek and the mountains beyond. In less than a mile the trail leaves the creek and heads uphill to Crow Creek Road. There, a small parking area (mile 1.6 of Crow Creek Road) provides another access point to the trail.

Cross Crow Creek Road and pick up the Iditarod Trail on the other side and slightly to the right. This stretch of the trail, a little over a mile long, is often in the forest but opens abruptly on a meadow with wonderful views of the glaciers and mountains at the back of Girdwood valley. Beyond the meadow the trail recrosses Crow Creek Road. Pick it up again on the other side, about 50 feet to the left. Shortly after the trail enters the woods there is a fork to the left that leads back to the road and another parking area and access to the trail (mile 2.8, Crow Creek Road). To reach the tram, take the right fork, which terminates in an old road. Turn right toward the creek and in a few minutes you will reach the top of a steep hill. A choice of trails leads straight downhill or to the right. Both go to the same place; the trail to the right reaches the bottom in a long switchback. Here is the tram and a much more lush world of ferns and alders as well as spruce and hemlock.

The tram takes upper body strength and is easiest with two people, one in the tram and one on the platform, both pulling. Take gloves. The view upstream from the tram midpoint is magnificent and worth a pause.

From the tram it is about a 5-minute walk to Winner Creek. Follow the main trail. From the Winner Creek gorge, follow the trail back to the hotel (see description above).

Winter Trails

Winner Creek Trail makes good skiing, although it is not groomed. Tracks are usually set by users. The Forest Service does not recommend winter use of this trail because it runs below slopes where avalanche control work is done with explosives. Check with the Ski Patrol or Alyeska Resort for avalanche control times. Upper Winner Creek is not recommended because of potential avalanches (see "Avalanches," in the Introduction). Most skiers, especially when snowfall is lean, prefer to ski the groomed Moose Meadows below the hiking trail, starting at the edge of Girdwood at the first curve in Arlberg Avenue. Park at Alyeska Resort, near the base of the chairlifts, or at the Alyeska Prince Hotel rather than along the street. These meadows connect with Winner Creek Trail to form a possible ski loop. As on any ski touring trail, be careful not to destroy the center ridge between the ski tracks, and please keep boots, snowshoes, and dogs off ski trails that others work hard to maintain.

A special treat for the coldest part of the coldest winters is a ski trip up Glacier Creek. Park at the school as described above and make your way to the creek. From the tram area upstream, the creek flows through a canyon where the ice will often be solid even though there is open water near the Alyeska Highway. The most scenic part of the canyon is upstream of the confluence with Crow Creek, and beyond the Narrows the valley opens to the headwaters of Glacier Creek with mountains and hanging glaciers all around. Your weight is so well distributed on skis that the danger of breaking through the ice is slight if it has been cold enough, but beware of thin ice, testing any questionable spots. You can ski up to 12 miles round trip. Dress warmly; it is cold in the canyon.

Still another treat for strong track skiers, those who can make telemark turns, and winter hikers is the snowcat trail that leads from Moose Meadows across Winner Creek and up onto the slopes above.

22 | CROW PASS AND EAGLE RIVER TRAVERSE

Distance: to pass 8 miles round trip; traverse 26 miles
Hiking time: round trip to Crow Pass 4–6 hours;
    traverse 2–3 days
High point: 3,550 feet
Total elevation gain: 2,000 feet northbound, 3,050 feet
    southbound (traverse)
Best: mid-June–September
Maps: USGS Anchorage A6, A7
Agencies: Chugach National Forest and Chugach State Park

The hike to Crow Pass offers a pleasant day trip into a beautiful mountain wilderness with gold mine relics, glaciers, alpine lakes, and wildflowers. The route follows a dogsled route once traveled by mail carriers, explorers, and prospectors. Experienced hikers can take a 2- or 3-day point-to-point trip on the old Iditarod Trail through Chugach State Park to the Eagle River Nature Center.

In the early 1900s, the trail over Crow Pass was part of the Iditarod winter sled trail through the mountains between Turnagain Arm and Knik Arm, en route from Seward to Knik, and thence to Interior goldfields. It was used by pack animals as well as dogs and was used alternately with Indian Pass

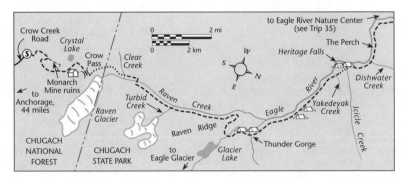

Trail (Trip 24), the preferred route. Steady use of both trails probably ended in the early 1920s when regular railroad service began between Seward and Fairbanks.

The old mail trail over Crow Pass continued down Raven Creek and Eagle River. Today, this is a well-traveled hike popular on long weekends. It can be done faster; during the annual Crow Pass Crossing mountain run, top athletes manage the trail in 3 to 5 hours, despite its obstacles.

Driving directions. To reach the Crow Pass trailhead, drive to mile 90 of the Seward Highway (37 miles south of Anchorage) and turn north onto Alyeska Highway toward the community of Girdwood. As the highway rounds a curve to the right at mile 2, turn left onto Crow Creek Road, a minimally maintained gravel road. Continue 5 miles to a bridge and, immediately thereafter, a fork. Go right and uphill another mile to the road's end at the trailhead parking area (elevation 1,550 feet). The trail begins at the far end of the parking area. Driving directions for the southern end of the trail appear under Trip 35, The Perch. Reasonably priced van service for backpackers may be available in Anchorage and is especially helpful to those completing the traverse.

On foot, follow an old mining track as it climbs in switchbacks to brushline. As the trail nears 2,500 feet elevation and the ruins of the Monarch Mine, 1.7 miles from the parking area, the trail forks. The left hand fork leads to the mine, a hard rock gold mine that operated from 1906 to 1948. This fork passes remains of what were once a mill and crew's quarters; above in the cliffs are mine adits. Maintaining elevation, walk along the hillside behind the mine ruins for a short side trip into the beautiful canyon through which Crow Creek cascades. Stay on the trails to help prevent erosion and for safety; people have fallen trying to scramble off the path here.

To reach Crow Pass, take the right fork (a switchback) shortly before the mine. This trail is *much* less steep than the old route above the mine ruins and safer. It also provides spectacular views down the valley. At mile 3 (3,500 feet elevation), a U.S. Forest Service cabin is available for public use in the summer by permit only (see Appendix for information on making reservations). The cabin is not rented during winter and early spring because of avalanche danger.

Nearby Crystal Lake, nestled beneath a steep mountain wall and rimmed by wildflowers in July, is a splendid destination for many. West of the lake lies the tip of Crow Glacier. To see Raven Glacier, about a mile farther, hike past the cabin, following rock cairns through the pass (elevation 3,600 feet). While Dall sheep are common in the Chugach Mountains near Anchorage, this is one of the few places where hikers may also see mountain goats.

Camping spots abound in both the mine and pass areas, although snow often persists well into June at the pass. Water is available. Campfires are not permitted. Snow showers and strong winds are possible any time, so

View to south from mile 1.7 of Crow Pass Trail (Gayle Nienhueser)

take a parka, cap, and mittens. The trail is extremely hazardous in winter because of avalanche danger (see "Avalanches," in the Introduction).

To complete the traverse to Eagle River, follow the trail and giant cairns from the Raven Glacier overlook down along the moraine bench on the southwestern side of the glacier. Cross Clear Creek at its junction with Raven Creek; expect wet feet except in early spring when it is possible to cross on a snow bridge. In about ¾ mile, cross Raven Creek on a bridge over a gorge. Note the natural stone arch at the bottom of the waterfall in the gorge. From this point to the Eagle River Nature Center, hikers often sight black bears (see "Moose and Bears," in the Introduction). The frequency of encounters is increasing, and bears have destroyed unoccupied tents.

The trail parallels the east side of Raven Creek for about 3 miles, staying on the hillside above the creek. Clear drinking water is not likely to be available in this stretch. From the crest of Raven Ridge, there is a view of Eagle Glacier and, with binoculars, the area marked for fording Eagle River.

Near the base of the ridge, the trail turns and heads up Eagle River Valley (toward the glacier) to a good river crossing area (elevation 850 feet), which is well marked, half a mile downstream from Glacier Lake. Although instructions on how to ford are posted, practice crossing streams before taking on this swift glacial river (see "Stream Crossings," in the Introduction). Expect knee-deep water. Although of glacial origin, the river's water level does not rise greatly late in the day. Heavy rain will cause the water level to rise rapidly; if the river is too high to cross safely, camp, and wait.

From the ford, the trail generally parallels the river, passing Thunder Gorge in about a mile. It is about 7 miles to Icicle Creek from the river crossing and about 13 miles to the Eagle River Nature Center and the trail's end (elevation 500 feet). The mountain walls make a fine backdrop along this stretch of trail. Near Dishwater Creek, the trail connects with Trip 35, The Perch. The path through the upper valley is narrow and has some tricky footing hidden by tall grass, but after descending from Crow Pass, the grades are mostly easy. The trail along the river is subject to flooding and is managed as a semi-primitive trail. Hikers should be prepared to navigate around the obstacles nature may present. In one area, the route climbs a short ladder. Many good campsites appear along the way, including designated campsites with minimal facilities. Take a stove for cooking; campfires are permitted only in metal fire pits at the campsites or on the gravel bars of upper Eagle River. Firearms may be carried for self-protection; target shooting is prohibited.

The entire trail is closed to off-road vehicles, including snowmobiles. The state park section of the trail is closed to horses and bicycles year round. The portion in Chugach National Forest is closed to horses from April 1 through June 30 and is too steep for mountain bikes. Contact the Chugach State Park office for current trail information and to file a trip plan if desired (see Appendix for contact information).

23 | BIRD RIDGE

Round trip: 2–12 miles
Hiking time: 1–8 hours
High point: 4,650 feet
Total elevation gain: 4,600 feet
Best: April–October
Map: Imus Geographics "Chugach State Park"
Agency: Chugach State Park

This is the classic spring conditioning hike, snow-free earlier than many other places because of its southern exposure. The earliest spring flowers can be found here too.

Take a picnic lunch, climb as high as you like, stretch out on the ground, and enjoy the warm sunshine and rich smell of earth—all while surrounding mountains remain cloaked in white. The hike is steep but worth the effort because of its sweeping view of fjord-like Turnagain Arm.

Driving directions. To reach the trailhead (elevation 50 feet), drive to mile 102.1 of the Seward Highway, about 15½ miles southeast of the Rabbit Creek Road overpass on the edge of Anchorage. Turn northeast into a large parking area (marked).

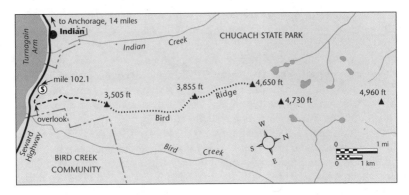

The lower Bird Ridge Trail, paralleling the Seward Highway for about ¼ mile, is a combination of pavement and boardwalk with an easy grade of less than 8 percent. It leads through birch and spruce forest to handicapped-accessible outhouses and an overlook of Turnagain Arm. To continue up Bird Ridge, turn left at the outhouses onto the unpaved Bird Ridge Trail (marked). Follow the trail to the ridge crest and another trail sign. Ahead lie the valleys of Bird and Penguin Creeks. The upper Bird Ridge footpath continues left, climbing steeply up the crest of the ridge.

You will soon leave brush behind. The first high point (elevation 3,505 feet) is about 2 miles from the trailhead, and is a good destination for a short trip. In spring it may be necessary to skirt or cross snow patches. The energetic can continue 4 miles farther to point 4650, overlooking the headwaters of Ship Creek. The ridge culminates at 4,960 feet. Several of the peaks beyond point 4650 are difficult and require mountaineering experience.

Whether you gain the high points or stop at a lower viewpoint, the views of the surrounding mountains and Turnagain Arm are magnificent. Turnagain Arm was named by Captain James Cook in 1778 when he explored these waters as part of his search for the Northwest Passage.

Turnagain Arm has one of the world's greatest tide differentials with a range of as much as 37 feet. Watch for the bore tide, the well-defined leading wave of an incoming tide. The Arm was scoured out by glaciers and has since been filled by silt carried by streams from the retreating rivers of ice. At low tide these mud flats are clearly visible. Because of the speed of the tide as it pours into and out of the narrow Arm and because of frequent high winds, the waters are dangerous for boats.

Look for the season's first Jacob's ladders and anemones, followed by the flowering of the whole cycle of dry tundra plants. Ptarmigan and Dall sheep are frequent visitors to the ridge, and bald eagles ride the winds.

The footing is generally good, and though the hike is steep in spots, especially in the beginning, it is not unpleasantly so. No water is available along the trail. The best camping is at Bird Creek Campground; campfires are permitted only in the campground in metal campfire rings. Winter

Bird Ridge, May (Ginny Hill Wood)

hiking on the ridge can be excellent, but stay on the ridge crest to avoid avalanches (see "Avalanches," in the Introduction) and avoid the overhangs of snow cornices on the leeward side of ridges. The trail is closed to off-road vehicles and bicycles year round.

24 | INDIAN VALLEY

Round trip: 12 miles; traverse 21 miles
Hiking time: 5–8 hours; winter traverse 1–3 days
High point: 2,350 feet
Total elevation gain: 2,100 feet to the pass; traverse 1,250 feet southbound
Best: May–mid-October; winter February–March
Map: Imus Geographics "Chugach State Park"
Agency: Chugach State Park

Indian Valley offers a good family hike along Indian Creek through a delightful combination of forests and meadows to alpine tundra and tiny lakes high in the mountains. In the early 1900s, dog mushers drove their dog teams from Indian to Ship Creek. They crossed over Indian Creek Pass, a part of the Iditarod Trail system between Seward and Interior goldfields.

Leaving treeline on the Indian Valley trail, August (Helen Nienhueser)

The route over Indian Pass was used alternately with the route over Crow Pass (Trip 22). The Indian Creek section of the trail has been cleared and is generally easy to find; the Ship Creek section is brushy, often boggy, and difficult to find. The traverse is most often done in winter by strong cross-country skiers.

Driving directions. To reach the trailhead, drive to the community of Indian, about 15 miles southeast of the Rabbit Creek Road overpass on the southern edge of Anchorage. At mile 103.1 of the Seward Highway, turn north onto Ocean View Road just west of the Turnagain House Restaurant and Indian Creek. After 0.5 mile take the right fork and continue another 0.5 mile to the trailhead (elevation 250 feet), just before a powerline crosses the road. A pipeline carrying natural gas to Whittier from Anchorage also crosses the road at this point.

The trail begins on the left (west) side of the road and heads upstream along Indian Creek. After about a 5-minute walk, there is a bridge. Do not cross the stream. The bridge leads to Powerline Trail (see Trip 29). The trail to Indian Pass continues on the right-hand side of the stream for about a mile before the first crossing; all crossings are on bridges. Follow this trail upstream through tall conifer trees and across delightful meadows created by winter avalanches. (Beware of these open places in winter and spring during periods of high avalanche danger. See "Avalanches," in the Introduction.) The trail can be wet and slippery; waterproof or well-greased boots with good traction are recommended. In late summer, the trail may be overgrown with tall grass. Ahead, high tundra beckons. The entire trail climbs gently with few steep ups or downs.

At the pass, knobs and dips formed by glacial action are today well vegetated by scrub hemlock and crowberries. Nearby ridges and side valleys with tiny alpine lakes invite exploration. Camping in the pass is lovely from mid-June through September, although there are few flat places.

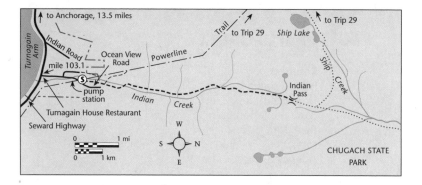

Water is available. Campfires are not permitted, so bring a stove. For a longer trip, head for Ship Lake, about 3½ miles from Indian Pass. To find Ship Lake, walk over the pass and in about a mile bear left (west, then southwest) up Ship Creek to the lake. This off-trail route connects with The Ramp (Trip 29).

This valley is a good place to spot Dall sheep. The valley is open to sheep hunting beginning August 10.

A backcountry winter trip for strong cross-country skiers is the traverse from Indian Valley to Arctic Valley. The Ship Creek trailhead (elevation 1,950 feet) is at mile 6.5 of Arctic Valley Road (see map of Trip 33). Look for a bulletin board at the parking area. A trail drops nearly to the level of the creek and then parallels the creek to Indian Pass. In winter, the 21-mile trip can take 3 days if extensive trail breaking is necessary, although if spring snow conditions are good, strong skiers can make the trip in 1 day (7 to 12 hours). The preferred direction of travel is south to north. With a heavy pack, southbound skiers will have difficulty descending initially to Ship Creek and, later, negotiating tight turns in wooded Indian Creek. In addition, it is necessary to carefully watch for the valley of the center fork of Ship Creek when going south. A number of skiers have unwittingly followed the north fork and ended up in alder-choked Bird Creek canyon.

In spring there will often be a ski track left by others (unless there is fresh snow). After mid-April the segment that parallels Ship Creek may require frequent backtracking because of collapsing snow bridges across the creek. Beware of avalanches, especially in the narrow valley just below Indian Creek Pass.

A summer traverse, from Arctic Valley to Indian or vice versa, is a difficult bushwhack and rarely done.

Powerline Trail, described in Trip 29, terminates in Indian Valley at the Indian Creek trailhead. It is open to mountain bikes. Do not attempt Powerline Trail in winter due to extreme avalanche hazard. Indian Creek Trail is closed to off-road vehicles, including bicycles, year round.

25 | FALLS CREEK

Round trip: 5¼ miles
Hiking time: 4–7 hours
High point: 3,000 feet
Total elevation gain: 2,900 feet
Best: June–September
Map: Imus Geographics "Chugach State Park"
Agency: Chugach State Park

Climb a narrow, stream-cut valley, unusual for the Chugach Mountains, from the seaside to an alpine lakeshore. Less well known than other valleys near Anchorage, the Falls Creek valley leads quickly to alpine country, nicely framed views of Cook Inlet, and impressive rock outcrops and cliffs that rise above the lake.

Driving directions. To reach the trailhead, drive to mile 105.6 of the Seward Highway, about 12.1 miles south of the Rabbit Creek Road interchange on the edge of Anchorage. A hiking sign alerts drivers that the trailhead is imminent. Find a small pullout next to Falls Creek, which tumbles out of the forest at the start of the trail.

There are minor informal trails near the beginning that present some potential for confusion. The Falls Creek Trail starts to the right of the creek and stays to the right of it until near the end of the hike. Follow the main trail, roughly paralleling the creek, as it heads into the mountains. Don't cross the creek or parallel the highway.

About 10 or 12 minutes after starting, the main route will leave the bluff just above Falls Creek and make a switchback to the right at a rock outcropping. Follow this, and continue steeply uphill through the forest, now away from the creek. Eventually, the path pops into a small, level open area lying between the lowland forest and the alder zone. Here, at a large rock, is a natural spot to catch your breath and take in a bit of view. There is an old fork in the trail here. Follow a trail sign directing hikers to the left and slightly downhill. The old right fork climbs directly and very steeply through alder to the rock face visible above and peters out.

The left fork is thankfully cut through thick brush as it works its way back to the creek. At occasional open spots, scan the cliffs above for sheep. The creek is a marvelous traveling companion, always there although it is going the other way. It jumps and tumbles its way downhill, one small waterfall after another. The trail soon leaves the alders in favor of grass and wildflowers, which in turn give way to tundra. The trail is less steep than it was near the beginning, and the valley is less V cut, showing instead a more typical U-shaped cross section that proves the glacial origin of the upper valley. This is a good lesson in geomorphology, demonstrat-

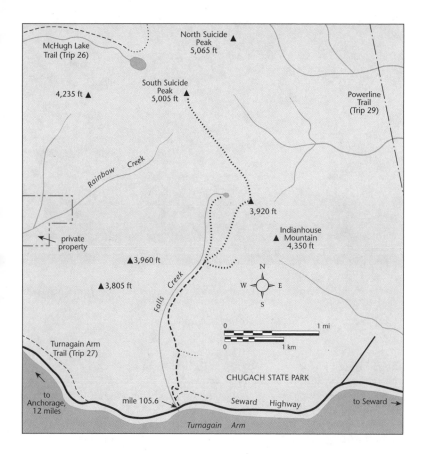

Map labels:
- McHugh Lake Trail (Trip 26)
- North Suicide Peak 5,065 ft
- South Suicide Peak 5,005 ft
- 4,235 ft
- Powerline Trail (Trip 29)
- Rainbow Creek
- 3,920 ft
- private property
- Indianhouse Mountain 4,350 ft
- 3,960 ft
- 3,805 ft
- Falls Creek
- N W E S
- Turnagain Arm Trail (Trip 27)
- 0 1 mi
- 0 1 km
- CHUGACH STATE PARK
- to Anchorage, 12 miles
- mile 105.6
- Seward Highway
- to Seward →
- Turnagain Arm

ing the vast difference in how flowing water and ice carve away at the "solid" rock of mountains.

Ahead, the valley divides. The mountain tarn destination is in a higher valley to the left. The lower right-hand valley leads to the base of Indianhouse Mountain (elevation 4,350 feet), the blocky cliffs of which are obvious as you walk up the valley. Between the forks, a ridge leads upward. Mount a short steep knob at the base of the dividing ridge. This knob, where the trail begins to peter out, makes a nice destination in itself. To continue, hike left (north) over tundra into a small side valley. Flat areas in this side valley invite camping, although for most, this trip will be just a day hike. Follow this side valley about ⅔ mile until the valley dead-ends at a cirque and the lake. If you are alone and won't be bothering others, let go a yodel; the cliff faces all around will answer. Kick back in this south-facing reflector oven on fine days and enjoy the best of the Chugach Mountains.

Headwaters of Falls Creek, October (Helen Nienhueser)

The dividing ridge leads, with minor scrambling, to point 3920 and far-reaching views from on high. Via the left-hand skyline, it also leads to the summit of South Suicide Peak (elevation 5,005 feet). There is a steep stretch of talus slope on the way to the top, and no trail, but this ascent is just long, not complicated.

Map note: The "Anchorage and Vicinity" Road and Recreation Map includes this area, but the trail shown is not entirely accurate.

26 | MCHUGH AND RABBIT LAKES

Round trip: 13 miles
Hiking time: 6–10 hours, or allow 2 days
High point: 3,150 feet
Total elevation gain: 3,050 feet
Best: June–September
Maps: USGS Anchorage A7, A8 SE
Agency: Chugach State Park

With its blue-black waters set below 2,000-foot walls of the Suicide Peaks, Rabbit Lake is a scenic beauty. Smaller McHugh Lake is just next door. The lakes make good destinations for an overnight or a long day hike.

Camping is good, and there are several options for additional hikes and climbs from the lakes.

Driving directions. To reach the trailhead, drive to mile 111.9 of the Seward Highway, 6.4 miles south of the Rabbit Creek Road interchange on the southern edge of Anchorage. Turn into the McHugh Creek Picnic Area. Expect to pay a fee for parking. Follow the McHugh entrance road uphill to the back of the last and highest parking lot. The picnic area is closed with a gate at 9 P.M.; alternate parking space is provided near the highway for nighttime and early morning hikers.

To reach Rabbit Lake, start on the trail, marked "Turnagain Arm Trail" (Trip 27), which begins at the far end of the parking area (elevation 100 feet). Follow the path about 150 yards to an intersection. Go left, following signs for "Potter" along the Turnagain Arm Trail. Within 10 to 15 minutes' walking time from the parking lot, beyond two boardwalks and a mileage marker (mile 3 from Potter), find the McHugh Lake Trail (marked) heading to the right.

Follow this trail to the base of the hillside and up a long series of easy switchbacks to about 1,000 feet elevation. The rock outcrop above the trail is Table Rock, which affords grand views. (Pass below the rock outcrop cliffs and look for a steep side trail up to Table Rock. The silver waters of Turnagain Arm and Cook Inlet spread out to the horizon. An intermittent footpath continuing uphill from Table Rock is a very steep route to the skyline ridge.)

The main McHugh Lake Trail passes Table Rock and enters the McHugh Creek valley, well above the creek itself. About an hour from

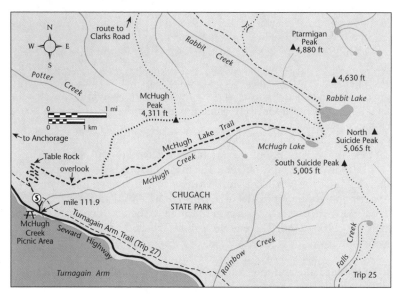

McHugh Lake Trail and North Suicide Peak, August (Helen Nienhueser)

the car, another small rocky outcrop appears on the right overlooking the creek, the Arm, the Kenai Mountains, and the parking lots far below. This is a good goal for hikers with limited time or energy.

The main trail continues up the valley, traversing the hillside and gradually climbing. About 10 minutes beyond the overlook, a much steeper trail of loose gravel departs uphill to the left. This is a route to McHugh Peak. The main trail eventually passes through the alder zone to a spectacular area of alpine tundra surrounded by grand ridgelines and lofty summits. Snow remains at this elevation (near 3,000 feet) well into June. The first good camping is on a flat gravelly area to the right, below an obvious notch in the ridge across the valley. This is somewhat less than 2 miles from the lakes, where many more campsites are available.

McHugh Lake (2,930 feet) and the much larger Rabbit Lake (3,082 feet) lie at the bases of the Suicide Peaks (elevations 5,005 and 5,065 feet), which are separated by a high saddle called Windy Gap. On windless days, camping at lake level is delightful, and swimmers have been known to try the lakes. But Windy Gap is aptly named; winds can be fierce, so take warm clothes even in midsummer.

The Suicide Peaks have nontechnical routes, but neither is an easy ascent. Several other options for day hikes or alternate routes back to town will be more tempting for hikers. The most obvious is the low, easy ridge that separates the two lakes. Head westward up this ridge for better views or a trip to the summit of McHugh Peak (about 2¾ miles distant). Another 2 to 3 miles on, down the flanks of McHugh to the northwest, are possible exits on Clarks Road. There is no well-established trail. Scout a route to avoid clumps of alder. Clarks Road connects to upper Rabbit Creek Road.

Another hike is to walk about 1½ miles down Rabbit Creek valley from Rabbit Lake and then angle northward and uphill 700 vertical feet to Ptarmigan Pass (elevation 3,585 feet). The steep north side of this pass allows access to and from the South Fork of Campbell Creek, the Powerline Trail in that valley, and the Glen Alps entrance to Chugach State Park (see Trip 29). Above this pass to the east is 4,880-foot Ptarmigan Peak. The Rabbit Creek side of the ridge from the pass to the peak is the easiest way up this steep mountain.

Although a trail continues down Rabbit Creek to Upper DeArmoun Road, a state court determined that it does not provide legal public access across private property. Watch for bears on the trail from McHugh Creek Picnic Area and follow the usual precautions (see Introduction).

27 | TURNAGAIN ARM TRAIL

One way: 9.4 miles
Hiking time: 4–8 hours
High point: 900 feet
Total elevation gain: 1,130 feet eastbound, 1,375 feet westbound
Best: April–November
Map: Imus Geographics "Chugach State Park"
Agency: Chugach State Park

The Turnagain Arm Trail, which follows an old wagon road through the woods high above Turnagain Arm, offers good walking much of the year, spiced with occasional spectacular views of Turnagain Arm and the mountains on the Kenai Peninsula. Watch for white beluga whales, Dall sheep, bears, and the first wildflowers of spring. The trail predates Anchorage (it was reportedly developed in 1910 as a telegraph line) and was used as an alternate trail from Seward to Knik when snow conditions necessitated. The main winter trails went over Crow Pass (Trip 22) and Indian Pass (Trip 24).

Turnagain Arm Trail offers opportunities for good family outings and can be hiked in short or long segments. South of McHugh Creek, during periods of new and full moons, watch for bore tides 45 minutes to an hour after the Anchorage low tide (check tide books, available at grocery stores and banks, for tide times). Snow is seldom deep enough for skiing, so the trail often provides good winter hiking. Historically, the trail extended beyond Girdwood, but southeast of Windy Corner the trail is now obscured by natural land sloughing and highway construction.

Driving directions. To reach the western trailhead near Potter Creek (marked 1 on the map), drive to mile 115.1 of the Seward Highway, 2.9 miles south of the interchange at Rabbit Creek Road. Turn toward the mountains into the Potter Creek trailhead for the Turnagain Arm Trail (marked) and park (elevation 312 feet).

To reach McHugh Creek trailhead (marked 2 on the map), drive to mile

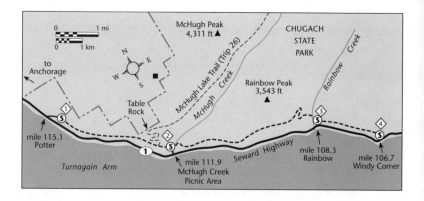

111.9 of the Seward Highway. Follow the paved road uphill. If hiking south to Rainbow, go right, to the lower parking lot beside the creek. To hike to the Potter Creek trailhead (3.3 miles, elevation gain 325 feet) take the left fork to the upper parking area.

The Rainbow Valley access (marked 3 on the map) is at mile 108.3 of the Seward Highway. Park in the area provided north of the highway and east of Rainbow Creek. Walk west to the trailhead (marked) on the bank of Rainbow Creek. McHugh Creek Picnic Area is 4.2 miles away (elevation gain 850 feet).

The Windy Corner trailhead (marked 4 on the map) is at mile 106.7 of the Seward Highway. Park at the pullout on the north side of the highway, and follow the trail up the boulder-covered slope to connect with the obvious old trail at the base of rock cliffs. Rainbow Creek is 1.9 miles to the north (elevation gain 200 feet).

This description outlines a hike beginning at the north (Potter) end of the trail. The first 200 feet of the trail are paved. For the next ⅓ mile, the route is on a good gravel trail that heads uphill. Along the way in this first section are interpretive signs. After that you are on the old trail, a mostly-level, earthen footpath through the woods, laced with roots. Portions of the trail are wet in spring. McHugh Creek Picnic Area (marked 2 on the map) is 3.3 miles southeast (elevation gain 180 feet). Stop at the viewpoint at mile 1.9 for a glorious view of Turnagain Arm. About 10 minutes before McHugh, a trail branches off to the left. It leads to Table Rock and ultimately to McHugh and Rabbit Lakes (Trip 26).

At McHugh Creek Picnic Area (elevation 100 feet), follow the signs for Rainbow and the trail that bypasses the picnic area. Rainbow is 4.2 miles away. Cross McHugh Creek on a bridge. Just beyond the first switchback, a marked trail goes right to Rainbow (marked 3 on the map; elevation gain 800 feet). From McHugh Creek, the trail climbs high above Turnagain Arm, emerging from the cottonwood forest to a panoramic view. Here the trail passes under high, rocky, rotten cliffs. Be sure no one is on the cliffs above, watch for natural rockfalls, and take care not to dislodge rocks because people may be below. While the trail is safe enough, cliff scrambling here is dangerous; at least one person has been killed by losing his footing when scrambling up a slope of loose rock off the trail.

Beyond the cliffs the trail enters pleasant woods. There are side trails, but the main trail should be obvious. A little more than 2 miles from McHugh, the trail again begins to climb, to about 900 feet. Here the trail crosses a ridge of Rainbow Peak, offering a route to its summit (3,543 feet). The trail then descends in switchbacks, crossing the gravel Rainbow Valley road and continuing downhill along Rainbow Creek to the Rainbow trailhead.

From the Rainbow trailhead, the trail climbs a gentle grade and continues 1.9 miles to Windy Corner (elevation gain 200 feet), offering some nice views along the way. Near the end there is a right fork heading downhill, a somewhat steep but short descent to the Windy Corner trailhead.

The trail is closed to off-road vehicles, including bicycles, year round. Be alert for the occasional bear, especially during berry season.

Bird Point to Girdwood Bike Trail

Ten miles father east is, in effect, an extension of the Turnagain Arm Trail, a 6-mile-long, paved bike trail along an abandoned stretch of the Seward Highway. Known informally as the "Bird to Gird" trail, it begins at the Bird Point Wayside, mile 96.7 of the Seward Highway, ducks under the highway, and climbs uphill briefly before leveling off. The trail technically ends at the Alyeska Highway in Girdwood, near the U.S. Forest Service Glacier Ranger District building. However, it connects with the Girdwood bike trail system, which runs from the small shopping center at the intersection of the Alyeska and Seward Highways (mile 90 of the Seward Highway) to the Alyeska Prince Hotel in Girdwood. There is also a bike trail between the communities of Indian and Bird, on the Turnagain Arm side of the highway, that runs through the Bird Creek Campground and offers nice views. Eventually this trail will connect with the "Bird to Gird" trail, but presently there is a 3- to 4-mile gap between them.

View from Turnagain Arm Trail (Pete Martin)

ANCHORAGE BOWL

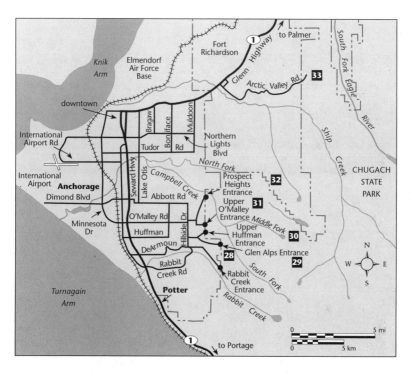

Anchorage sits on a triangle of flat land surrounded by ocean (Turnagain and Knik Arms of Cook Inlet) on two sides and the Chugach Mountains on the third side. Those mountains rise abruptly east of the city and are protected as Chugach State Park, the second largest state park in the nation. It is a hiker's paradise. All hikes in this section are within Chugach State Park.

Opposite: *Tikishla Peak (Trip 32) from Tikishla Park in Anchorage* (John Wolfe Jr.)

28 | FLATTOP

Round trip: 3 miles
Hiking time: 2–5 hours
High point: 3,510 feet
Total elevation gain: 1,260 feet
Best: June–October
Map: USGS Anchorage A8 SE
Agency: Chugach State Park

Thanks to easy access, Flattop is probably the most frequently climbed peak in Alaska, and the trip to its broad summit has long been the classic afternoon hike near Anchorage. The view from the top extends from Denali (Mount McKinley) in the northwest to Mount Redoubt volcano in the southwest. Although parts of the climb are steep, most of the ascent is not difficult. Novices may have problems, however. Do not take small children unless they are cautious, experienced hikers. Boots with good traction and ankle support are recommended for safety.

On the shortest and longest nights of the year, the Mountaineering Club of Alaska holds overnight outings on the summit (despite the lack of water). Flattop is a good winter climb for those properly equipped, but avalanches have killed people here on the north and southwest slopes and even on the low hills leading up to Flattop (see "Avalanches," in the Introduction). Check with the Chugach State Park office about current snow conditions before making a winter or spring climb. People have been injured in the main, snow-filled gully, either in winter avalanches or by sliding out of control on leftover snow in summer.

Driving directions. From the interchange of the Seward Highway and O'Malley Road in south Anchorage, turn uphill on O'Malley. Drive toward the mountains about 4 miles to the intersection with Hillside Drive. Turn right onto Hillside Drive, and continue 1 mile to Upper Huffman Road and a sign for Chugach State Park. Turn left, go 0.7 mile, and turn right onto Toilsome Hill Drive. (In winter, studded snow tires are necessary, and tire chains or four-wheel-drive are recommended.) This road, which becomes Glen Alps Road, climbs steeply uphill for about 2 miles to the Glen Alps entrance to Chugach State Park. Leave your car here (elevation 2,200 feet). Expect to pay a fee for parking.

The trail begins up an obvious stairway, winds through a grove of short mountain hemlock trees, and then emerges onto alpine tundra on the side of Blueberry Knoll. Stay on the trail to protect the fragile vegetation. When the main trail forks, head right on the loop around Blueberry Knoll, as directed by signs. This brings you to a saddle (elevation 2,500 feet) on the opposite side of Blueberry Knoll. In winter, use caution, because the north-facing slope of this saddle becomes loaded with windblown snow, and human-triggered avalanches have caught more than ninety people here. At the saddle, the much steeper trail to Flattop takes off to the right. Continuing straight ahead takes you around Blueberry Knoll to rejoin the path you started.

The Flattop Trail climbs via rock cuts, steps, and switchbacks to a second, higher saddle. From the second saddle, the trail follows switchbacks through talus to a rocky promontory. From this point, the route is steep, exposed, and could be subject to falling rocks knocked loose by hikers or pets (do not take pets). In spring and early summer, parts of the upper route are covered by snow. Wind sculpted snow on the last stretch to the

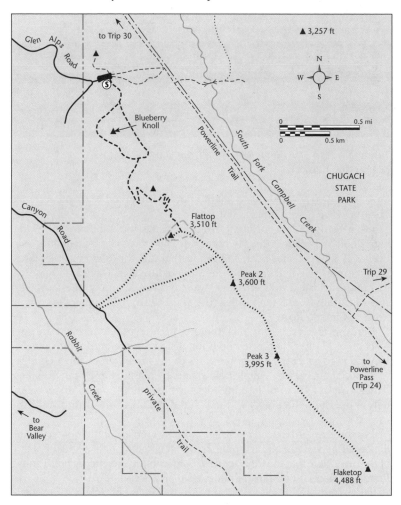

Turnagain Arm and Kenai Peninsula from Flattop, August
(Helen Nienhueser)

top can be nearly vertical and should not be attempted without an ice ax. The top (3,510 feet) is, in fact, flat.

From Flattop, the continuing ridge can take you another 3 miles to a high point at 4,488 feet (locally known as Flaketop). The route passes over Peak 2 (3,600 feet) and Peak 3 (3,995 feet) and is exposed in some places, but an experienced hiker will encounter no difficulty. There are also informal routes up the draw between Flattop and Peak 2 and up the southwest side of Flattop from Rabbit Creek (use Hillside Drive to Upper DeArmoun Road to Canyon Road).

Because Flattop is popular, there is greater potential on the upper reaches of Flattop than elsewhere for dislodged rocks to injure people. Never roll rocks down any of the sides of the mountain or allow children to do so. There may be people below, and even a small rock can become a lethal weapon. Avoid dislodging rocks while walking, and if one accidentally falls, immediately yell "Rock!" and repeat the warning until the rock is at rest.

For those not interested in the summit, the loop around Blueberry Knoll makes a fine walk of about 1 mile, with hill climbing only a small fraction of the hike. Note that the trails for this route on the "Anchorage and Vicinity" Road and Recreation Map are not particularly accurate.

These trails are closed to motorized vehicles and bicycles year round.

29 | THE RAMP

Round trip: 12½ miles
Hiking time: 7–9 hours
High point: 5,240 feet
Total elevation gain: 3,000 feet
Best: June–September
Map: Imus Geographics "Chugach State Park"
Agency: Chugach State Park

On a sunny summer day, take a delightful hike to Ship Lake Pass. Then climb a 5,240-foot peak. From the pass the mountainside does indeed resemble a ramp. The walk up is a moderately steep climb, gaining 1,200 feet elevation in about half a mile. From the top are fine views, especially of the Ship Creek headwaters, and the drop toward Williwaw Lakes takes your breath away. An easier summit is The Wedge (4,660 feet) southwest of the pass. The pass is a nice destination for a hike or a ski trip, and the trip toward the pass makes a good hike or overnight backpack for children.

Driving directions. From the interchange of the Seward Highway and O'Malley Road in south Anchorage, turn uphill on O'Malley. Drive toward the mountains about 4 miles to the intersection with Hillside Drive. Turn right onto Hillside Drive, and continue 1 mile to Upper Huffman Road and a sign for Chugach State Park. Turn left, go 0.7 mile, and turn right onto Toilsome Hill Drive. (In winter, studded snow tires are necessary, and tire chains or four-wheel drive are recommended.) This road, which becomes Glen Alps Road, climbs steeply uphill for about 2 miles to the Glen Alps entrance to Chugach State Park. Leave your car here (elevation 2,200 feet). Expect to pay a fee for parking.

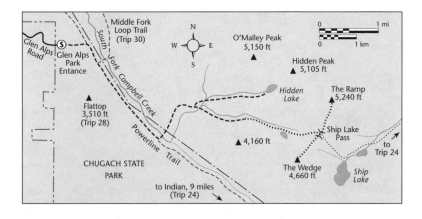

From the Glen Alps parking lot, take either of two trails that begin to the left of the wooden stairs. Walk or bike ½ mile to Powerline Trail. Turn right and follow Powerline Trail about 2 miles, past twelve power poles, to an obvious trail that takes off to the left. A sign for Hidden Lake Trail marks this turnoff. (The trip time can be shortened by riding a mountain bike to this point, but bicycles are not allowed off Powerline Trail.) Follow the trail down to the South Fork of Campbell Creek. Sometimes the stream can be crossed on rocks, but wading may be necessary. The trail climbs gradually uphill beyond the creek, in and out of brush, to the stream draining the valley ahead. To reach The Ramp and Ship Lake Pass, cross the stream and follow the footpath on its south side that aims for the back of the valley. To reach Hidden Lake, walk the little ridge north of the main stream.

Ship Lake from The Ramp (Evan Steinhauser)

The footpath on the south side of the stream climbs gradually toward Ship Lake Pass. Before long a path is no longer truly necessary and there is easy, brush-free walking in all directions. The pass (elevation 4,050 feet, elevation gain 1,800 feet) is a fine destination, offering dramatic views of emerald green Ship Lake below and the mountains rising abruptly above it. From the pass it is a little over a half mile up the ridge to The Ramp to the north or The Wedge to the south.

Walking in this alpine valley is freedom itself. The brush has been left behind, and firm, dry tundra, laced with occasional springs, makes distances seem short. Look for wildflowers in season, ground squirrels, and Dall sheep. Enjoy the summer smell of heather on a warm sunny day. Visit Hidden Lake. Camping is inviting, but carry a cooking stove; campfires are prohibited.

Traverse

A 16-mile traverse from the Glen Alps trailhead to the Indian Valley trailhead is possible via Ship Lake Pass (total elevation gain 1,900 feet). Descend the east side of the pass steeply to Ship Lake (2,700 feet). Follow its outlet 1½ miles downstream, veer right around the toe of the ridge, and follow the center fork of Ship Creek upstream to Indian Creek Pass (elevation 2,350 feet). The trail from the pass to Indian is described in Trip 24.

Powerline Pass to Indian

Another traverse to Indian Valley is 13 miles long over Powerline Pass (elevation 3,550 feet, elevation gain 1,300 feet). Attaining the pass is an easy walk or somewhat challenging bike ride up Powerline Trail. From the pass, the trail switches back and forth down the slope into Indian Valley, steeply enough to make a difficult mountain-bike descent. The trail ends at the trailhead for Indian Valley Trail (Trip 24). The pass remains snowy into July, but, when snow-free, there is good camping near the streams on its southeast side. The Campbell Creek drainage and the Powerline Trail north of a metal gate, 2½ miles from Indian, are closed to motorized vehicles during snow-free months. Bicycles are allowed on the entire Powerline Trail. Because the descent to Indian is steep, some prefer to start at Indian and push bicycles uphill rather than ride down.

Winter

Skiing and snowshoeing in the Campbell Creek drainage are inviting, but the South Fork drainage is open to snowmobiles upstream of Middle Fork when snow cover is sufficient. Under the right conditions, most of the slopes could avalanche, and snow-filled gullies pose a serious hazard, even when surrounding slopes are bare (see "Avalanches," in the Introduction). The route over Powerline Pass should not be taken in winter because of extremely high avalanche hazard.

30 | WILLIWAW LAKES

From Prospect Heights
Round trip: 14 miles to largest lake
Hiking time: 8–12 hours
High point: 2,600 feet
Total elevation gain: 1,600 feet

From Glen Alps
Round trip: 11 miles to largest lake
Hiking time: 8–11 hours
High point: 2,600 feet
Total elevation gain: 960 feet in, 575 feet out

Traverse
One way: 18 miles (from/to Prospect Heights trailhead)
Hiking time: 2 days
High point: 3,750 feet
Total elevation gain: 3,850 feet

Best: June–early October
Maps: USGS Anchorage A7, A8
Agency: Chugach State Park

Alpine gems of different sizes, colors, and shapes, and in various settings, the lakes at the base of Mount Williwaw (elevation 5,445 feet) lie in a mountain paradise. Walk amid a wide variety of alpine flowers in grassy meadows studded with scrub hemlock; pick blueberries, cranberries, and crowberries in season. Watch for Dall sheep. Families with older children who are experienced hikers will enjoy this as an overnight trip. Or take the traverse past the Williwaw Lakes, over a pass, down the North Fork of Campbell Creek, then over Near Point and back to the Prospect Heights trailhead.

Williwaw Lakes can be reached from either the Prospect Heights or Glen Alps trailheads. The Prospect Heights route is longer but *much* drier than the traditional route from Glen Alps. Chugach State Park staff hope to develop a dry summer route from Glen Alps, but, until there is a dry route, the Prospect Heights access is recommended for summer use.

Driving directions, Prospect Heights trailhead. From the interchange at the Seward Highway and O'Malley Road in south Anchorage, turn uphill on O'Malley. Drive about 4 miles to Hillside Drive. Turn left, then immediately right onto Upper O'Malley Road. Follow it 0.5 mile to a T intersection. Turn left onto Prospect Drive, and continue 1 mile to a stop

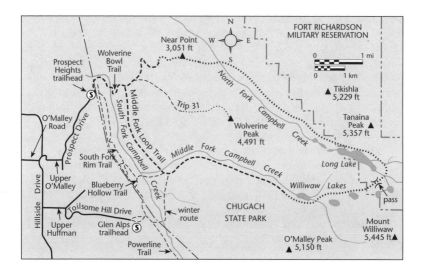

sign. Turn left, and drive 0.1 mile. Then turn right at the Prospect Heights entrance to Chugach State Park (elevation 1,100 feet). Expect to pay a fee for parking here.

On foot, follow the trail (an old homestead road) that heads east from the end of the parking area to the Powerline Trail. Turn left and continue on the main trail as it bends away from the powerline, becomes the Wolverine Bowl Trail, and descends to the South Fork of Campbell Creek. Cross a bridge, and continue around a sharp switchback and up a hill. At the top of the hill, take a sharp right-hand turn onto Middle Fork Loop Trail. Follow this trail across the lower slopes of Wolverine Peak a little less than 2 miles to a bridge across the Middle Fork of Campbell Creek. Across the stream, the trail forks. Follow the left fork (marked) about 3½ miles to the first large lake. The right fork goes to the Glen Alps trailhead.

The first large lake (elevation 2,600 feet) is a fine destination for a day trip or overnight and offers good camping nearby. If the weather is good, linger here enjoying the magnificent scenery. For a slightly longer trip, continue upvalley about 1½ miles to the beautiful lake in a cirque (3,250 feet elevation) below Mount Williwaw. The pass to the North Fork of Campbell Creek is 500 feet higher and less than an hour away to the northeast.

Driving directions, Glen Alps trailhead. At the intersection of O'Malley Road with Hillside Drive (see above) turn right onto Hillside Drive, and continue 1 mile to Upper Huffman Road and a sign for Chugach State Park. Turn left, go 0.7 mile, and turn right onto Toilsome Hill Drive. (In winter, studded snow tires are necessary and tire chains or a four-wheel-drive vehicle are recommended.) This road, which becomes Glen Alps Road, climbs steeply uphill for about 2 miles to the Glen Alps entrance to Chugach State Park. Leave your car here (elevation 2,200 feet). Expect to pay a parking fee.

For a winter ski trip or the "wet-foot" route from the Glen Alps trailhead, take either of two trails that begin to the left of the wooden stairs in the parking lot. Walk ½ mile to Powerline Trail and turn right. Walk about 300 yards, and then turn left at the sign for Middle Fork Loop Trail. Follow this trail across the South Fork of Campbell Creek, up the other side, and north (left), more or less paralleling the stream. In about 1½ miles you will reach the fork in the trail just before the Middle Fork of Campbell Creek. From this point, follow the directions above to Williwaw Lakes.

Williwaw Lakes Loop

A 2-day, 18-mile loop trip continues from the pass beyond Williwaw Lakes to Long Lake and the valley of the North Fork of Campbell Creek. This valley can be followed around Long Lake (on either side of the lake) and past Tanaina, Tikishla, and Knoya Peaks. Map-reading skills are essential to find the way out. This is a wonderful wilderness trip at Anchorage's back door. Because it is not easy to get to the North Fork valley, relatively few people go there.

To complete the loop and return to the Prospect Heights entrance, follow the North Fork of Campbell Creek downstream about 2½ miles beyond the last lake. Begin climbing diagonally up and across the northwest ridge of Wolverine Peak on your left before there is much brush. Aim for a notch in the ridge southeast of a bump called Near Point. It is a steep climb with about 800 feet of elevation gain. Once on top, follow the ridge over Near Point and pick up a narrow trail that descends from Near Point to the end of the old homestead road. Look for a trail that heads down the southwest ridge of Near Point. The more obvious trail starts down the northwest ridge and goes to the same place but via a valley that is sometimes very wet. Follow the trail back to the Prospect Heights trailhead.

Campfires are prohibited in the park, so bring a stove. The trip to Williwaw Lakes also makes a good ski trip via Middle Fork Loop Trail from either the Glen Alps or the Prospect Heights entrance. Be aware of avalanche danger (see "Avalanches," in the Introduction). The Glen Alps route is closed to bicycles except for the portion on the Powerline Trail. The trail from Prospect Heights is open to bicycles on the old homestead road to its end at the base of Near Point (2.4 miles). The entire area north of the Middle Fork is closed to motorized vehicles year round. The Campbell Creek drainage upstream (south) of Middle Fork is open to snowmobiles when snow cover is sufficient.

Blueberry Hollow and South Fork Rim trails

A network of trails between the Glen Alps and Prospect Heights trailheads provides several options for short hikes. Combining the Blueberry Hollow Trail with parts of the Powerline and South Fork Rim trails makes a nice loop from the Glen Alps trailhead. To find the Blueberry Hollow Trail, follow the directions above from the Glen Alps trailhead to

Long Lake, North Fork of Campbell Creek, August (Helen Nienhueser)

Powerline Trail. Turn left and after 15-20 minutes, turn right on the Blueberry Hollow Trail. Follow this to the South Fork Rim Trail; from here, you can turn left and follow the South Fork Rim Trail back to the Powerline Trail and back to Glen Alps.

31 | WOLVERINE PEAK

Round trip: 11 miles
Hiking time: 4–8 hours
High point: 4,491 feet
Total elevation gain: 3,500 feet
Best: June–September; winter, November–April
Maps: USGS Anchorage A7 NW, A8 NE
Agency: Chugach State Park

Wolverine Peak, the broad triangular mountain on the skyline east of Anchorage, makes an excellent one-day trip, offering views of Anchorage, Cook Inlet, and the Alaska Range and glimpses of the lake-dotted wild country behind the peak. An old homesteader's road, now part of the Chugach State Park trail system, makes a fine access to tree line for hiking and ski touring. Watch for ground squirrels, spruce grouse, moose, and, on rare occasions, a wolverine. Pick blueberries and cranberries in season.

Driving directions. From the interchange at the Seward Highway and O'Malley Road in south Anchorage, turn uphill on O'Malley. Drive toward the mountains about 4 miles to Hillside Drive. Turn left, then immediately right onto Upper O'Malley Road. Follow it 0.5 mile to a T intersection. Turn left onto Prospect Drive and continue 1 mile to a stop sign. Turn left, and drive 0.1 mile to the Prospect Heights entrance to Chugach State Park (elevation 1,100 feet). Expect to pay a fee for parking here.

On foot, follow the trail that heads east from the end of the parking area to the Powerline Trail. Turn left, and continue on the main trail as it bends away from the powerline, becomes the Wolverine Bowl Trail, and descends to the South Fork of Campbell Creek. Cross a bridge and continue around a sharp switchback and up a hill. A side trail that turns sharply right is Middle Fork Loop Trail. Continue past this trail to the next trail entering from the right, a little over a mile beyond the creek and 2⅓ miles from the parking area.

Follow this trail as it angles off uphill, starting at an elevation of 1,330 feet. The distance from here to the peak is about 3 miles. The trail quickly narrows to a footpath through alder, then emerges above brushline. The mountain reaches out toward Anchorage with two ridges that are like

North Fork Campbell Creek from Wolverine Peak summit, June (John Wolfe Jr.)

Wolverine Peak from Anchorage, March (John Wolfe Jr.)

welcoming arms. The route heads uphill between these ridges, climbing gradually onto a lower center ridge. Follow the crest of this center ridge to the skyline ridge, and follow this main ridge to the peak. The summit (elevation 4,491 feet) is not obvious much of the way. The hike to brushline is a pleasant evening outing with a fine view of Denali (Mount McKinley).

Winter

Climbers may want to tackle the peak in winter, although some avalanche hazard may exist (see "Avalanches," in the Introduction). The upper slopes are likely to be windpacked or windswept, and crampons may be necessary. The last part of the climb generally does not have enough snow for skiing.

A network of about 20 miles of ski trails is accessible from Prospect Heights and three other entrances to Chugach State Park. Ski the old road to its end beyond the Wolverine turnoff, take Middle Fork Loop Trail or follow the Powerline Trail. The Loop Trail connects this entrance with the Glen Alps park entrance and can be skied as a circular trip using the Powerline Trail. Shorter loops extend from the Powerline Trail. Other access points include the Upper O'Malley and Upper Huffman entrances to Chugach State Park. Maps of the trail system are available from the park office (see Appendix for the address) and are posted at some trailheads. Some of the trails are packed for winter use. (See also the Trip 30 map.)

The area is closed to motorized vehicles year round. Bicycles are allowed on the main trail, from the Prospect Heights parking lot to the turnoff for Wolverine and beyond to the end of the homestead road (2.4 miles) at the base of Near Point (see Trip 32).

32 | NEAR POINT AND TIKISHLA PEAK

Near Point
Round trip: 8.5 miles
Hiking time: 4–5 hours
High point: 3,051 feet
Total elevation gain: 2,150 feet
Best: June–September
Map: USGS Anchorage A8 NE

Tikishla Peak
Round trip: 15 miles
Allow: up to 2 days
High point: 5,229 feet
Total elevation gain: 5,200 feet
Best: late June–September
Map: Imus Geographics "Chugach State Park"

Agencies: Chugach State Park, Fort Richardson Military Reservation

Two climbs—one easy, one long and hard—begin with the same access. Lower, closer, and easier, Near Point is a knob overlooking east Anchorage. It is suitable for long summer evenings. Tikishla Peak is across the North Fork of Campbell Creek from Near Point. Because the North Fork valley has difficult access, Tikishla sees little traffic. Hikers may wish to explore the valley, perhaps connecting with Trip 30 to make a loop back to their starting point.

Driving directions. The primary access to these destinations is via O'Malley Road in south Anchorage. For access that is closer to east Anchorage but is more complex and harder to find, see the end of this description. For the main access, turn uphill from the interchange at O'Malley Road and the Seward Highway, and drive about 4 miles up O'Malley Road to Hillside Drive. Turn left then immediately right onto Upper O'Malley Road. Follow it 0.5 mile, turn left onto Prospect Drive, and continue 1 mile to a stop sign. Bear left, and go 0.1 mile to the Prospect Heights entrance to Chugach State Park (elevation 1,100 feet). Expect to pay a fee for parking.

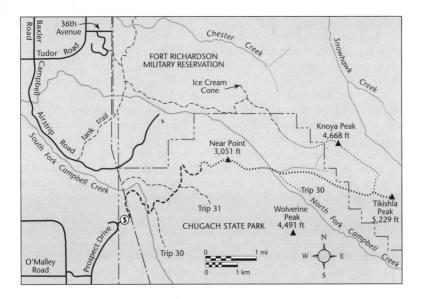

Near Point

On foot, follow the trail that heads east from the end of the parking area to the Powerline Trail. Turn left, and continue on the main trail as it bends away from the powerline, becomes the Wolverine Bowl Trail, and descends to the South Fork of Campbell Creek. Cross a bridge, and continue to the end of the old road, 2.4 miles from the parking area. There are trails that branch to the right; ignore them except to note that the main route's name officially changes to Near Point Trail after passing the fork to Wolverine Peak (Trip 31).

At the base of Near Point, where the old roadbed ends, the route becomes a footpath. At this transition, the path doubles back to the right for a short distance and becomes a boardwalk. From the end of the boardwalk, the trail heads uphill toward a lone spruce tree. At the tree, the preferred trail heads to the right and uphill. The left fork, which appears to be the main trail, continues straight but becomes mucky. The trail to the right is quite steep at first, but the angle eventually eases, and the route is dry and pleasant (after rain, it can be slippery). The trail is faint near the top. Note your approach to the ridge crest and summit (elevation 3,051 feet) so you can find the trail upon descent. Avid mountain bikers may like to pedal the 2.4-mile approach to the base of Near Point, where the old roadbed ends. Only this initial part of the trail is open to bicycles.

Map note: The route on the "Anchorage & Vicinity" Road and Recreation Map shown traversing around the base of Near Point and leading into the North Fork of Campbell Creek is not accurate and does not provide reasonable access. The route goes over Near Point.

Tikishla Peak

To reach Tikishla Peak, climb to the top of Near Point and continue along its ridge. The trail peters out, but follow the ridge to a low point and then drop off the ridge into the valley of the North Fork of Campbell Creek. Tikishla Peak is across the valley and a little upstream. As you descend, avoid mountain hemlock and brush directly below by angling upvalley toward the base of an inviting ridge that rises from the creek to Tikishla. Once at the creek, it is about 3,000 feet of climbing up the ridge to the summit (elevation 5,229 feet). For most, this trip is probably best as an overnight. Carry a stove, because campfires are not permitted.

From the top of Tikishla, it is possible to walk the main ridge northwest to Knoya Peak (elevation 4,668 feet) before dropping back into the valley. There are several other variations on this trip, as described below.

Alternate Access Routes

East Anchorage access to Near Point. From Tudor Road in east Anchorage, turn south on Campbell Airstrip Road and proceed until you pass under a powerline. Park, and then walk away from the city on a hilly trail under the powerline to Campbell Creek canyon. Turn left, and follow an informal but well-worn footpath along the edge of the canyon and gradually uphill to the Wolverine Bowl Trail. At one point, the trail descends and intersects the Wolverine Bowl *Loop* Trail (primarily a winter trail). Go left on this trail and after several yards turn off it to the right. You soon intersect the much more substantial Wolverine Bowl Trail. Go left to reach Near Point. Note that this alternate access is on unmarked and unmaintained trails. It is possible to become disoriented.

East Anchorage access to Tikishla Peak. Another route to Tikishla is via a bump marked "Ice Cream Cone" on the Chugach State Park map. It is more hill than mountain but rises above tree line and has a fine view. The trail to this hilltop is on Fort Richardson Military Reservation, and the Army requests that hikers call the military police (see Appendix for phone number) to inquire about military maneuvers in the area.

It is possible to find this trail from two different points. One access is from mile 2.4 of Campbell Airstrip Road in Far North Bicentennial Park. Park on the left (north) side of the road, and hike or bike from a red gate across the base of the mountains on an old army tank trail. Cross a major powerline, enter military land, and step gingerly on a rotting bridge over the North Fork of Campbell Creek.

Take a right fork beyond the creek. At the next right (a walk of 7 to 10 minutes past the bridge and about 2 miles from the red gate), find a narrower, unmarked 4-mile trail that twists and winds uphill through wonderful forest to Ice Cream Cone. The turn may be marked with a ring of paint around a tree trunk. This trail roughly parallels the North Fork of Campbell Creek (often at some distance) and then enters steep switchbacks. To

Tikishla Peak and North Fork Campbell Creek, September (Helen Nienhueser)

continue 3 miles beyond Ice Cream Cone to Tikishla, hike up the ridge and over Knoya Peak. This makes an 18-mile round trip.

The trail to Ice Cream Cone is also accessible from the Chugach Foothills subdivision. Take East 36th Avenue east from Muldoon Road, turn right on Pioneer Drive, and follow it 0.5 mile. The trail lies between 8450 and 8470 Pioneer. Parking is limited. The trail follows a drainage ditch upstream between houses to military reservation land. Beyond the houses, go right and follow a powerline to a major four-way intersection of powerlines. At this intersection, go left toward the mountains along a powerline, and pick up a distinct path through the woods. It lets hikers out on the tank trail. Go right, and follow the tank trail about 5 minutes. Then go left on the trail to Ice Cream Cone. The tank trails are perfect for mountain bikes, but on the trail to Ice Cream Cone, all wheeled vehicles are forbidden.

33 | RENDEZVOUS PEAK

Round trip: 3.5 miles
Hiking time: 2–5 hours
High point: 4,101 feet
Total elevation gain: 1,500 feet
Best: anytime
Map: Imus Geographics "Chugach State Park"
Agencies: Chugach State Park and Anchorage Watershed

Rendezvous Peak is a perfect first summit. It's short enough for kids, and adults will enjoy the pleasant, uncomplicated climb. There are spectacular views of Denali (Mount McKinley), Mount Foraker, Mount Susitna, Cook Inlet, Turnagain and Knik Arms, Anchorage, and the valleys of Ship Creek and the South Fork of Eagle River. In winter, when snow conditions are good, the trip to the pass is fun on cross-country skis.

Driving directions. From the Muldoon Road interchange in the northeast corner of the Anchorage Bowl, drive northeast on the Glenn Highway 1.6 miles and take the first exit. This is Arctic Valley Road. Southbound traffic must take the exit for Fort Richardson at mile 8.1 of the Glenn High-

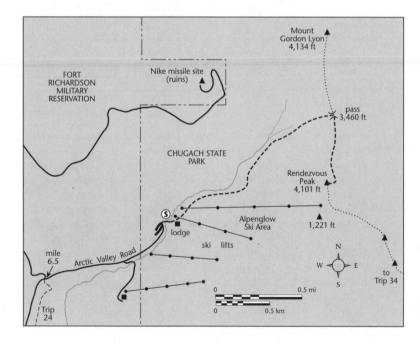

South Fork Eagle River from Rendezvous Peak (Gayle Nienhueser)

way and then follow signs to Arctic Valley. The road becomes gravel. Drive about 7½ miles from the exit to the end of the road at Alpenglow Ski Area. Stay on the main road; do not take a right-hand fork near the ski area. In winter, studded tires, four-wheel drive, or chains may be required for the steep ascent to Arctic Valley. When the ski area is closed, the lodge parking lot may be gated. There is ample parking outside the gate (elevation 2,600 feet). Expect to pay a parking fee (not included in the annual Chugach State Park pass). Note that to return to the Glenn Highway, drivers must use the Fort Richardson interchange.

If you parked outside the gate, walk into the lodge parking lot, crossing a small stream. Pass under ski lifts as you begin to head up the valley to the northeast. A footpath leads to the pass along the right-hand side of the

The authors sliding down the heather on Rendezvous Peak, ca. 1970
(Nancy Simmerman)

stream. Some parts of the trail are wet. The entire route is on tundra above
tree line. The area is popular for blueberries in late summer—so popular
that it is best to count on not finding any berries within easy reach of the
trail.

The pass (elevation 3,460 feet) has fine views, but those from the top of
Rendezvous Peak (elevation 4,101 feet) are even better. A steep but short
ascent up the ridge to the right (south) of the pass leads to the craggy summit. Sit for a while to enjoy the view. The odd structures on the ridge top to
the northwest are the asbestos-laden ruins of an old Nike missile site. From
the top of Rendezvous Peak, the ridge extending southeast beckons, promising a walk in the clouds high above the valleys of Ship Creek and the
South Fork of Eagle River. Be sure to carry water if you go very far. From
Rendezvous Peak choose your own descent route. In winter stay on windblown ridges to minimize avalanche hazard (see "Avalanches," in the Introduction).

An alternate trip is north of the pass to the summit of Mount Gordon
Lyon (elevation 4,134 feet), slightly higher but also relatively easy. In winter,
the ski up and back down Gordon Lyon is somewhat gentler than a ski on
Rendezvous Peak.

A one-way trip is possible from Arctic Valley to the South Fork of Eagle River. From the summit of Rendezvous Peak, follow the ridge southeast toward the head of the South Fork valley for about 2 miles to a low pass, climbing over or around about four high points with elevations to 4,000 feet. From the last of these high points, descend to the low pass between the Ship Creek and South Fork drainages (shown as elevation 2,861 feet on the Chugach State Park map). From the pass, descend the steep hillside about ½ mile to the South Fork Trail, an elevation loss of about 700 feet. When you intersect the trail, turn left to reach the trailhead, about 5 minutes away. See Trip 34 for driving directions to the trailhead.

Because the access road to Arctic Valley is on military land and subject to military control, civilian travel may be restricted due to military training or for security reasons, but such closures are a rarity. If in doubt, check with Chugach State Park or Fort Richardson (See Appendix). Alpenglow Ski Area buildings and equipment are the private property of a non-profit ski club. Please respect this property, and report any vandalism. The area is closed to off-road vehicles year round.

At mile 6.5 of Arctic Valley Road is a pull-off that serves as the trailhead for the route from Ship Creek to Indian (Trip 24). Look for a bulletin board in the parking area. The trail descends into the Ship Creek valley bottom but in summer becomes a bushwhack. The route is used in winter by experienced cross-country skiers. The preferred direction of travel in winter is from south to north. See Trip 24 for further description.

NORTH OF ANCHORAGE

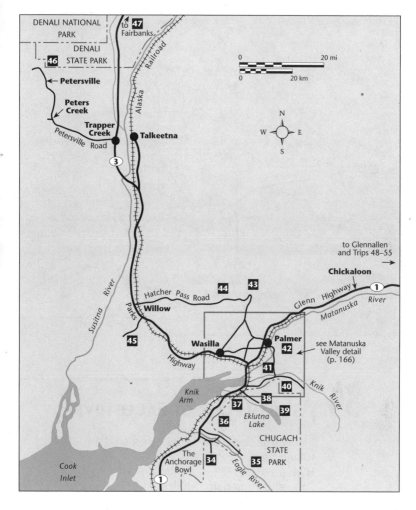

The area north of Anchorage stretches from Eagle River, which lies 14 miles from downtown Anchorage, to the Matanuska and Susitna Valleys. The Glenn Highway heads northeast out of Anchorage paralleling, but mostly out of sight of, Knik Arm. Along the way it provides access to trips on the north side of Chugach State Park, with emphasis on Eagle River and Eklutna Valleys and the mountains that rise above them. North of Palmer and Wasilla lie the Talkeetna Mountains and the lovely alpine area of Hatcher Pass. West of the Talkeetna Mountains, the Parks Highway takes hikers to and through Denali State Park, with several hikes and great views of Denali (Mount McKinley), North America's highest peak. *(See Matanuska Valley detail on page 166.)*

Opposite: *Iditarod Trail in Eagle River Valley (Trip 35), July* (Helen Nienhueser)

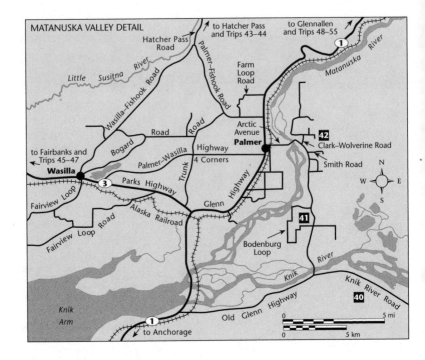

34 | SOUTH FORK OF EAGLE RIVER

Round trip: Eagle Lake 9 miles, Symphony Lake 11 miles
Hiking time: 4–8 hours
High point: 2,588 feet (Eagle Lake)
Total elevation gain: 740 feet
Best: June–early October
Maps: USGS Anchorage A7 NE, NW
Agency: Chugach State Park

For a backcountry treat, visit the valley of the South Fork of Eagle River. Head for shimmering, glacier-fed Eagle Lake, then wander through meadows of alpine flowers to nearby clear-water companions. Beyond lies a wilderness of rugged mountain peaks. Eagle Lake is an easy day trip, but more than a day is needed to explore this lovely valley. Look for blueberries in season.

Driving directions. From the Muldoon Road overpass at the northeast edge of Anchorage, drive 7 miles on the Glenn Highway to the Eagle River Loop Road/Hiland Road exit. Turn right (east) toward the mountains onto

Eagle Lake and Eagle Peak, July (Helen Nienhueser)

Eagle River Loop Road; in 0.1 mile turn right onto Hiland Road. Drive about 7 miles on Hiland Road into the valley of the South Fork of Eagle River, crossing the South Fork once, to South Creek Road (marked) and a Chugach State Park sign, both on the right. Follow South Creek Road across the river again, and turn right onto West River Drive. The park entrance is on the left (elevation about 1,950 feet). There is limited parking available in a small parking lot. In winter, Hiland Road can become icy, and a four-wheel-drive vehicle may be needed. At minimum, studded tires are recommended.

Past access problems in this valley have caused conflicts between landowners and hikers or skiers. Respect private property, and use the Chugach State Park access only.

The trail begins as a boardwalk and then climbs to and follows a bench for about a mile. The trail then descends to a bridge across South Fork (about 2 miles from the trailhead). Once across the river, follow the trail across the valley, then up the east side of the valley to Eagle Lake, about 9 miles round trip from the trailhead. Some spots in the trail are wet.

Other Trips

From Eagle Lake (elevation 2,588 feet), hikes and climbs abound. Some boulder-hopping is necessary to reach Symphony Lake (elevation 2,687 feet), 11 miles round trip from the trailhead. Extend this trip, if you like, into the valley behind Symphony Lake or around the south side of Eagle Lake. These valleys have no trails, and some bushwhacking is necessary. The two tarns high in a valley above and behind Symphony Lake are pretty, and the ridge between the tarns leads to a high plateau (elevation 4,500 feet) overlooking the North Fork of Ship Creek. Challenging peaks in the area, for experienced mountaineers only, include Cantata (6,391 feet), Calliope (6,820 feet), and Eagle Peak (6,909 feet).

Hanging Valley and Eagle River Overlook. A side trip for another day is Eagle River Overlook. From the parking lot, follow the trail across the bridge and across the valley. When the trail turns south toward Eagle Lake, continue straight up the slope to the hanging valley above. A well-worn footpath leads through brush about halfway up the valley on its south side, then becomes intermittent. Cross the creek when you can.

About 2½ miles from the South Fork Trail bridge, climb the steep, grassy slope on the left to a pass at 3,770 feet. From here, stroll to points 5065 and 5137 ("Eagle River Overlook"), both of which provide spectacular views of Eagle River valley and the mountain wilderness beyond. From the trailhead to the overlook is about 12 miles round trip.

An alternate destination is a gemlike alpine lake hidden in a cirque that opens off the south side of Hanging Valley, near the back of the valley and about 250 feet above the valley floor. A stream tumbles down the slope out of this cirque. Sheer peaks rise around this emerald-colored lake on three sides, and the tundra-covered valley floor makes this a wonderful picnic spot.

Rendezvous Peak Ridge. About 5 minutes from the trailhead a footpath heads uphill off the main trail. This leads, steeply, to a saddle at 2,861 feet in the ridge between Ship Creek and the South Fork of Eagle River. From the saddle, Rendezvous Peak is about 2 miles to the north (see Trip 33). Or walk the ridge to the south for miles, climbing up and down several small peaks and enjoying outrageous views in all directions. An alternate route to the ridge heads steeply uphill just before the South Fork trail turns downhill toward the bridge. This route leads to a second saddle at 3,169 feet.

Camping is unrestricted on parklands, but campfires are not permitted; take a stove. Watch for moose, black and grizzly bears, Dall sheep, and raptors, including merlins. Chugach State Park lands in the South Fork drainage are closed to off-road vehicles and bicycles year round.

35 | THE PERCH

Round trip: 8 miles
Hiking time: 4–6 hours
High point: 800 feet
Total elevation gain: 300 feet
Best: May–October
Map: Imus Geographics "Chugach State Park"
Agency: Chugach State Park

The walk to The Perch is an easy introduction to the stunningly beautiful Eagle River valley, just 40 minutes from Alaska's largest city. The walk is on a well-maintained, mostly level trail through a wooded canyon with 6,500-foot mountain walls shooting skyward all around. This is a good family hike anytime but is especially welcome in early spring or late fall when other hikes are closed by snow. The route lies along the Iditarod National Historic Trail, which in its heyday ran between Seward and the Interior goldfields. Ambitious backpackers can follow it well beyond The Perch to the Crow Pass trailhead near Girdwood, 26 miles distant (see Trip 22).

Driving directions. From the Muldoon Road overpass on the Glenn Highway at the northeast edge of Anchorage, drive 7 miles on the Glenn

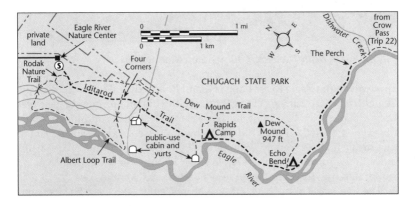

Mount Yukla from The Perch, July (Helen Nienhueser)

Highway to the Eagle River Loop/Hiland Road exit (1.8 miles south of the Eagle River exit). Turn right (east) toward the mountains onto Eagle River Loop Road. At the first light, bypass Hiland Road and continue on Eagle River Loop Road 2.6 miles until the highway crosses Eagle River and comes to a major intersection at Eagle River Road. Turn right, and proceed 10.8 miles to the road's end at the Eagle River Nature Center. Expect to pay a fee for parking; this is not included in State Parks' annual pass.

The trail starts at the back of the Nature Center (elevation 500 feet) and is marked Crow Pass/Historic Iditarod Trail. Check the public information bulletin board before starting on the trail—when bears fish for salmon in streams near the trail, a cautionary notice may be posted. There are several other trails that branch off the main route on both sides of the trail. Stay on the main route, which is generally well marked and obviously the main path. Follow signs for Crow Pass or the Iditarod Trail, and see the map for help in navigating these trails or finding alternate destinations or loops.

The main trail wanders through birch and spruce; lichens and mosses cover the rocky ground. Shortly after the Four Corners intersection a side trail to the right leads to a public-use cabin (rent it through the Eagle River Nature Center; see Appendix for address and website). About 2 miles from the Nature Center, the main trail reaches Rapids Camp on a knoll above Eagle River. The trail follows the river for the next 10 to 15 minutes, followed by some uphill and downhill. The cliffs of Dew Mound are visible to the left. About 3 miles out are wonderful gravel bars, great views of Mount Yukla, and a campsite beside the river at Echo Bend. Continue another mile to The Perch (marked), a massive, smooth rock outcropping. With a fine view up the Eagle River canyon to the snowy glaciated peaks beyond, this is the perfect spot for a photo and a sandwich. Eagle, Polar Bear, and Yukla Peaks rise overhead to 7,500 feet and are among the most impressive peaks to be found along a trail in southcentral Alaska.

The energetic may want to extend their walk another mile or so to a view of lovely Heritage Falls on the west side of Eagle River. The less energetic may wish to stick near the Nature Center. The Rodak Nature Trail, a ¾-mile loop, includes a salmon-viewing platform that doubles as a mountain-viewing and sunning deck. The 3-mile Albert Loop Trail leads to the gravelly banks of Eagle River in about 45 minutes and comes back by a different route (closed seasonally in late summer because of bears feeding on salmon). Both trails are forks off the main trail (see map).

The Dew Mound Trail is a more primitive trail that parallels the Crow Pass/Historic Iditarod Trail to Echo Bend and connects with it in several places, offering several options for loop trips. It leaves the main trail across from the second intersection with the Rodak Nature Trail. Check with the Eagle River Nature Center for current conditions.

Along any of these popular trails, open fires are generally not allowed. Along the Iditarod Trail, fires are permitted only in metal fire pits at Rapids Camp and Echo Bend. The park encourages campers to sleep away from these fire pits, because the food odors around the pits attract black bears. Camp stoves are generally better for cooking. In addition to the public-use cabin, two yurts are available for rent through the Nature Center.

These trails can be skied in winter when there is enough snow to cover the rocks. After the river freezes, it makes a grand ski highway. Check with park rangers for ice conditions, then follow either end of the Albert Loop Trail to the river. All trails mentioned here are closed year round to horses, other pack animals, mountain bikes, snowmobiles, and other vehicles.

36 | ROUND TOP AND BLACK TAIL ROCKS

Meadow Creek Access
Round trip: 8 miles to Black Tail Rocks, 10 miles to Round Top
Hiking time: 6–8 hours
Total elevation gain: 2,750 feet to Black Tail Rocks, 3,500
feet to Round Top

Ptarmigan Valley Access
Round trip: 11 miles to Round Top, 13 miles to Black Tail Rocks
Hiking time: 7–10 hours
Total elevation gain: 4,600 feet to Round Top, 5,000 feet
to Black Tail Rocks

High point: Round Top 4,786 feet
Best: June–September
Map: Imus Geographics "Chugach State Park"
Agency: Chugach State Park

A panoramic view from Mount Redoubt volcano to Denali (Mount McKinley) rewards the hiker who makes the steep climb to Round Top's summit. All around are the Chugach Mountains, including Bold Peak in the Eklutna area, the high Chugach behind it, and Eagle and Polar Bear Peaks in the Eagle River area. This day trip takes the urban dweller into an alpine wonderland.

Two approaches are possible: via Meadow Creek and via the Ptarmigan Valley Trail. Meadow Creek offers the most elevation gain by car but crosses private land; call Chugach State Park for current access information (see Appendix for phone number). The Ptarmigan Valley Trail is longer, gains more elevation on foot, and offers pleasant forest at its lower end.

Meadow Creek Access
Driving directions. From the Muldoon Road overpass on the Glenn Highway in northeast Anchorage, drive 7 miles on the Glenn Highway to the Eagle River Loop/Hiland Road exit. Turn right (east) toward the mountains onto Eagle River Loop Road and follow it 3.4 miles, across Eagle River Road, to West Skyline Drive on the right (just before Eagle River Loop Road turns left).

Southbound traffic should take the second exit for Eagle River and cross to the east side of the freeway. From the first stoplight, drive 0.7 mile on the Old Glenn Highway to Eagle River Loop Road; turn right. In 1.1 miles, where Eagle River Loop Road bears right, turn left onto West Skyline Drive.

Follow West Skyline Drive (also known simply as Skyline Drive) 2.4 miles to a gate and park (elevation 1,700 feet). The name of the road

Ridge on Round Top, September (Helen Nienhueser)

changes several times. Stay on the paved road until its end at the gate.

You can choose to climb a ridge north of Meadow Creek directly from the parking area or follow a more gradual route up the little valley beyond the ridge. The ridge route gains 1,600 feet elevation in less than a mile and offers good views of Eagle River. The valley route takes nearly 2 miles to gain the same amount of elevation and offers some protection from the wind and a greater sense of having left the city behind. Both trails are simply footpaths worn by hikers, and the less-used valley route may require a bit of bushwhacking in places.

The ridge route begins in the back left corner of the parking area and heads steeply uphill to a radio tower. Follow a trail left of the tower. Ignore a turn to the right. Aim instead for an obvious trail up the ridge to the summit of Baldy. Follow the ridge over Baldy onto the broad plateau (elevation about 3,100 feet) that leads to Black Tail Rocks.

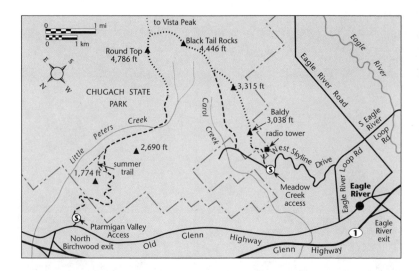

For the valley route, follow the road past the gate a little less than a mile. About 250 yards before a cluster of buildings, look for a trail through alder at the base of a lone spruce tree (well before you can see the buildings). The first few feet of this trail are wet and may require bushwhacking, but the trail breaks out of the alder in about 50 yards and from there is easy to follow. A short distance up the slope, the trail intersects an old roadbed overgrown with alder. Go left, entering a tunnel of alder, and then immediately right and gradually uphill toward Carol Creek. Follow the trail up the valley, toward the broad plateau.

Follow the south edge of the plateau for ¾ mile to Black Tail Rocks (elevation 4,446 feet). The last part of the climb is fairly steep. From Black Tail Rocks it is a relatively easy traverse along the ridge to Round Top (elevation 4,786 feet) 1 mile north.

Ptarmigan Valley Access

Driving directions. Take the Glenn Highway to the North Birchwood exit (16 miles from Muldoon Road in northeast Anchorage) and turn east toward the mountains. In 0.3 mile, turn right onto the Old Glenn Highway. Drive 0.6 mile and turn left onto a gravel road and parking lot (elevation 410 feet). The turn is marked with a sign for Ptarmigan Valley trailhead.

The trail was designed for snowmobiles and is wide and easy to follow. It twists its way through wooded topography, sometimes steeply up and down, occasionally level. Spruce and birch frame views of Knik Arm, Mount Susitna, Denali, and other peaks in the Alaska Range. The route splits at one point; the forks rejoin shortly. There is a second fork about 15 minutes beyond the first at mile 1.8. The left-hand trail is marked "summer trail" and leads up to and along a ridge, passing through pretty open forest and meadows studded with spruce and wildflowers. The summer trail parallels the winter route, which is wet in summer. Overall, the route climbs 1,200 feet in a little over 2 miles before cresting a broad ridge near tree line and dropping slightly into Ptarmigan Valley, the drainage of Little Peters Creek. The summer and winter routes rejoin at mile 2.5, and the trail soon intersects the original Ptarmigan Valley Trail, an old road now closed to public use at its lower end.

From the intersection of the new and old trails, follow the old trail up valley nearly another 2 miles to tree line and beyond. Once above the trees, pick a route up the slope to your left to Round Top's northwest or west ridge, then follow the ridge to the broad, lichen-covered summit (elevation 4,786 feet). Little Peters Creek is the last water. Look for blueberries in late August.

From Round Top, ambitious hikers can follow the ridge southeast to Vista Peak (elevation 5,000 feet). South and slightly west of Round Top are Black Tail Rocks, which can be climbed by following Round Top's southeast ridge and then veering south and west.

Both Round Top and Black Tail Rocks can be climbed in winter, but because of avalanche hazard, use ridge approaches to both and avoid gullies (see "Avalanches," in the Introduction). Because the final steep parts may be wind packed, crampons will probably be necessary. The Ptarmigan Valley Trail is popular with snowmobilers in winter.

37 | THUNDER BIRD FALLS

Round trip: 2 miles
Hiking time: 1 hour
High point: 330 feet
Total elevation gain: 200 feet in, 130 feet out
Best: late April–October
Map: USGS Anchorage B7 NE
Agency: Chugach State Park

A pleasant outing for families with small children, this easy trail leads through woods to a rushing stream and a view of a pretty waterfall. Although snow patches may linger deep in the gorge near the falls well into May, the walk is good any time snow cover permits. Under birch trees, the forest floor is laced with wild roses and ferns. Along the trail, children can learn to recognize and stay away from devil's club, a prickly, large-leafed shrub up to 6 feet tall.

Thunder Bird Falls, August (Marge Maagoe)

Driving directions. The trail begins off the Glenn Highway near Eklutna. From Anchorage, drive northeast on the Glenn Highway to mile 25.2, and take the Thunder Bird Falls exit. Drive 0.4 mile to a parking area on the right just before the Eklutna River bridge. The trailhead (elevation 130 feet) is marked. Southbound traffic should exit at Eklutna (mile 26 of the Glenn Highway), cross the bridge over the freeway to the east side, and turn right onto the Old Glenn Highway. Drive 0.6 mile to the trailhead parking area on the left. To return to the southbound freeway lanes from the Thunder Bird Falls parking area, turn right as you leave the parking lot, and drive 0.6 mile north on the Old Glenn Highway, crossing the Eklutna River bridge. Follow the freeway entrance signs.

An inviting broad trail leads 1 mile to Thunder Bird Creek and the falls. The first part of the trail passes a subdivision. About half a mile from the trailhead, there is a viewing deck overlooking the gorge of Thunder Bird Creek. The view down is impressive and provides instant understanding of the signs warning hikers to stay away from the cliffs. Near the end, the trail forks. The right-hand fork becomes a boardwalk that leads to a deck and a good view of the falls. A long, white water ribbon hidden in the back of a narrow gorge, the falls are in sunlight only a few hours each day.

The left fork of the trail leads down to the creek. You cannot see the falls when you reach the stream. A trail leads upstream about 100 yards toward the falls but stops before there is a good view. Do not go beyond the fence at the end of the footpath, and do not allow children to explore the cliffs, where they would be in danger of falling. Several deaths have occurred in this manner.

The trail is closed to off-road vehicles and bicycles year round.

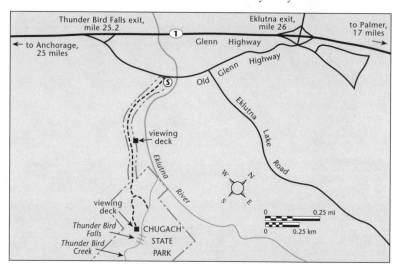

38 | EAST TWIN PASS

Round trip: 7–8 miles
Hiking time: 5–8 hours
High point: 4,450 feet (pass), 5,050 feet (knob)
Total elevation gain: 3,650 feet (pass), 4,250 feet (knob)
Best: June–September
Map: Imus Geographics "Chugach State Park"
Agencies: Chugach State Park and Anchorage Watershed

Follow the Twin Peaks Trail to tree line, and continue on a footpath through alpine tundra to East Twin Pass and a sudden, magnificent view over the Matanuska Valley to the Talkeetna Mountains. On the way up, shimmering Eklutna Lake is visible southward far below. The trail wraps around a broad ridge, leaving the lake vista behind, and climbs into a confined valley, with the dramatic rocky ramparts of the Twin Peaks containing the view until vistas break open again at the pass. With these peaks often in sight during the ascent, the hike is mysterious on gray days when clouds swirl around the summits. Chances of seeing Dall sheep are good, and the route crosses well-defined sheep trails near the pass, opening possibilities for easy traverses and further exploration of the upper bowl.

Driving directions. Drive to mile 26 of the Glenn Highway, 26 miles northeast of Anchorage, and take the Eklutna exit. Turn toward the mountains and then immediately right onto the frontage road (see the map for Trip 37). Drive 0.4 mile to a left turn for Eklutna Lake (marked). Follow this road about 9.7 miles to a ranger fee station. Beyond the fee station, drive

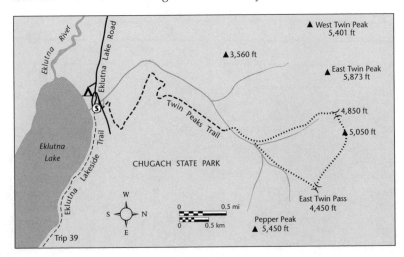

East Twin Peak from East Twin Pass, September (John Wolfe Jr.)

another 0.6 mile (past turns for a picnic area and campground) to a day-use parking area near the lake. Drive through the first parking lot, to the second parking area and trailhead (elevation 900 feet). There is a fee for parking.

From the southeast corner of the parking area, walk across a bridge. Turn left to find the Twin Peaks Trail (marked). Don't be confused by the Eydlu Bena Trail that begins in the same area (it is a short, less difficult option). Follow trail signs. Twin Peaks Trail crosses a service road and then climbs uphill, winding through woods on an old four-wheel-drive track. There are occasional views of the lake below, and about 1½ miles from the trailhead, a bench appears with a fine view of the lake.

Brushline, at the end of the old vehicle track (elevation about 2,700 feet), may be destination enough (2½ to 3 hours round trip and 1,800 feet elevation gain). There is another bench here from which to take in the view of the alpine bowl and East and West Twin Peaks across the valley. From this terminus of the maintained trail, there are two main footpaths worn in by use. A downhill path leads toward the pass. An uphill trail leads steeply up to a ridge crest and expansive views over Eklutna Lake but does not lead to the pass. A less-used third path leading straight ahead from the bench appears to go nowhere.

The downhill route traverses diagonally across the slope through high grass to a sparkling stream, crosses it, and then follows the valley toward East Twin Pass. Once in the base of the valley, hikers will find water rushing through small canyons in the alpine bowl. Picnicking is tempting on tundra among grasses and wildflowers. Camping is possible; level sites are limited. The narrow footpath leads along the west side of the stream toward East Twin Pass, which is the low point on the ridge to the northeast. The path crosses one draw that comes down from the northwest and then twice traverses to the right to stay near the edge of the main draw coming down from the pass. Eventually, the path begins to peter out in open tundra. If you lose the path, head for the pass (elevation 4,450 feet).

For the best Matanuska Valley vistas, extend the trip along the ridge crest northwest from the pass to a 5,050-foot knob. To make a circular route, continue west to a second pass at 4,850 feet and then go down the steep south slope, staying west of the stream below this pass, to rejoin the path you ascended.

Climbing either of the peaks requires experience and mountaineering equipment. The usual approach to East Twin Peak (5,873 feet) is from the 4,850-foot pass. The trail is closed to off-road vehicles and bicycles year round.

39 | BOLD PEAK VALLEY

Round trip: 17 miles from parking lot,
  7 miles from mile 5 of Lakeside Trail
Hiking time: 9–11 hours from parking lot
High point: 3,700 feet (moraine), 4,456 feet (ridge)
Total elevation gain: 2,800 or 3,556 feet
Best: late June–early October
Map: USGS Anchorage B6
Agency: Chugach State Park

The hike to Bold Peak valley, good all summer, is an unsurpassed September outing when Bold Peak is topped with white, the alpine valley is carpeted in red, the lower hillsides are sheathed in gold, and Eklutna Lake shines far below. Look for marmots, ground squirrels, hawks, magpies, and ptarmigan. In season, you will find beautiful wildflowers, high-bush cranberries, and blueberries. If you are lucky, you may see moose, Dall sheep, or bears.

Driving directions. Drive to mile 26 of the Glenn Highway, 26 miles northeast of Anchorage, and take the Eklutna exit. Turn toward the mountains and then immediately right onto the frontage road (see map of Trip 37). Drive 0.4 mile to a left turn for Eklutna Lake (marked). Follow this road about 9.7 miles to a ranger fee station. Beyond the fee station, drive another 0.6 mile (past turns for a picnic area and campground) to a day-use parking area near the lake. Drive through the first parking lot to the second

Eklutna Lake from Bold Peak valley, August (Helen Nienhueser)

parking area and trailhead (elevation 900 feet). There is a fee for parking.

From the southeast corner of the parking area, walk across a bridge (see map of Trip 38). Turn right and follow Lakeside Trail (an old road) around the lake about 5 miles to the Bold Creek bridge. About 100 feet beyond the bridge, take a trail to the left (marked "Bold Ridge Overlook 3.5 miles"). Bicycling to this point takes about 30 minutes, substantially reducing the time needed for this hike.

Hike the trail, another old road, as it climbs steeply through deciduous forest to brushline. The old road, in places overgrown with a narrow band of alder, goes another ¾ mile to a knob at about 3,400 feet. The knob is only a little more than 2 miles from the lake and may be destination enough. The view is spectacular in all directions.

From the knob, a choice of footpaths beckons the hiker. The easiest leads about a mile along the almost-level valley floor to the glacial moraine at the head of the valley and a superb view of Bold Peak (7,522 feet). Another trail climbs Bold Ridge to the south of the knob. On top of the ridge, walk the heights about a mile to point 4456. The views of Bold Peak, Eklutna Lake, Eklutna Glacier, and surrounding mountains are magnificent. The return can

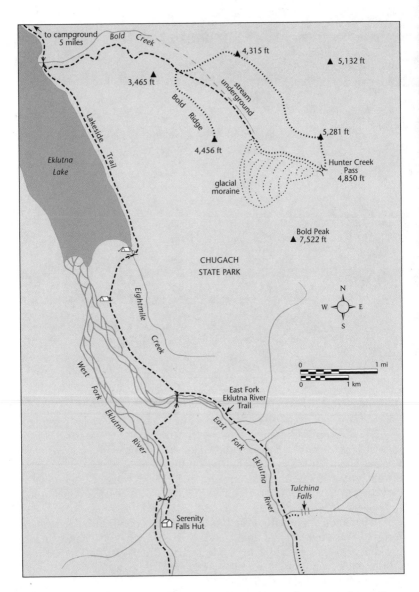

be via the same route or by descending the steep, tundra-covered east slope of the ridge to the valley and following the valley floor back to the knob.

The really energetic can climb the steep scree slope at the head of the valley to Hunter Creek Pass (elevation 4,850 feet), then follow the ridge up to point 5281. There are good views of the relatively inaccessible Hunter Creek valley and the mountain wilderness rising behind it. For a 6-mile loop, follow the northwest ridge from point 5281 back to the lower end of the valley and descend to the knob and the end of the old road. Bold Peak should be attempted only by experienced climbers.

Note that the stream shown on the USGS maps draining the valley is partially underground, limiting access to water. The stream runs on the surface at the head of the valley near the gravel moraine and then goes underground and does not reappear until it is north of point 3465. Good campsites can be found near the stream.

Lakeside Trail

The Lakeside Trail continues past Bold Creek for another 8 miles around the lake to the head of Eklutna Valley. It is a good mountain bike trip. Motorized, all-terrain vehicles are permitted, on the road surface only, Sundays through Wednesdays. All other areas are closed to all-terrain vehicles. Bicyclists can avoid the motorized vehicles by following a narrower trail that hugs the lakeshore. Its condition, not as good as the main trail, is adequate in most places. Near mile 8 the trail crosses the path of a major avalanche that covered the trail in February 2000. Look for views of retreating Eklutna Glacier here and at mile 11.2. From the end of the old road, Glacier Trail continues for about ⅓ mile through glacial debris and requires some rock scrambling. It leads to a narrow canyon but ends before there is a view of the glacier. Technical equipment and skills are required to go farther. For a view of the glacier, climb the rock mound to the right of the trailhead (and return by the same route).

East Fork Eklutna River Trail

Another adventure lies along the East Fork of the Eklutna River. A trail leaves Lakeside Trail at the East Fork bridge (mile 10.5) and winds back into the mountains for about 6 miles, following the narrow river valley. The trail to Tulchina Falls, 2½ miles one way, is generally level and easy walking in most places. However, side streams are not bridged and must be crossed on logs or forded. Occasional fallen trees must be climbed over, roots can trip the unwary, and a steep scree slope must be crossed. The trail is in the woods with occasional views of the steep mountains lining the valley. There are great views and good camping and picnicking spots on the cottonwood-studded gravel banks of the creek below Tulchina Falls. Beyond the falls the "trail" is more of a route, paralleling the creek and eventually leading to the upper, alpine valley.

Public-Use Cabins and Campgrounds

There are two public-use cabins in Eklutna Valley. Yuditnu Creek Cabin is on the lake with access at mile 2.7 and mile 3 of the Lakeside Trail. (*Yuditnu* is Athabascan for "Golden Eagle Creek.") Serenity Falls Hut is reached from mile 11.8 of Lakeside Trail. The first multiparty hut in Chugach State Park, this cabin has bunks for 12 to 15 people. See Appendix for information on how to make reservations. There are also three camp-grounds.

A park concessionaire, located across the bridge from the parking lot, rents bicycles and kayaks. They may also offer a shuttle for people or equipment to the far end of the lake, opening the potential to boat one way and bike back. See Appendix for contact information.

40 | PIONEER RIDGE

Round trip: 9 miles
Hiking time: 7–10 hours
High point: 5,300 feet
Total elevation gain: 5,100 feet
Best: June–September
Map: Imus Geographics "Chugach State Park"
Agencies: Matanuska-Susitna Borough and Alaska Division
of Mining, Land, & Water

Pioneer Peak rises 6,400 feet over the Matanuska Valley, its rocky ramparts intimidating even to experienced mountaineers. But try the Knik River–Pioneer Ridge Trail for steep but easy access to the upper reaches of this magnificent peak. From up high, view the expanse of the Knik Glacier and elusive 13,176-foot Mount Marcus Baker, highest of the Chugach Mountains.

Driving directions. To reach the trailhead, start by taking the Old Glenn Highway exit off the new Glenn Highway at mile 29.3 (about 25 miles from Muldoon Road in Anchorage, and just south of the Knik River). With Pioneer Peak hanging overhead, drive 8.7 miles on the Old Glenn to its intersection with Knik River Road. Find a parking area, marked with an inconspicuous wooden sign for the trailhead, at mile 3.9 of Knik River Road. This trailhead (elevation about 200 feet) is around the back side of Pioneer, where the intimidating slopes have moderated to merely steep and the peak is not even visible.

The trail starts upward immediately. Within an hour, Knik Glacier and 10,610-foot Mount Goode are visible, the glacier 4 miles wide and more than 25 miles long, the peak sharp and ice-covered. This lower trail can be thick with grass after midsummer and can be muddy in a few places anytime.

Soon, the trail breaks out of the brush and—for a moment—levels off, inviting a rest stop. But save the picnic for higher up. Improbably placed, on small flat spots carved by the glacier and surrounded by wildflowers and some of the best views in southcentral Alaska, is a succession of four sturdy picnic tables. The first is near 2,000 feet and about a third of the way to the ridge crest, both in elevation gain and distance. The second and third tables are slightly off the trail to the north and possible to miss—the second

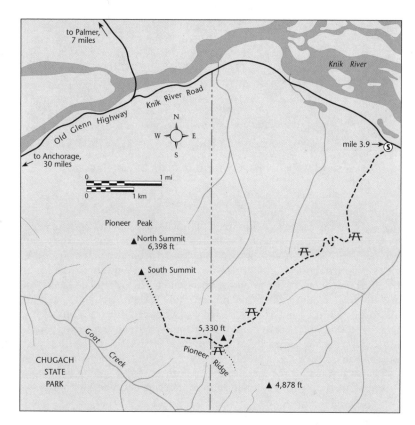

at the last bit of brush, the third only several hundred vertical feet below the upper trailhead where the trail is level for a while. Any of these makes a fine destination in its own right, with full views of either 13,176-foot Marcus Baker to the south or Denali (Mount McKinley) far to the north, as well as the Knik River and the Matanuska Valley.

At upper elevations, the route is intermittently marked with orange fiberglass stakes and is not always completely obvious on the ground because vegetation is sparse. Clouds often swirl in, even on fine days, so pay close attention to the stakes and the general lay of the land to aid in finding the route while descending. People have become disoriented, and the prospect of bushwhacking back to the road through thick alders on the lower slopes is not pleasant.

Beyond the third picnic table about 45 minutes hiking time, the trail crests the broad back of Pioneer Ridge at 5,300 feet. Suddenly another 180 degrees of view opens up (and there is the fourth table). This view, across Goat Creek valley, is of Bold Peak, Eklutna Glacier and the ice field beyond, and other familiar mountains in Chugach State Park. The ridges

Knik Glacier and the inner peaks of the Chugach Mountains, July
(John Wolfe Jr.)

above Goat Creek are home to Dall sheep, usually visible in the area. Reaching this goal can easily take 6 hours, but nowhere else in the Chugach does a footpath take hikers so high. For those with energy remaining, the gently rolling ridge top offers easy walking in either direction.

The south summit of Pioneer lies approximately 1½ miles and 1,100 vertical feet northwest of the upper trailhead along the ridge. The peak itself and the ridge leading to it is in Chugach State Park. Although the summit appears as intimidating as ever, it is accessible with a little rock scrambling to experienced hikers confident in their footing. Sheep trails lead around most rocky promontories, but routefinding is necessary. The south peak is pleasing in its own right, but it is a few feet lower than the north peak (6,398 feet). A deep col separates the two peaks, and crossing this gap is recommended only for experienced mountaineers equipped with ropes.

41 BODENBURG BUTTE

Round trip: 3 miles
Hiking time: 1½ hours
High point: 886 feet
Total elevation gain: 900 feet
Best: May–October
Map: USGS Anchorage C6 SE
Agencies: Matanuska-Susitna Borough and Alaska
    Division of Mining, Land, & Water; private land of
    the Sandvik family

In May of 1935, Midwest farming families hurt by the Great Depression arrived by ship at Seward. They were the colonists of the Matanuska Colony. With government sponsorship they were bound for a new life of farming in the north. While their families waited that May at the port of

Seward, the men drew lots at what is now Palmer for rights to farm the soils at the junction of Matanuska and Susitna River valleys. Ingolf Sandvik and Paul Nelson were among them. They drew land they didn't want. But they successfully traded it for land they'd had their eyes on. It was fine, flat land—flat except for an 886-foot fist of rock today called Bodenburg Butte.

One side of the butte is still in the Sandvik family, which may be the only Matanuska Valley family still farming its original land three and four generations later. There has been a trail up the south side of the butte on the Sandvik land for decades. Randy and Patty Sandvik have opened it to the public and have created a parking area and brought in a portable toilet. For this, they request a small donation. Meanwhile, the Matanuska-Susitna Borough, with help from Americorps, has created a trail up the north and west sides on public land, and this is likely to become the preferred route. A trail grand opening was scheduled for 2003.

The butte's dry conditions, perhaps coupled with enough height to stand above a late glacial advance without being overtopped, give the butte unique vegetation for the area. Sage is most obvious. There are also Serviceberries and tiny, quite rare flowers called *Draba caesia*. It is also one of few areas in southcental Alaska with grasshoppers. Kids will love chasing them.

Driving directions, north trailhead. Both trailheads are off Bodenburg Loop Road. To reach the newer, north trailhead, drive the Glenn Highway to mile 29.3, and take the Old Glenn Highway exit (29 miles from Anchorage). Drive 12.4. miles on the Old Glenn, past Bodenburg Butte, prominent to the west), and turn toward the butte on Bodenburg Loop. Drive 0.5 mile, and turn left on Mothershead Road. After nearly 0.2 mile, at a powerline, find a parking area on the right. The trailhead itself (elevation 130 feet) is a bit farther along Mothershead Road. Park in the parking lot and walk around the curve in the road to find it. The trail begins along the base of the butte on an easement granted by property owners. Respect private property here.

Glacier scoured summit, September (John Wolfe Jr.)

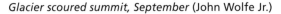

The trail winds along below the impressive northern face of the butte, at first gaining elevation only in short spurts. Then it climbs 500 vertical feet all at once, much of it on steps, up the steep western side of the butte. On this approach, the best views—Pioneer Peak, Knik Glacier, and the high, glaciated, inner peaks of the Chugach Mountains—appear only near the end, a fitting reward for the effort.

The lower trail presents fine panoramas over the Matanuska River and surrounding farm fields, with the Talkeetna Mountains prominent in the background. The top is rolling grassland with views in all directions. Standing on top, looking at the distant face of the Knik Glacier, and imagining such ice overtopping the butte and filling the entire width of the Knik and Matanuska Valleys is awesome indeed. This is a marked contrast to the idyllic pastoral farming scene laid out around the butte today.

Expect high grass along this route and potential wet spots on the lower trail. Parts of the trail do not get sun until after noon even in summer.

Driving directions, south trailhead. To reach the old Sandvik trailhead, follow the Old Glenn Highway to mile 11.5 (measured from milepost 12), where there is a four-way intersection with a blinking light. Turn left toward the butte on the south end of Bodenburg Loop (Plumley Street is to the right). Drive 0.6 mile to a small gravel parking area on the right.

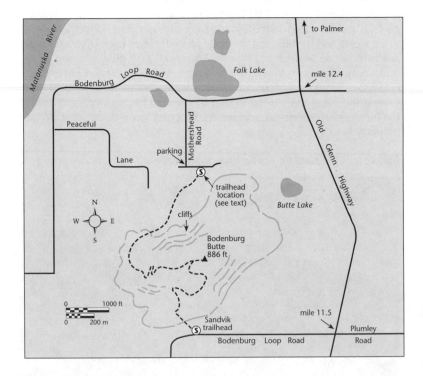

The trail starts upward steeply near the entrance to the parking lot. In a few steps, hikers can turn and look over telephone poles at the view of Knik Glacier.

At the summit is obvious erosion from years of informal foot traffic. There are virtual canyons eroded into the surface, a visible reminder that hiking boots have impact. Follow the switchbacks built into this trail (and all trails) to minimize future erosion. These eroded trenches are educational; they reveal an amazing depth of loess. This silty soil from the Knik Glacier lies on top of the rock and is likely almost all deposited by notorious Knik River winds. The very top of the butte has large areas of exposed rock (much of it also revealed because of erosion), and striations are evident where the glacier ground over the top of this resistant rock knob.

The butte, especially its south and east sides, is typically quite dry. It is one of the first areas good for spring hiking, because wind and sun keep snow to a minimum. The south (Sandvik) side, especially, sometimes can be good in early to mid-April. Tinder-dry conditions and carelessness have caused the butte to burn three times since the 1930s. Don't use fireworks, light fires, smoke, or otherwise threaten this special spot.

The Sandviks and others on Bodenburg Loop sometimes have you-pick vegetables or berries, a worthwhile diversion after the hike, and there is a herd of reindeer to watch either from the slopes of the butte or from the fence along Bodenburg Loop on the south side of the butte.

42 | LAZY MOUNTAIN AND MATANUSKA PEAK TRAIL

Round trip: 5–7 miles (trip extensions possible)
Hiking time: 5–6 hours
High point: Lazy Mountain 3,720 feet
Total elevation gain: 3,120 feet
Best: May–October
Map: USGS Anchorage C6 NE, SE
Agencies: Matanuska-Susitna Borough and Alaska Division of Mining, Land, & Water

Lazy Mountain is a steep hike with a nice summit that lets hikers know they are finished. The Matanuska Peak Trail in the adjacent McRoberts Creek valley is somewhat easier but has a less distinct hiking goal. These primitive trails, with variations on the same fine views, are close enough to connect, and a loop trip is possible. Looming beyond both is Matanuska Peak, a summit for the truly hardy.

The trails are suitable for children, although kids will take more time. The views are principally of the Matanuska Valley farming district, the silver

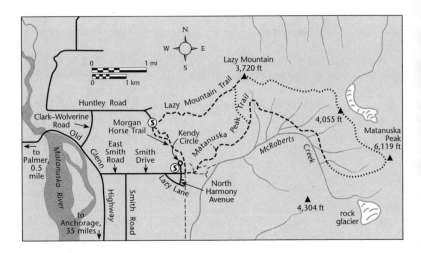

waters of Cook Inlet, and Pioneer Peak jutting above the Knik River. The lower portions of both trails wind through tall grass, which, even on a clear day, may be wet with dew, so take rain pants. Wildflowers abound; new species introduce themselves with every hundred feet of elevation gained, culminating on the Lazy Mountain ridge crest and at the upper end of McRoberts Creek in minute lichens, with brilliant pinhead-sized sporangia, clinging to the rocks. Three hike variations and the Matanuska Peak climbing routes are described here. Lazy Mountain Recreation Area also offers winter skiing and hiking opportunities.

Lazy Mountain

Driving directions. To reach the Lazy Mountain trailhead, drive to Palmer at Glenn Highway mile 42.1 (36 miles northeast of Anchorage). Turn east at a stoplight onto West Arctic Avenue, easily identified by a Tesoro gas station on the corner. Follow this road, which becomes the Old Glenn Highway, 2.3 miles through Palmer and across the Matanuska River to Clark–Wolverine Road (marked). Turn left, continue 0.7 mile to a T junction, and then turn right onto Huntley Road (marked). Drive 1 mile to the crest of a hill and a Y intersection. Go right, downhill, 0.2 mile to the Lazy Mountain Recreation Area and a parking area (elevation 600 feet).

The 2½-mile Lazy Mountain Trail begins at the left (northeast) side of the parking area across a culvert. A level, wider, gravel trail that starts between large boulders at the southeast side of the parking lot, the Morgan Horse Trail, leads to the Matanuska Peak Trail, nearly 1½ miles or about 35 minutes away.

Start up the Lazy Mountain Trail. Ignore an indistinct fork in the path a dozen yards up the trail; go right on the more distinct right-hand trail. It is well defined all the way to brushline.

The path becomes steep and is muddy and slippery when wet. Beyond the first of several false summits, where the growth gives way to low berry bushes, the grade is gentler. From here pick your own route up the tundra-covered slopes. The last 200 feet of the summit ridge of Lazy Mountain are narrow and exposed; children will need help. Carry drinking water.

In winter the Matanuska-Susitna Borough grooms ski trails that begin at the Lazy Mountain Recreation Area parking lot. Parts of these trails are steep. Hikers often use the Lazy Mountain trail all winter.

Matanuska Peak Trail

Driving directions. To reach the Matanuska Peak Trail, start in Palmer as described above, but bypass Clark-Wolverine Road and proceed 0.4 mile from the Clark-Wolverine intersection to an intersection with East Smith Road (marked). Turn east (uphill) on East Smith Road, and continue *straight* 1.4 miles until the road ends at a T intersection with Kendy Circle and North Harmony Avenue. (At 0.6 mile Smith Road turns right and Smith Drive goes straight. Go straight on Smith Drive.) At the T, turn left and park off the road in the small parking lot (elevation 525 feet).

The trail, which starts as a vehicle track, is marked Matanuska Peak Trail. It heads east up McRoberts Creek valley toward the mountains from the end of Smith Drive. Within a couple of minutes, the Morgan Horse Trail crosses at right angles. The trail to the left connects with the Lazy Mountain trailhead 30 to 40 minutes away. Parking there and hiking the Morgan Horse Trail to this intersection is an alternative.

To continue up the McRoberts Creek valley, hike about 15 minutes on the main route to the top of a long, straight, steep hill and an iron gate. Just past the gate, an all-terrain-vehicle trail heads uphill on the left. It forks immediately. Take the right fork and then a left fork that leads uphill. This is the Matanuska Peak Trail, which leads to the upper McRoberts Creek valley. A couple of minor routes join or diverge; bear right and uphill to tree line (about 1½ hours). Much of this part of the trail is quite steep. At brushline, the path dips through a deep ravine. Beyond the ravine, the path underfoot eventually becomes less obvious, but the route is marked with orange fiberglass stakes. This upper section between miles 2 and 4 has only gentle grades. A reasonable end point for a hike is in the upper valley where the route begins to steepen again.

Lazy Mountain–Matanuska Peak Trail Loop

To make a 7-mile loop trip, start up the Matanuska Peak Trail. As the trail heads into the ravine at brushline, diverge to the left and head cross-country uphill over tundra. It is about 1,000 vertical feet and ⅔ mile to the Lazy Mountain Trail. Reaching it, continue another several hundred vertical feet to the top of Lazy Mountain. Then descend Lazy Mountain Trail to the parking lot, and return to the Matanuska Peak trailhead on the Morgan Horse Trail (described above). There are several small loops near the north

Pioneer Peak and Twin Peaks from Lazy Mountain, June
(Helen Nienhueser)

end of the Morgan Horse Trail. All paths lead to the same place, but the quickest is probably the lowest trail.

Matanuska Peak

Those with boundless energy may want to continue from either trailhead to Matanuska Peak (6,119 feet), the real mountain, looming at the head of McRoberts Creek and 4 miles along the undulating ridge to the east of Lazy Mountain. The hike is a long one—10 to 14 hours round trip from either trailhead. From Lazy Mountain, follow the ridge crest, and head to the right up the northwest ridge of Matanuska Peak. From the top of this ridge, approach the summit rock pile up a loose scree slope. Go right at the final rocks. A climbing rope probably is not necessary if the route is carefully chosen.

The route to the summit via the Matanuska Peak Trail is shorter (11 miles round trip instead of 13), although the last 2,000 feet are very steep and include a stretch of loose talus (blocks of rock) that could be dangerous. Orange route markers continue from the end of the trail to near the summit. Because of the length of either summit route, consider taking headlamps on all but the longest days of summer. The summit usually has snow until July.

43 | REED LAKES

Round trip: Lower lake 7 miles, upper lake 9 miles
Hiking time: 5–7 hours
High point: 4,250 feet
Total elevation gain: 1,850 feet
Best: July–September
Map: USGS Anchorage D6
Agencies: Alaska Division of Parks and Outdoor Recreation and Alaska Division of Mining, Land, & Water

At the foot of towering granite spires reminiscent of the high Sierra, plunging cascades feed alpine Reed Lakes. On the edge of the vast wilderness of the Talkeetna Mountains, this mountain world is unlike any other near Anchorage. Watch for ptarmigan, marmots, ground squirrels, pikas, northern shrikes, and golden eagles.

Driving directions. Reach the trailhead from mile 49.5 of the Glenn Highway by turning west on a road marked "Fishhook Road." (This road is also known as Palmer–Fishhook and Fishhook–Willow Road; see the Matanuska Valley detail map.) This paved road begins 1.5 miles beyond Palmer's West Arctic Avenue, the farthest north Palmer stoplight. It is the road over Hatcher Pass. Follow it to elevations above tree line. Nearly 15 miles from the Glenn Highway, it rounds a sharp switchback at the Motherlode Lodge. Proceed another 0.8 mile to Archangel Road (also called Fern Mine Road), which begins with a sharp switchback to the right off the Hatcher Pass Road. Archangel Road is marked, but inconspicuously and well before the intersection. Drive 2.3 miles on this unmaintained road to a pullout on the right, marked as the Reed Lakes trailhead (elevation 2,400 feet).

The road is rutted and quite bumpy but mostly level. It requires fording a small stream. Standard passenger cars with good clearance generally can make it if driven carefully. In winter, park in a plowed turnout along the Hatcher Pass Road near the beginning of Archangel Road or at the Gold–Mint trailhead, and take a shovel in case your car gets stuck.

From the summer trailhead, walk the eroded Snowbird Mine road about 1½ miles to its end at an ill-kept cabin (elevation 2,700 feet). This is at the site of the old Snowbird Mine village. Building foundations and other scraps of history are buried in the brush here. The mine itself was high on the mountainside to the northwest up Glacier Creek. From the cabin, Lower Reed Lake is 2 miles away, and Upper Reed Lake is a mile beyond that.

Reed Creek valley is not obvious from the cabin. While the main valley appears to head back to the right (northeast) of the cabin, Reed Creek comes down more steeply from the north; look for cascades part way up. From

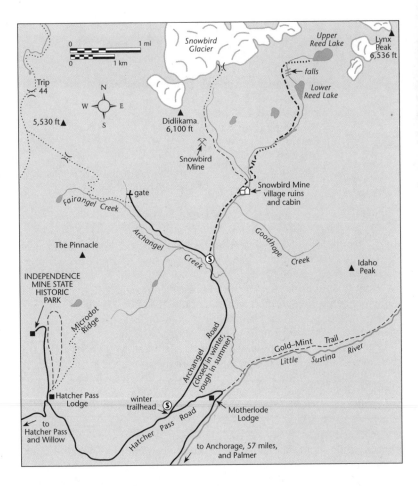

the cabin, follow a footpath to Glacier Creek, and cross it on a bridge. About 100 feet farther, cross Reed Creek on a second bridge. The main trail heads left up Reed Creek.

The trail climbs uphill in switchbacks painstakingly prepared by the British Schools Exploring Society as a service project. The project included replanting the old, direct trail that was eroding badly. Please do not cut corners and create further erosion on this popular but little-maintained trail. The trail contours left below the hilltop to an area of granite boulders. Boulder-hopping is necessary, a difficult task for less-experienced hikers, young children, and dogs. Beyond the boulder field, follow sparkling Reed Creek through grassy meadows and past small clear pools that reflect the surrounding mountains. Cross on boulders to the north side of the creek as you approach these pools. The aqua beauty that is Lower Reed Lake lies

200 vertical feet above (at elevation 3,750 feet), although the trail stays high on the left above the lake. Beyond, a lovely waterfall cascades over rock slabs.

To reach Upper Reed Lake (elevation 4,250 feet), a mile from the lower lake, skirt the falls to the left, crossing rocks and grassy meadows. Beyond a shallow pond, the vivid upper lake appears at the base of Lynx Peak (elevation 6,536 feet). Granite spires and sheer faces rise high above talus and glaciers. The lakes are often ice-covered into July, and ice forms again by

Super Bowl Sunday on Reed Lakes Trail, January (John Wolfe Jr.)

mid-September. Nonetheless, hardy types swim in these chilly waters on hot days. Good campsites are available after the snow melts (sometimes not until July). Bring a stove for cooking.

The ill-kept cabin on the way to Reed Lakes is open for public shelter but is unpleasant. From the cabin, the hanging valley of Glacier Creek makes a nice alternate hike and leads by steep trail to the flattened buildings of Snowbird Mine (½ mile) and beyond to an overlook of the Snowbird Glacier (2 miles).

It is possible to connect Archangel Road with Trip 44 via a high and rocky or snowy but otherwise not technical pass accessible via Fairangel Creek. Look for an informal trail near an old mining cabin about 1.7 miles beyond the Reed Lakes trailhead. Another nearby option is the Gold–Mint Trail, which begins across the road from the Motherlode Lodge. It leads 9 miles to the head of the Little Susitna Valley.

Winter Activity in the Area

The trip from the Hatcher Pass Road to the old cabin on the Reed Lakes Trail is a good winter ski or snowshoe tour over gently sloping terrain. Snowmobiles use Archangel Road and the area west of the road but are prohibited on the Reed Creek side. The Gold–Mint Trail that begins across from the Motherlode Lodge also offers ski touring in a nonmotorized area, although the trailhead can be noisy with snowmobilers heading toward Hatcher Pass.

Farther up the road toward Hatcher Pass are other winter opportunities. The Hatcher Pass Lodge and Independence Mine State Historic Park, where road maintenance ends in winter, is good for skiing and closed to recreational snowmobiling. Popular ski options are touring on groomed tracks in the valley (pay a fee at the lodge), or touring uphill to telemark back down (no fee, but no guarantee of a trail). Popular telemark destinations are Microdot Ridge and April Bowl. Microdot Ridge lies across the valley from the buildings of Independence Mine, and skiers usually start from the lodge A-frames. April Bowl lies immediately above and south of Hatcher Pass proper. While skiers have attempted most slopes in the area, all are steep enough to avalanche under the right conditions (including portions of Microdot Ridge and April Bowl—see "Avalanches," in the Introduction). Make sure you have the proper equipment and training before tackling the slopes.

The unplowed stretch of road over Hatcher Pass and into Willow Creek can make a grand ski tour. The route climbs about 1½ miles to the pass and descends about 12½ miles and 2,300 vertical feet to a parking area about 3 miles east of the Willow Creek bridge and about 18 miles east of the Parks Highway. The road to the east side of the pass and all areas west of the pass are open to snowmobiles. Reach the Willow end of the road to Hatcher Pass (Fishhook–Willow Road) at mile 71.2 of the Parks Highway.

44 | CRAIGIE CREEK

Round trip: 3–9 miles (trip extensions possible)
Hiking time: 2–7 hours
High point: 4,250 feet
Total elevation gain: 950 feet–1,500 feet
Best: mid-July–early October
Map: USGS Anchorage D7
Agency: Alaska Division of Mining, Land, & Water

Take a picnic lunch to a blue-green alpine lake at the base of precipitous peaks and spires. The short walk is just right for families with children, but don't overlook this easy hike to Dogsled Pass as an entrance to outstanding, if more-difficult, wilderness hiking deep into the Talkeetna Mountains.

Driving directions. To reach Craigie Creek, drive to mile 49.5 of the Glenn Highway (43.5 miles northeast of Anchorage and 1.5 miles north of Palmer's West Arctic Avenue stoplight), and turn west onto a road marked "Fishhook Road." (This is also known as Palmer–Fishhook Road and Fishhook–Willow Road; see the Matanuska Valley detail map.) Fishhook Road is the road over Hatcher Pass. It is a narrow, steep, and winding route unsafe for trailers and large campers. Drive about 18.8 miles from the Glenn Highway, through the scenic gorge of the Little Susitna River and uphill past the road to Independence Mine State Historic Park, to the crest of Hatcher Pass. About 1.4 miles beyond (west of) the pass, the road forks; take the left fork. Continue another 3.2 miles to a side road that turns right into the valley of Craigie Creek and may be marked "Craigie Creek Trail." The total distance from the Glenn Highway to this point is 23.4 miles.

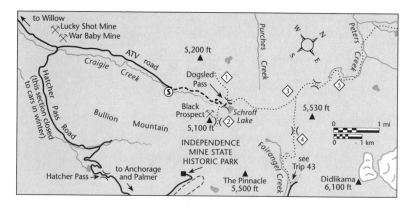

Upper Peters Creek, July (John Wolfe Jr.)

Craigie Creek Trail is a very narrow, very rocky, unmaintained old road. It is passable for about 3 miles by vehicles with good clearance and four-wheel drive. The first mile or so is extraordinarily rough. Nearly level and lined with wildflowers, it makes a great hike and presents mountain bikers with some good technical challenges (rocks). Note that walking it makes the entire hike about 9 miles instead of 3 miles round trip.

Because of deep snow, the road over Hatcher Pass is almost never open before the third week in June, and often later. Craigie Creek Trail should be free of snow by late June but may have wet and soft spots. Those who drive should park well off the road. One possible parking spot (elevation 3,300 feet) is on the right where the ruins of a cabin are visible across the creek, about 2.8 miles from the main road.

At the beginning of Craigie Creek Trail, note the adit entrances of Lucky Shot and War Baby Mines high on the mountains to the left. Gold mining in the Craigie Creek area began prior to 1919 and continued at least through 1930. On-again, off-again mining activity has taken place in recent years. If there are signs posted against trespassing in certain areas, respect the signs. The route may cross private property, although hikers have used this access for years without complications. Do not disturb buildings or equipment, and leave rocks or other minerals where they lie.

From the possible parking areas on this old road, continue on foot as the track climbs gently, passing old buildings and waterfalls. The road then becomes a foot trail leading high above brushline to Dogsled Pass (elevation 4,250 feet) and a lovely tarn locally known as Schroff Lake. The north side of the pass is covered by acres of granite boulders, which make both walking and camping difficult near the pass and lake.

Hikes and climbs abound, but the boulder field makes further access more difficult than the initial route to the pass. Several possibilities are outlined here. Numbers are keyed to the map.

1. From Dogsled Pass, an easy walk leads up the west ridge to several high points.
2. A rock scramble up the gully to the southeast next to the old Black Prospect Mine entrance leads to a ridge crest and a view of the historic Independence Mine buildings far below.
3. The upper end of Purches Creek awaits on the far side of Dogsled Pass. A traverse around the upper end of Purches Creek leads to a bowl with good camping on flat tundra, a welcome change from negotiating large boulders while descending to the north and east from the pass.
4. From the tundra bowl in Purches Creek, a difficult, rocky pass (elevation 4,850 feet) leads southeast to a high valley containing the Talkeetna Mine. Descend to Fairangel Creek, pick up a trail, and follow it to Archangel Road (see Trip 43 for driving directions to this area). The descent requires good routefinding skills and is steep.
5. North of the tundra bowl in upper Purches Creek is another pass that leads to upper Peters Creek. There, find even grander scenery and finer camping opportunities. The pass into Peters Creek is steep but has fewer boulders than Dogsled Pass. From the pass crest (elevation 4,500 feet), it is least steep to head a few hundred feet east before dropping into the Peters Creek drainage. Still farther to the north is yet another pass. It is strewn with boulders, especially on the north side, but leads to views down unnamed streams to the Kashwitna River drainage.

The Craigie Creek Trail area is also accessible from Willow on the Parks Highway at mile 71.2. In winter, the Hatcher Pass road is not plowed between the Hatcher Pass Lodge A-frames (Independence Mine area) and a parking area on the Willow side about 3 miles upstream from the Willow Creek bridge and 18 miles from the Parks Highway. Good ski touring can be found here (see also Trip 43), but the entire west side of Hatcher Pass is open to snowmobiles.

45 | NANCY LAKE CANOE TRAILS

Lynx Lake Loop: 8 miles
Allow: 7 hours–2 days
Best: late May–early October
Maps: USGS Tyonek C1; for Little Susitna River, Anchorage C8
Agency: Nancy Lake State Recreation Area

The Nancy Lake State Recreation Area offers a lovely, tranquil, popular canoe trip, Lynx Lake Loop, through a chain of fourteen forest-rimmed lakes. The twelve overland portages are on good trails and are well marked. Loons dot the lakes, bears occasionally use the portages, and fishing is good in several of the lakes. Some of these lakes are actually warm enough for swimming! In the relatively recent past Tanaina Indians lived here, supporting themselves by subsistence hunting, fishing, and trapping.

Driving directions. Take the Parks Highway to mile 67.3 (from Anchorage). Turn west onto Nancy Lake Parkway, a wide gravel road that is rough when not recently graded. You will reach a fee station in a little over a mile where you must pay a fee for parking and camping. Drive 4.6 miles from the Parks Highway to the canoe trailhead at Tanaina Lake.

Pick up the pamphlet "Summer Guide to Nancy Lake State Recreation Area" at the trailhead if not before. The map is helpful for finding the portages. The loop can be taken in either direction, but going by way of Milo Pond, in a counterclockwise direction, puts the longest portages at the beginning of the trip. Begin the trip by paddling to the south end of Tanaina Lake and portaging to Milo *Pond*. Note that the second lake in the opposite direction is named Milo *Lake*.

All of the portages are under a half mile, and most are considerably shorter. They are marked by orange, diamond-shaped signs. Some have boardwalks over wet spots. Several require carrying the canoe uphill. The portage between Frazer and Jackknife Lakes is by water.

The best camping spots are at designated campsites: between Little Noluck and Big Noluck Lakes (a little over an hour from the trailhead); on the northwest corner of Lynx Lake (a little over 4 hours from the trailhead via Milo Pond and a little over 2 hours via Milo Lake); and at either end of Ardaw Lake (about an hour from the trailhead). Each of these campsite areas has an outhouse. There are also four public-use cabins on Lynx Lake Loop: one at James Lake (the nicest) and three on Lynx Lake. Make reservations to rent a cabin with Alaska State Parks Mat-Su/Copper Basin Area office or with the Department of Natural Resources (DNR) Public Information Center (see Appendix for addresses).

All of the lakes except Lynx are surrounded by public land. Lynx Lake has some private land and private cabins around it, and camping is permitted

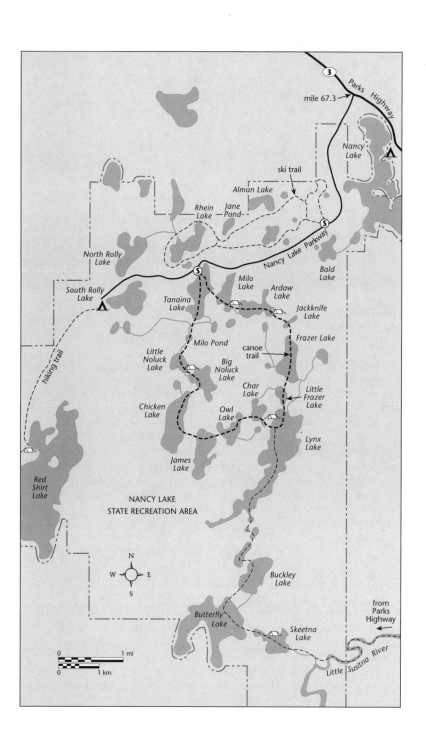

3
Parks Highway

mile 67.3

Nancy
Lake

ski trail

Alman Lake

Rhein
Lake
Jane
Pond

S

Nancy Lake Parkway

North Rolly
Lake

Bald
Lake

S

South Rolly
Lake

Milo
Lake
Ardaw
Lake
Jackknife
Lake

Tanaina
Lake

Frazer Lake

Milo Pond

canoe
trail

Little
Noluck
Lake
Big
Noluck
Lake

Char
Lake
Little
Frazer
Lake

hiking trail

Chicken
Lake

Owl
Lake

Lynx
Lake

James
Lake

Red
Shirt
Lake

NANCY LAKE
STATE RECREATION AREA

N
W   E
S

Buckley
Lake

from
Parks
Highway

Butterfly
Lake

Skeetna
Lake

Little Susitna River

0   1 mi
0   1 km

Chicken Lake, June (Helen Nienhueser)

only at the designated campsites. Airplanes and boats with outboard motors are allowed on Lynx Lake, but not on the other lakes.

Several variations on the standard loop trip are possible. You can extend the trip by heading south from Lynx Lake to Butterfly and Skeetna Lakes, then returning via the same route. There are several campsites on Skeetna Lake, and Butterfly Lake has good fishing.

It is also possible to enter the canoe system via the Little Susitna River. Access is from mile 57 on Parks Highway. It takes 4 to 5 hours on the river to reach the portage for Skeetna Lake (marked). The river portion requires more canoeing experience than do the lakes.

In addition to those cabins on the Lynx Lake Loop, Nancy Lake State Recreation Area offers public-use cabins on Nancy, Red Shirt, and Bald Lakes. See the State Parks website for information. There is a campground at the end of the road at South Rolly Lake and a campground on the northeast shore of Nancy Lake, accessible from mile 66.5 of the Parks Highway.

Bring binoculars for watching birds and spotting portages. Rubber boots will keep feet dry, and a head net is nice to have for the portages. Canoes can be rented nearby and may be available at the trailhead (see Appendix for addresses). To ensure availability and access to the locked canoes at the trailhead, it is best to arrange the rental ahead of time. However, there is a canoe rental office near the boat launch at the South Rolly Campground, and it is generally staffed daily until 5 or 6 P.M. during summer (except Wednesdays).

In winter, 10 miles of maintained cross-country ski trails loop through the rolling, lake-dotted country north of Nancy Lake Parkway. The area north of the Parkway is closed to snowmobiles. Pick up a copy of the pamphlet "Winter Guide to Nancy Lake State Recreation Area" at the State Parks Mat-Su/Copper Creek Area office or the DNR Public Information Center (see Appendix for addresses) for a map of the ski trails. The winter trailhead is at mile 2.2 of the Parkway. The Bald Lake Cabin is nearby, and the Nancy Lake cabins are only about a mile away. When the lakes freeze solid before the snow falls, the lakes also offer the opportunity for overnight ice-skating trips. Take a light plastic sled for gear, and reserve a cabin for a novel weekend. Take warm boots for the "portages."

46 | PETERS HILLS

Round trip: 4–14 miles
Allow: 3 hours–3 days
High point: 2,840 or 3,929 feet
Total elevation gain: 1,000–2,550 feet
Best: July–September
Map: USGS Talkeetna C2
Agencies: Alaska Division of Mining, Land, & Water and
Denali State Park

The majestic white mountain known as Denali (Mount McKinley) looms over the Peters Hills, making its presence, 40 miles away, felt whether it is visible or not. When Denali is out, the views of it and its consorts, Foraker and Hunter, are superb. When Denali is shrouded with clouds, you may still be able to see the Kanikula and Tokositna Glaciers and the jagged black peaks of the Tokosha Mountains—and there is always the chance of a glimpse of Denali later in the trip. No matter what the weather, this trip offers wonderful walking on alpine ridges, great camping beside alpine lakes, blueberries and low bush cranberries in season, and the possibility of glimpsing a grizzly bear or a wolf.

The hike is particularly scenic in early September when the rich reds and golds of autumn foliage are at their best. But, beginning in late August, the area is also popular with hunters, particularly on weekends, and many hunters use all-terrain vehicles (ATVs) near the beginning of this hike.

A few cautions: The trip described here is a cross-country hike, much of it without any trail. The first part follows an ATV trail through brush. The footpath that branches off the ATV trail peters out and eventually disappears

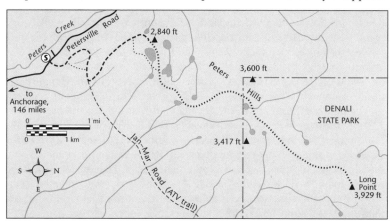

Clouds open to a view of the Tokositna Glacier and Tokosha Mountains, August (Helen Nienhueser)

entirely. You are on your own to find the best route. There is no developed trailhead, there is no trail maintenance, and there are no signs. Finding the point where the ATV trail leaves the road can be a challenge. Some off-trail experience is necessary to ensure that you can find your way back to your car. A map and compass and the ability to use them are essential in the event that the clouds settle down on these hills, as they often do. The last 12½ miles of the access road are rough.

Driving directions. At mile 114.8 of the Parks Highway (115 miles north of Anchorage), turn west onto Petersville Road at the tiny community of Trapper Creek. The Peters Hills are 31 miles away. The first 3 miles of the Petersville Road are paved and the remaining 15+ miles to the Forks Roadhouse and Peters Creek are fairly good gravel. Bear right at the roadhouse. From this point the road narrows, is poorly maintained, and may have deep mud holes during spring and early summer. When the road is dry, usually by July, cars with normal clearance should be able to reach the trail, although a few eroded sections may challenge driving skills. Allow nearly 2 hours to drive the 31 miles from Trapper Creek. Contact the Alaska Department of Transportation for a road condition report (see Appendix for phone number).

The hike begins on an ATV trail called Jan-Mar Road, a little more than 12 miles north of the Forks Roadhouse. To find Jan-Mar Road watch for the buildings of the Petersville placer mine a little over 11 miles north of the Forks Roadhouse, in the bottom of a small valley. Drive 1 mile farther and find gravelly Jan-Mar Road leaving the right side of the road. Jan-Mar Road may or may not be marked by a sign. Look for an open gravel area to the left of the Petersville Road and below it, a few yards past Jan-Mar Road. Park here (elevation 1,825 feet).

The first viewpoint, point 2840, is 2 miles away. On foot, follow Jan-Mar Road uphill. It bends to the left and follows the dry crest of a low ridge, then makes a broad U turn to the right and traverses a hillside. This arc makes an end run around a small drainage and is pleasant walking. As an option, a muddy shortcut crosses the drainage.

Beyond the arc, the trail climbs a short hill, levels, and heads northeast. It then descends slightly to a small creek and climbs the hill on the other side. On the far side of this second hill there is a second, larger stream. Fewer than 100 feet before the second stream another ATV trail branches off Jan-Mar Road to the left, uphill. A yellow metal sign may mark the intersection. Follow this side ATV trail through the brush a little over a mile up a long ridge. New ATV trails are continually being created. If in doubt, stay on the low ridge heading northwest, paralleling the stream on your right.

The side ATV trail peters out at the top of the ridge near a small pond. Shortly before the end of the trail, a well-worn footpath heads to the right, uphill. Follow this path toward point 2840, which offers a wonderful view of Denali and makes a good destination for a day hike.

Hikers heading toward Long Point will find no trail but have a choice of routes. One is to follow the directions above to point 2840. From there continue around the ridge north of the lake on the east side of point 2840. Follow this ridge past the outlet of the lake.

An alternate route to Long Point is to leave the side ATV trail before its end, just before it goes very steeply uphill. Head cross-country to the right, across a brushy depression, to a low point on the rocky ridge above. Cross the ridge and contour left to reach the lake below and east of point 2840. Walk around the lake on its south side, cross its outlet, and head northeast.

To reach Long Point (5 miles away) via the least brushy route, weave through the lakes and high points along the ridge as shown on the map. From the outlet of the lake east of point 2840, head northeast, and contour around the eastern end of the heart-shaped lake on a dry, low ridge. Cross the brushy valley between two tiny lakes. The northern of these lakes, labeled 2545 on the USGS maps, is nearly dried up. The easiest route is north of the southern and most obvious lake, which drains southeast and is not shown on the USGS map.

Then climb toward point 3600, following dry-looking, brownish patches on its south ridge. Head for the top or contour to the right above the brush and cross a small saddle at about 3,400 feet. From here the rest of the route to Long Point is a comparatively easy, gently rising 2-mile walk.

Follow this tundra-covered ridge as far as time permits. Sunlight, clouds, and storms sweeping through the mountains to the north are hypnotic. Watch the sunset, the sunrise, and the northern lights play with the continent's highest peak and its consorts. Famed Alaska artist Sydney Laurence painted many of his canvases of Denali from just below Long Point.

Camp anywhere. Water is easily available, but take a stove for cooking. The eastern half of the ridge lies in Denali State Park.

47 | KESUGI RIDGE (CURRY RIDGE)

Traverse: 37 miles (Little Coal Creek to Byers Lake: 28 miles)
Allow: 3–6 days
High point: 3,550 feet
Total elevation gain: 6,100 feet (southbound)
Best: late June–September
Maps: USGS Talkeetna C1 and Talkeetna Mountains C6, D6
Agency: Denali State Park

With superlatives in scenery, weather, and physical challenge, Kesugi Ridge captures the diversity of southcentral Alaska backpacking on one route. The name "Curry Ridge" is often applied to this hike. This may be a holdover from previous decades, before Parks Highway construction, when railroad passengers would stop to hike to the Curry Lookout on Curry Ridge for the view. The lookout, an historic structure, sits on Curry Ridge, an extension of the Kesugi Ridge system, but there is no trail there now.

Trending north–south between the Alaska Range and the Talkeetna Mountains, Kesugi Ridge offers miles of walking on alpine tundra along its broad, rolling top. This Kesugi-Curry ridge system is the central feature of Denali State Park. The hike comes complete with wee tundra flowers, outrageous rock formations, shining tarns, and tumbling streams. But it is not only an alpine ridge. The traverse drops into stands of beautiful old birch trees, open cottonwood groves, and spruce forests.

On clear days, none of these features, fine as they are, likely will gain hikers' attention as much as the view of the towering dark cliffs of Moose's Tooth and the brilliant ice peaks of 20,320-foot Denali (Mount McKinley). The view of these peaks is arguably best from Kesugi Ridge, which offers the right combination of elevation (up to nearly 3,600 feet) and setback to allow views between and over the lesser peaks to the heart of the Alaska

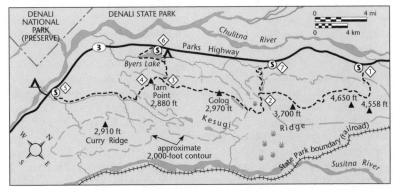

Range. Denali presents a particularly dramatic profile from this vantage.

The ridge may offer the promise of perfection, but it comes at a price. Four routes from the Parks Highway to the ridge top are evenly spaced for abbreviated traverses along the ridge top, but all include a steep hike. Except at the north end, the ridge-crest trail tends to climb over high points rather than traversing around them. It winds through all the best visual features even if that means greater effort, can be quite wet in spots, and is characterized often by taking grades head-on instead of wasting time with switchbacks. Also, weather here can be terrible. Some of the trail at the highest elevations is nearly indecipherable without the many cairns placed along the way. In foggy, rainy, windy weather, picking out these stone piles from the backdrop of natural stone can be impossible. It is imperative that any party have 1:63,360 topographic maps and a compass with them, know how to use them, and be prepared to turn around or sit tight and wait when the weather is poor.

The four trailheads are called Little Coal Creek, Ermine Hill, Byers Lake, and Troublesome Creek. Park rangers recommend hiking the trail from north to south. The description below covers the full traverse and assumes this favored direction of travel. Note, however, that the Troublesome Creek Trail is closed from approximately July 15 to September 1 each year when salmon reach the creek and attract many black bears and some grizzlies. During that time, the full trip must be truncated with an exit to Byers Lake. Even then, if the weather is good, it is worthwhile going beyond the junction leading to Byers Lake at least to Tarn Point before descending. The following table lists points of interest, keyed to the map, and basic mileage.

Number on Map	Point of Interest	Approximate Mileage cumulative	from previous
1	Little Coal Creek trailhead	0	0
2	Ermine Hill Trail junction	14	14
3	Cascade Trail junction	24	10
4	Tarn Point	25	1
5	Troublesome Creek trailhead	37	12
	Side Trails	**Mileage**	
6	Cascade Trail, Byers Lake Campground to ridge-crest junction	3.4	
7	Ermine Hill Trail, Parks Highway to ridge-crest junction	2.7	

Driving directions, Little Coal Creek. To reach the northern access, follow the Parks Highway to the Little Coal Creek trailhead (marked; elevation 1,350 feet) at mile 163.9, about 164 driving miles north of Anchorage and about 74 miles south of the Denali National Park entrance.

Driving directions, Ermine Hill. The Ermine Hill Trail begins at a pull-out on the east side of the highway at mile 156.4 (elevation 1,375 feet). As of this writing, trailhead information was posted on a sign a few dozen yards into the woods and was not visible from the pullout. The park was considering making it more obvious.

Driving directions, Byers Lake/Cascade Trail. Byers Lake Campground is at milepost 147. The official trailhead (elevation 850 feet) is on the campground loop where there is no parking (unless you have paid for a campsite), but a trail along the lakeshore connects to this main trail. Parking is available at Public-Use Cabin Number 1 and at a boat launch.

Driving directions, Troublesome Creek. To reach the southern access, stop at the Upper Troublesome Creek trailhead on the east (Kesugi Ridge) side of the highway at mile 137.6 (elevation 650 feet). Do not confuse the trailhead with the Lower Troublesome pullout and campground on the opposite side of the highway at mile 137.2.

On Foot

The Traverse. From the Little Coal Creek trailhead, the trail climbs quickly out of the trees in about 1½ miles and continues uphill for a total ascent of about 2,200 feet to the high point on the entire Kesugi Ridge Trail at 3,550 feet. Ready access to water is lacking along much of this initial ascent. Beyond the high point, the route is level for several miles along the western edge of the ridge—prime view territory—before climbing again to another high point, this time along the eastern edge. Camping spots with good views and water are plentiful, but this segment of the route has sustained exposure to weather. The Ermine Hill Trail junction is in a somewhat protected depression near a lake.

The segment of the ridge trail from Ermine Hill to the Cascade Trail (Byers Lake) has perhaps the greatest variety, but if you have just come up the Ermine Hill Trail, know that the route toward Byers Lake only stays high for a short distance before dropping steeply 900 feet to forest and wetlands only to ascend again. Camping is good near the Ermine Hill Trail junction but poor for at least 3 miles through the lowland.

From the wet lowland, the route ascends over granite slabs and outcrops, passing by Skinny Lake and over a rounded 2,970-foot summit called Golog. The rolling route continually reframes views of the big peaks across the valley and provides good camping options. The junction with the Cascade Trail is over the edge a bit on the western side, above Byers Lake.

The segment from the Cascade Trail junction to the Troublesome Creek trailhead passes over 2,880-foot Tarn Point. The route to Tarn Point sees day-use traffic from Byers Lake via the Cascade Trail (about 8.5 miles round trip). The route south of Tarn Point sees little traffic at all. The alpine portion, extending at least another 2 miles southward, has scenery as beautiful as any other portion of the ridge, and camping is good. The trail here is less distinct than previous segments. Ultimately, it drops into the Troublesome Creek valley and its beautiful, if buggy, forest. The trail parallels this creek,

Denali (Mount McKinley) from Kesugi Ridge, June (John Wolfe Jr.)

which carves its way through granite buttresses. The stream is loud; be diligent in letting wildlife know you are coming. The forested portion is best for transit and not for camping and is closed during salmon and bear activity, July 15 to September 1, each year.

Ermine Hill Trail. The Ermine Hill Trail winds through the woods at the base of the ridge for about 1½ miles before crossing Giardia Creek and mounting the ridge side in switchbacks. This route provides perhaps the easiest access to alpine country, only about 1,000 vertical feet from the trailhead.

Byers Lake Loop and Cascade Trails. The Byers Lake Loop Trail leads to the Cascade Trail, which climbs past a waterfall and up steeply about 1,700 vertical feet to join the ridge-crest trail. Byers Lake Loop encircles the lake in 4.8 miles, is flat, and combines woodland and shoreline scenery.

On any of these trails, hikers should be prepared for mud, eroded areas, slippery and rocky footing, snow crossings, minor stream fords, and—in forest areas—blown-down trees.

A Denali State Park visitor information center sits at the Alaska Veterans Memorial, immediately north of the Byers Lake Campground. It is open every day in summer. Allow time here to:

• Draw the route from posted USGS maps onto your maps.
• Hear recent trail conditions.
• Pick up bear-proof food containers (free use with a deposit and driver's license).

The information center is the only place the entire trail is mapped on 1:63,360 maps. You may also pick up a brochure on site or at State Parks offices elsewhere. There is no phone service at the information center. There is no ranger station at Denali State Park. The best source of telephone information is the Finger Lake State Parks office (see Mat-Su/Copper Basin Area office in Appendix for phone number).

This point-to-point trek requires a car shuttle, or you might leave your car at the Troublesome Creek or Byers Lake trailheads and get a ride from motorists stopping at the Troublesome Creek wayside or the Veterans Memorial. Another option is a shuttle (for a fee) run by Susitna Expeditions, a park concessionaire based at Byers Lake (see Appendix for contact information). Byers Lake also includes two public-use cabins, which must be reserved in advance (see Appendix), and a hike-in or paddle-in campground on the back side of the lake.

CHICKALOON – NABESNA – VALDEZ

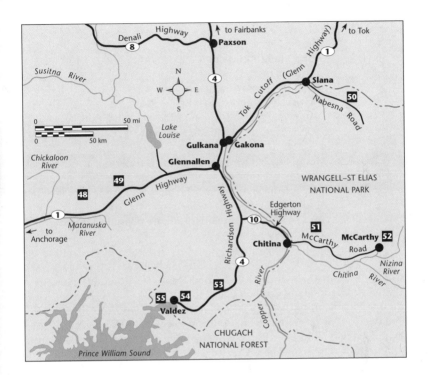

The vast, relatively unpeopled eastern half of southcentral Alaska offers some of Alaska's most spectacular scenery. The Glenn Highway, from the small community of Chickaloon eastward, lies between the spectacular walls of the Chugach Mountains (to the south) and the Talkeetna Mountains (north). Here, and north and south of the high icy peaks in Wrangell–St. Elias National Park and Preserve, are a few of the most rigorous backcountry hiking trips described in this book. The Richardson Highway passes through the vast Copper River drainage, which roughly separates the Chugach Mountains from the Wrangell Mountains. The Wrangells rise to more than 16,000 feet from a base at less than 1,000 feet. Visitors must negotiate gravel roads to hike here, but the extensive wilderness makes the effort worthwhile. At the southern end of the Richardson Highway lies the city of Valdez, surrounded by mountains at the head of lovely Port Valdez, where there are several hiking options.

Opposite: *Monarch Peak in the Talkeetna Mountains (Trip 48)* (Helen Nienhueser)

48 | HICKS CREEK–CHITNA PASS

One way: 42 miles
Allow: 4–5 days
High point: 4,700 feet
Total elevation gain: 4,400 feet eastbound, 4,100 feet westbound
Best: late June–August
Maps: USGS Anchorage D2, D3, D4
Agencies: Alaska Division of Mining, Land, & Water and U.S. Bureau of Land Management

The Talkeetna Mountains, which invite endless wandering, are a fascinating wilderness of peaks, tundra, alpine valleys, and clear mountain streams, most of it far from civilization. The trip over Chitna Pass is nearly circular and includes unmaintained trails. Using the trails as access and topographic maps as a guide, many other trips are possible, limited primarily by time and food supply.

According to old-timers, prospectors traveled parts of this trail in the early 1900s. The route took them from Knik (which was accessible by boat from Seattle in the summer) and Chickaloon, up Boulder Creek, over Chitna Pass, and along Caribou Creek to Alfred Creek (see Trip 49). Their destinations were gold prospects and mines on Alfred and Albert Creeks. Today, many of these routes are all-terrain vehicle (ATV) trails, still used by miners and by hunters in the fall. The route described here starts on an ATV trail known as the Hicks Creek Trail or Pinochle Creek Trail and ends on an ATV trail known as the Purinton Creek Trail, connecting these with routes over Chitna Pass.

A caution: First, regarding aesthetics, the ATV use that keeps these trails open spoils the first several miles from either trailhead. Some who walk this area during wet weather when the trails are particularly muddy are deeply disappointed by the sometimes-boot-sucking muck and visual mess. For most, the deep backcountry and views of the spectacular Chugach and Talkeetna Mountains make up for these problems. It is probably best to plan this trip in midsummer, when the weather is drier and there is less use of the trails by hunters on ATVs.

A second caution: The route described here is on unmarked, unmaintained trails—and for short stretches it is without trails. The trip is not for novices; it is possible to become lost. A 1:63,360-scale USGS map is essential; help is far away. Do not go unless your party includes someone who is good at reading topographic maps. Experienced backpackers in good condition and able to follow USGS maps will find that these routes lead to delightful country.

Watch for caribou, moose, black bears, grizzly (brown) bears, Dall sheep, wolves, and coyotes.

Driving directions, Hicks Creek Trail. Take the Glenn Highway to about mile 99.7 (from Anchorage). This is about 3 miles east of the Hicks Creek bridge and 0.1 mile east of a large pullout on the north side of the Glenn Highway. Turn north onto Pinochle Lane, and drive 0.5 mile to an unmarked trailhead on the north side of the road. Park opposite the trailhead near powerline pole 7746 in an area defined by boulders (elevation 1,776 feet), or turn north onto a dirt road and park without blocking the road. Follow this dirt road, which becomes an ATV trail heading for a pass.

Driving directions, Purinton Creek Trail. To reach the Purinton Creek trailhead by road, drive to mile 89 of the Glenn Highway. Parking is available in a pullout by the Purinton Creek bridge (elevation 2,100 feet). About 75 yards east of Purinton Creek is a dirt road that starts northward and bends immediately to the east. Respect private property along the road. Soon, it bends north again and ascends a very steep hill. A new trailhead at mile 90.7 avoids private property but is more suitable for ATVs than hikers.

To complete the full trip, follow the dirt road north of the Hicks Creek trailhead. It quickly becomes an ATV trail that climbs above tree line to a

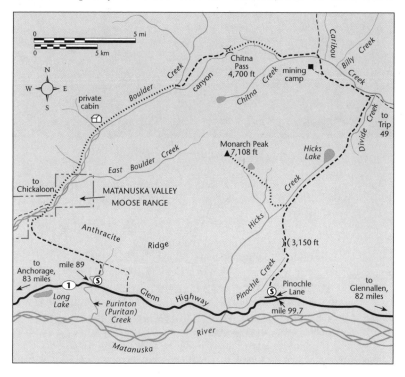

Swans along Purinton Creek Trail, August (John Wolfe Jr.)

3,150-foot pass. The trail over the pass is good, although the lower ground on either side of the pass is rutted and often mucky. The north side of the pass is especially wet.

Not far beyond the pass, the trail descends steeply to Hicks Creek, at 3,000 feet. An off-trail side trip from the creek heads northwest to a small alpine lake (5,000 feet) 3½ miles away, where there is good camping. Use maps to find your way there. Monarch Peak (7,108 feet), towering above the lake, is the highest in the area and is a steep but uncomplicated climb.

The main trail continues to Hicks Lake. Pick whichever side of the creek looks easiest. Camping is possible near the south end of the lake. Watch for muskrats in the water. Beyond Hicks Lake, the ATV trail becomes drier and pleasant. It crosses an indistinct 3,300-foot divide, then follows Divide Creek down to Caribou Creek at 2,800 feet elevation, about 4 miles from Hicks Lake.

Follow the trail up the south side of Caribou Creek, passing good camp-sites. Nearly 2 miles after leaving Divide Creek, follow the most distinct route as it climbs the bank to avoid cliffs and winds along higher ground roughly paralleling the creek (another track continues up the creek bank). Beyond a small ravine and upstream of the junction of Chitna and Caribou Creeks, the trail forks. Follow the right branch steeply down to Chitna Creek (the left fork climbs to a mining camp).

Chitna Creek is swift but usually not deep or difficult to cross. The trail up the opposite bank goes up two distinct levels. Follow it to the top of the second bluff. The ATV trail then continues north along Caribou Creek. *Do not follow it,* unless you are purposefully diverging from the route described here. Instead, pick up a narrow footpath that winds along the edge of the bluff, following the Chitna Creek valley upstream.

The trail blends with animal trails, but it does continue nearly to Chitna Pass and is worth staying on. About 2½ miles from Caribou Creek, turn northwest up a tributary of Chitna Creek toward Chitna Pass. Map-reading skills are essential to find this drainage that leads to the pass, because the trail disappears here for a while. Two separate creek channels come down this one valley, but only the larger ravine farther to the west shows as a creek on the map. You may not find much water in the smaller ravine, but it is an indication that this is the correct valley to ascend. Make your way uphill between these two channels, and rediscover the trail.

At 3,600 feet the vegetation changes from brush to open tundra. A gradual 2½-mile climb to Chitna Pass (elevation 4,700 feet) traverses fine country for camping and exploring. The trail mostly vanishes. Nearby 6,000-foot peaks are easily climbed. Water is available, but firewood is not.

Southwest of Chitna Pass, the route parallels a small creek, and a well-defined footpath reappears. Follow it to nearly level ground and a bend to the left. A short time later, about 2½ miles from the pass, the stream plunges into a small canyon. At that point, the trail leaves the creek, traverses out to the right, and descends a ridge all the way down to Boulder Creek. It does not drop steeply to Boulder Creek directly west of Chitna Pass as shown on the USGS map. The views of the Boulder Creek valley from the ridge crest make the whole trip worthwhile.

About 4 miles from Chitna Pass the well-defined trail ends when it enters the Boulder Creek gravel bars. If the water level allows, walking the riverbed, splashing across the braided channels, is by far the easiest mode of travel. At higher water, cross Boulder Creek once and stay on the northwest side where occasional stretches of trail alternate with occasional stretches of bushwhacking. Following the southeast riverbank requires scrambling over bluffs, necessary perhaps if Boulder Creek is flooding. Camping is good on the river bars.

Once on the gravel bars, it is more than 10 miles to Anthracite Ridge. The crest of Anthracite Ridge drops steeply to the riverbank. Find the Purinton Creek Trail on the east bank of Boulder Creek right at the base of the ridge. On some maps it may be labeled the Chickaloon–Knik–Nelchina Trail. Follow this trail south, then east to the Glenn Highway. This rolling trail has some very wet muck holes created by ATVs, but generally the walking is good. On a clear day, the approach to the Purinton Creek trailhead is spectacular with its panoramic view to the south of the rugged Chugach Mountains.

The two ends of the trail are reasonable for day trips by mountain bike in dry conditions, although each has a long steep hill that requires a tough stint of pushing the bike. Hicks Creek valley is too wet for cycling. The Purinton Creek Trail is hilly. Much more of the route can be used for ski touring, either for day trips from either trailhead or as a several-day trip for experienced skiers and winter campers. The route near the trailheads is likely to be packed by snowmobiles. In midwinter prepare for temperatures to -30°F or colder.

49 | SYNCLINE MOUNTAIN

Circuit: 26 miles, traverse 24 miles
Allow: 3 days
High point: circuit 4,350 feet; traverse 5,471 feet
Total elevation gain: circuit 2,400 feet; traverse 4,900 feet
Best: June–September
Maps: USGS Anchorage D1, D2
Agencies: Alaska Division of Mining, Land, & Water and
U.S. Bureau of Land Management

A network of trails around Syncline Mountain provides access into the backcountry of the Talkeetna Mountains, inhabited primarily by caribou, sheep, miners, and—during the last part of summer—hunters. Two different trips are possible, a circumnavigation of Syncline Mountain and a steep but otherwise straightforward traverse over it. In late June, watch for the Nelchina caribou herd migration through this area. And look for sheep, black bears, grizzlies, coyotes, wolves, and other wildlife any time. In season, there are blueberries and the gamut of Alaska wildflowers. Both trips are rugged and require routefinding skills and backcountry experience.

The part of the circuit that follows Alfred Creek lies along the route of the old Chickaloon–Knik–Nelchina Trail, which provided access to gold mines on Alfred and Albert Creeks before there was a Glenn Highway. In the early 1900s, prospectors traveled Alfred Creek, coming from Knik Arm by way of Chitna Pass (see Trip 48). Gold was discovered on Alfred Creek in 1911, but prospectors were also going beyond Alfred to Albert and Crooked Creeks. When the price of gold was deregulated in the mid-1970s, mining activity began again, and Alfred Creek valley contains an active operation. The ATV access trail on that side of Syncline Mountain is well used and has been maintained.

Driving directions. One trailhead is at Glenn Highway mile 118.5. Here, turn west (uphill) on Trailhead Road, and drive 800 feet to a parking area (elevation 3,245 feet). The turn off the highway is marked as part of the "Chickaloon–Knik–Nelchina" trail system. The parking area, outhouses, and access road are on a remnant of the old Glenn Highway. To begin the hike, follow the old pavement.

The other trailhead is off Martin Road: drive to Glenn Highway mile 123.3, and turn onto Martin Road (sometimes muddy but drivable by most cars). It is marked by a "Trail" sign. Follow Martin Road 1.4 miles to a substantial ATV trail known as Squaw Creek Road. Park about 0.2 mile along Squaw Creek Road, across a shallow stream ford. Because of mud holes, this "road" is not drivable by street vehicles much beyond the parking area. The ATV trail from Belanger Pass joins Squaw Creek Road another 0.2 mile beyond the parking spot.

The Circuit

The circuit of the mountain follows the valleys of Squaw, Caribou, Alfred, and Pass Creeks and climbs over Belanger Pass to complete the loop. The route follows ATV trails and mining roads most of the way, although one option at the west end of Syncline Mountain takes hikers off the trails for a high-country traverse with views overlooking vast, wild valleys.

The circuit can start and finish at the Squaw Creek Road parking area. The trip distance is about the same, the walking is easier, and there is no need to shuttle cars. However, because the Glenn Highway start offers greater scenic variety, that is the route described here. From the mile 118.5 parking area, walk the old Glenn Highway 0.8 mile west to a former gravel pit north of the road. An ATV track known as Meekins Trail begins at the right (northeast) side of the pit. Follow this sometimes-wet trail over the

Caribou Creek valley, June (John Wolfe, Jr.)

toe of Gunsight Mountain and down into the Squaw Creek valley at 2,700 feet, about 3 miles. Find reasonable camping in another mile in spruce woods just across Gunsight Creek, near where the ATV trail forks.

From the trail fork, the route to the left winds through a swampy area, and the right fork heads directly to Squaw Creek and fords it. Go right, and cross the creek (usually no problem). Then head uphill to the Squaw Creek ATV "road," which parallels the creek. Follow it west (left) about 3 miles. When it descends to the level of Squaw Creek, look for a smaller ATV trail on the right.

At this point, there are two options. The side trail leads to the high route around the end of Syncline Mountain (marked 1 on the map). This 3½-mile off-trail trek between the Squaw and Alfred Creek valleys, sometimes brushy and with only intermittent animal trails to follow, is the most difficult but most beautiful part of the circuit. It is also possible to hike from Squaw Creek valley to Alfred Creek valley on a little-used ATV trail that parallels Caribou Creek (marked 2 on the map) instead of crossing the mountain slope. This alternate route is about 2 miles longer, requires 6 to 8 crossings of Squaw Creek, and has some unavoidable boggy areas. It is somewhat easier but less scenic than the off-trail route.

To access the high route, find the ATV side trail about 200 yards before Squaw Creek Road crosses Squaw Creek for the first time. There is more than one trail; if in doubt, follow the road to the first crossing of Squaw Creek and walk back to the trail. Follow this ATV trail uphill and left (west) through brush onto a bench. Leave the trail at its high point, before it starts downhill. Strike out cross-country, heading for the pass between two bumps locally known as Twin Peaks. Stay at about 3,200 feet elevation while contouring around the northern Twin Peak. On your way toward Alfred Creek, look for occasional animal trails through the brush. Flat camping places are hard to find (but not impossible). Water is also difficult to find, as some streams are underground in spots. Listen for running water.

As you round the northwest flank of Syncline Mountain, pick a route and descend into forest to an ATV trail that traverses the base of the mountain at about 2,750 feet. Follow this ATV trail as it bends downhill, paralleling a drainage ravine, and descends to Alfred Creek.

To avoid the high traverse and follow the lower ATV trail around this end of Syncline Mountain, continue on Squaw Creek Road almost to Caribou Creek. The stream crossings are generally easy but cold. Just before a well-used campsite in spruce woods on the north side of the road (about ½ mile before Caribou Creek), follow an ATV side trail straight up the steep bluff. A slightly less steep alternate trail is immediately to the left. Once up the hill, this trail passes through delightful meadows and some very wet areas and is sometimes indistinct. Bear left at forks to stay near the bluff above Caribou Creek and to go west of the tiny lake shown on the map. After little more than 2½ miles, this trail intersects a more substantial ATV trail, placing you about halfway down a long straight grade. (Note: if coming around the mountain counter-clockwise, this junction is not at all

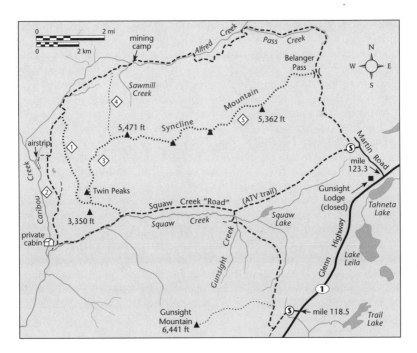

obvious.) A small stream runs in the ATV trail here. Turn right (uphill), and follow this trail as it bends away from the little stream and runs level along the base of Syncline Mountain. Approximately at the point it turns distinctly left and downhill, it becomes common with the off-trail traverse route described above. Paralleling the ravine of an Alfred Creek tributary, descend to Alfred Creek.

Follow the ATV trail a short way up Alfred Creek to a stream that drains the south side of a plateau, obvious on the USGS map. Turn on an ATV trail up this stream and then immediately turn very steeply (still on an ATV trail) up a narrow brushy ridge separating the smaller stream from Alfred Creek. This route gains the top of a plateau, at about 3,150 feet elevation, where the views are grand in all directions. The ATV trail cuts across the plateau's southern edge for a mile and drops to a mining operation near the confluence of Sawmill and Alfred Creeks (elevation 2,900 feet). Avoid the mine buildings, which are private property, and continue up Alfred Creek.

The ATV trail crosses Alfred Creek about six times in the 2 miles upstream of the buildings. Unless the water is high, the easiest option is to follow the trail and walk in wet boots. During high water, it may be preferable to reduce the number of crossings. Alfred Creek is potentially dangerous, as it can be at least knee-deep and very swift. In such conditions, cross at the first wide place upstream of the mining camp, as it becomes increasingly difficult upstream. Cliffs on the south bank appear to make continuing on that side impossible. Two miles from the buildings, the track (now almost a true road and popular with weekend four-wheelers) climbs up and over high bluffs on the south side of the creek. Recross where the route is visible winding uphill away from the stream, or walk the gravel bars another 1½ miles until the road again is visible descending from the high bluffs. Trying to minimize crossings will surely mean bushwhacking where gravel bars pinch out against vegetated banks.

In early summer, finding the route up Pass Creek may be difficult because ice may cover the ATV trail. The route crosses Pass Creek several times and then generally follows it on the north side. The climb to Belanger Pass (4,350 feet) is gradual. The view of the Chugach Mountains during the descent from the pass is magnificent, a fitting climax to the trip (elevation loss about 1,400 feet). The ATV trail drops to Squaw Creek Road 0.2 mile west of the parking area. Respect and avoid private property along the trail as it approaches Squaw Creek Road.

Note that Squaw Creek Road can be very muddy, particularly in the fall when the weather is wetter and the ATV hunter traffic is higher and churns up the surface. Parts or all of the circuit can be done on mountain bikes, but the routes are only pleasant bicycling when dry. Much of the ATV route on the bench above Caribou Creek likely will require pushing the bike.

The Traverse

The traverse over Syncline Mountain offers nice views of the Chugach and Talkeetna Mountains and avoids most of the mining areas. Hikers up high are more likely to see sheep and caribou. Hiking time averages about 1 mile per hour in this trailless terrain.

To do the traverse, follow the directions for the circuit to Twin Peaks. To climb the mountain (elevation 5,471 feet), head up its southwest ridge (marked 3 on the map). Animal trails make much of the route easy (though steep), and the ridge-top walking is delightful. From the pass between the Twin Peaks to the high point at 5,471 feet is a little over 2 miles. From point 5471, several trips are possible. Stay high, exploring ridges and watching wildlife, returning at day's end to camp. (Camping on the ridge requires carrying water or descending from camp to find water.) Or descend via the steep north ridge (marked 4 on the map) toward the plateau above Alfred Creek and continue the circuit around Syncline Mountain. Another possibility is to follow the ridge tops (marked 5 on the map) east and north to Belanger Pass, about 7 miles (no water), or to gain the ridge top from Belanger Pass as a grand day trip.

The trail up to Belanger Pass also may be used for access to intriguing country northeast of the trips described here. Possible explorations could head east and north from Pass Creek toward South Lake or could follow Alfred Creek toward its headwaters (see USGS maps). Another option in the area is an ascent of Gunsight Mountain (6,441 feet) from Meekins Trail. This may be done summer or winter but may be best in winter when low brush is covered.

50 | MENTASTA MOUNTAINS

One way loop: 21 miles
Hiking time: allow 3 days
High point: 6,050 feet
Total elevation gain: 3,050 feet
Best: June–August
Map: USGS Nabesna C5
Agency: Wrangell–St. Elias National Preserve

On the northern edge of Wrangell–St. Elias National Park and Preserve, the headwaters of the Copper River flow north before turning south to Prince William Sound, and two minor creeks begin gathering the water that will become Interior Alaska's Tanana River. A 6,000-foot pass divides these two creeks, Lost Creek and Trail Creek, and creates a traversable gap in the Mentasta Mountains. The creeks have carved valleys that make a fine, if mostly trailless and often rocky, trekking route in and out of the peaks. Both streams cross the quiet Nabesna Road within 2 miles of each other, making an attractive closed loop. Much of the walking on this loop is on gravel bars or easy tundra, but in places you may encounter brief stretches of tussocks or willows and will likely wade braided river channels several times. There is no one trail, though in places all-terrain vehicles (ATVs) or sheep have made segments of trails. Backcountry routefinding skills and an ability to read a topographic map are essential. Watch for Dall sheep, caribou, wolves, bears, moose, pikas, hares, lynx, and glimpses of the high, white Wrangell Mountains.

Driving directions. Take the Tok Cutoff/Glenn Highway to mile 59.8 near Slana (262 miles east of Anchorage), and turn southeast onto the

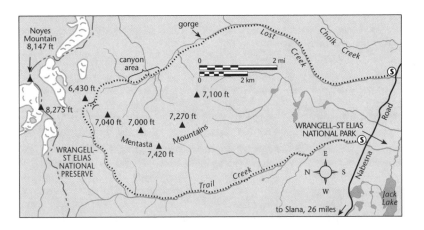

gravel Nabesna Road. Go ¼ mile, and turn right on the access road to the National Park ranger station, where information on road conditions is available (and recommended). Return to the Nabesna Road, and drive about 28.1 miles to Trail Creek and 29.8 miles to Lost Creek. There are no bridges over these creeks, and water levels affect the ability of cars to pass. The stream channels often change across wide gravel bars, and mileage could vary by more than a tenth of a mile. Either stream could have too much water to drive through, but either could be completely dry (especially Trail Creek). About 0.3 mile beyond the main channel of Lost Creek is a sign for Big Grayling Lake trailhead on the left. There is good camping here (but no facilities) and a place to leave a car off the road, but the safest thing to do is leave the car on the west side of Trail Creek because the creeks could rise and block your return. Park well away from the river.

The hike can start either on the Big Grayling Lake Trail (an ATV trail) or on the Lost Creek gravel bar itself. The Big Grayling Lake Trail heads north through brush and in about 5 minutes of hiking time emerges on the gravel bar. In a few hundred yards, you may follow the ATV trail back into the woods for perhaps another 10 minutes, roughly paralleling the stream, before returning again to the gravel bar. About 1½ miles from the road, the main ATV trail heads east toward Big Grayling Lake. This time, stay on the gravel bar, and do not follow the trail.

The route follows Lost Creek to the pass. Until the route enters the mountains, you will walk mostly on the gravel bar. Sometimes you may find yourself on the terrace above the creek walking through scattered dwarf birch and willow on animal trails. Ultimately, as you enter the mountains, the best route will be on the west side of the stream. Hikers usually can ford the creek. Logs may provide crossings where the creek cuts against forested banks. At the point where the creek leaves the mountains, it flows out of a steep-sided cut not suited to walking. A good route around this cut

Above Lost Creek, July (Dave Wolfe)

is on the west side of the creek and up, steeply, nearly 300 feet onto a bench where the walking is good. The route on the east is reportedly passable but requires side-hilling.

On the west, a rolling and discontinuous bench system parallels the stream for about 1½ miles. At one point, a ravine seems to force a descent, but it is possible to cross it on tundra just above a dramatic gorge and continue along the bench well above Lost Creek. Drop back to the creek beyond this ravine where convenient, and proceed upstream as the mountains press in and form a sort of canyon. At this point, approaching elevation 4,500 feet, it is best to cross back to the east side of the creek. Camping spots are scarce at this point in the circuit, but they do exist.

Finding the route out of the canyon area and to the pass is perhaps the trickiest part of the hike, especially if visibility is poor. Consult the map. Several streams come together out of several small canyons; follow the one that leads into Section 28 on the USGS map and then forks. You will likely have to cross the stream you are following more than once. When you round a bend to the right and the canyon opens up a bit (as you enter Section 28), you will see a steeper fork coming in from the left and the main valley continuing to the right at a shallower grade. Creating the divide between these forks is a steep but vegetated hill. The best walking to the pass is at the top of the hill. You may mount the hill directly (best), continue up the right fork until you see a notch on the left side that allows less-steep access toward the pass, or follow the left fork toward the pass (more direct but rocky, viewless, and likely to require walking directly in the stream). Once you are in the higher bowl, the views are fine and the walking good. Camping is possible, although it may be necessary to walk for water. Head to the back left part of this bowl and find the pass, where slatey gray gravel and rust-colored gravel meet at a distinct line.

The west side of the pass drops to a valley that leads about 2 miles to Trail Creek. The descent from the pass requires crossing steep scree and likely a snow patch or two. This may make some uneasy, but there are sheep trails. The trail to the right from the pass is best. The trail to the left eventually runs into rock bands. The broad, partially vegetated hump of a rock glacier in the valley bottom makes good walking, but stay toward the left (south) side to bypass an active ice face toward the right side. Find your way off the rock glacier and follow a pleasant stream back into the land of willows, knee-high grass, and wildflowers. As you enter the Trail Creek valley, the high white volcanoes of the Wrangell Mountains appear to the southwest. Camping is good in this junction area.

To complete the loop, follow Trail Creek valley—quite different than Lost Creek—nearly 7 miles. There is a trail along Trail Creek, but it is intermittent. Find the route that offers the best walking. Often it will be gravel bars, sometimes the ATV trail. Sometimes (especially in the lower stretches) you will face a choice between willow bashing for a short stretch or wading across the creek. Neither option is particularly difficult.

Experienced mountaineers can climb Noyes Mountain (8,147 feet) from the pass. The green tundra of upper Trail Creek invites exploration upstream if there is time. Note that the Trails Illustrated map "Wrangell St. Elias National Park and Preserve" covers this area, but the scale is insufficient to make the map useful for navigation. Hunting is allowed in the Preserve, with sheep season generally beginning August 10 and moose season beginning August 20.

51 | DIXIE PASS

Round trip: 21 miles
Hiking time: 3–4 days
High points: 5,150 feet (pass); 5,770 feet (peak)
Total elevation gain: 3,550 feet
Best: late June–early September
Maps: USGS Valdez C1, McCarthy C8
Agency: Wrangell–St. Elias National Park

Dixie Pass is one of the few backcountry trips in the Wrangell Mountains that can be done without an airplane. It offers the chance for a close-up view of massive, glacier-covered, 14,163-foot Mount Wrangell and of 16,390-foot Mount Blackburn. The hike follows beautiful, crystal-clear Strelna Creek along successively smaller branches until it disappears at its source just below the pass. The countryside is wild, rugged, big, and beautiful, changing from open spruce and willow forest at lower elevations to willow-covered gravel bars somewhat higher, and then becoming alpine tundra below the pass. Watch for bears, moose, Dall sheep, ground squirrels, and ptarmigan.

Although the hike is not long, it is not easy. There are no maintained trails. Part of the route has only intermittent animal trails, and the hiker must choose between walking the gravel bars, crossing and recrossing the stream, or following animal trails through thick willow. Map-reading and routefinding skills are necessary to find the pass. Despite this, the trip is popular with Alaska visitors because it is one of the few easily accessible routes in the Wrangell–St. Elias National Park.

Driving directions. Take the Richardson Highway to mile 82.6 and the junction with the Edgerton Highway (86 miles north of Valdez and 219 miles east of Anchorage). Follow the Edgerton Highway 33 miles to Chitina and from there follow signs for McCarthy. From the east (McCarthy) side of the Copper River bridge, drive about 13½ miles on the gravel McCarthy Road to the Kotsina/Nugget Creek Road on the left, across from the grass Strelna airstrip. (Local residents have erected their own mileposts; as measured by these the Kotsina/Nugget Creek Road is at mile 14.4.)

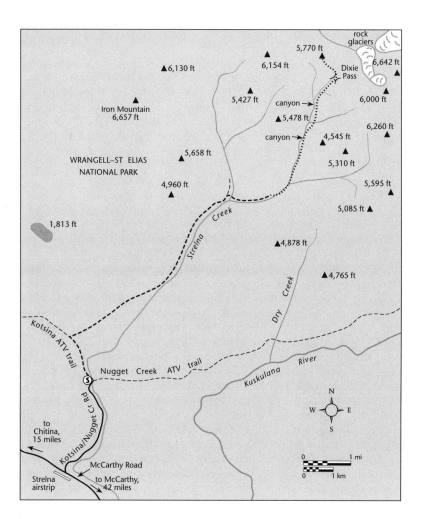

Follow the rough gravel Kotsina/Nugget Creek Road, 2.6 miles to the intersection of Nugget Creek and Kotsina ATV trails. This intersection is easily identified by the ford of Strelna Creek on the Nugget Creek trail just past the intersection. Most cars should park here. Four-wheel-drive vehicles with high enough clearance can continue another 1.3 miles on the Kotsina ATV trail to the Dixie Pass Trail on the right. The trail to Dixie Pass, a narrow footpath, may not be marked. A small clearing, across the road from the trail, helps locate the trail and provides a place to park.

The route winds through open woods of spruce and willow on a good trail for the first 2 miles. After the trail reaches Strelna Creek, it veers northward to follow the creek through much denser forest. The trail in this stretch is more difficult to walk as it is sometimes blocked by a fallen tree or heads steeply uphill to avoid a cliff.

It is about 5 miles from the Kotsina ATV trail to the confluence of the west and east forks of Strelna Creek, the first major confluence on the route. The route follows the east fork. Watch carefully for the valley of the east fork. The trail does not go within sight of the confluence, and it is easy to miss. The side valley containing the east fork of Strelna Creek is obvious, however, to those looking for it. Cross the west fork above the confluence where the water is generally less than knee deep and no problem to cross. Wearing boots or tennis shoes is advisable.

The route for the next 3 miles up the east fork is the most difficult part of the trip. There is a trail of sorts on the north (left) side of the creek for the first mile. Some may prefer to walk the creek bed. Cross the creek to the southeast (right) bank when the trail runs into a cliff.

The route for the 2 miles beyond the initial cliff is on gravel bars or intermittent animal trails through scrub willow, and it is necessary to cross the creek several times to avoid further cliffs. It may be possible to do these crossings on rocks, depending on the water level. Some of the tributary creeks are not shown on the USGS topographic map, which makes locating oneself more difficult. About a mile beyond the first tributary of the east fork that is shown on the USGS map, the creek goes through a canyon for about 100 feet. Here choose between climbing the steep hillside to get around the canyon or walking in the creek if the water level is low enough. Neither is easy. In the canyon, the water is very cold, and in one place hikers must clamber over a boulder overhung by a cliff to avoid a deep pool.

Just beyond the canyon, the valley widens into a broad gravel bar dotted with willow and laced with dwarf fireweed (elevation 3,600 feet). This is a popular campsite and could become overused. Water quality could be affected by careless toilet practices (see "Leave No Trace," in the Introduction).

The second tributary shown on the USGS map comes in at the north end of the gravel bar. To reach the pass (about 1½ miles farther), follow the obvious trail heading uphill between the two forks of the creek. (The left branch of the creek leads to the pass but goes through another canyon as a waterfall.)

When the trail peters out above the last willow, you may either climb to the ridge on your right or continue ahead at the same elevation. Either option leads again to a trail, although the paths are intermittent from this point to the pass.

There are beautiful views from Dixie Pass—of Strelna Creek drainage and the Chugach Mountains to the south, of Rock Creek valley and peaks reaching to 7,500 feet to the north, and, on clear days, glimpses of snowy Mounts Wrangell and Blackburn. But the best views by far are those from peak 5,770, a short climb along the ridge to the northwest.

Camping at Dixie Pass is possible, although water must be melted from snowbanks that linger most of the year on the north side or from the creek

Strelna Creek drainage, August (Helen Nienhueser)

down the slope. Camping at the pass provides the option of being there when the views open up, although bad weather and wind could make camping there unpleasant. Another option is to camp part way down Rock Creek valley on the other side of the pass.

There are many good campsites on gravel bars along the entire route. Strong, fast, experienced backcountry hikers can do this trip in 2 to 3 days. Leisurely hikers may prefer 5 or 6 days. Extra time allows a better chance of seeing the view.

Other Trips in the Area

The Nugget Creek ATV trail, an old mining road, makes a great back-country mountain-bike trip or hike. It is about 30 miles long, round trip, and leads to a public-use cabin on the east side of Nugget Creek (first come, first served), the rubble-covered base of the Kuskulana Glacier, and fine views of Mount Blackburn. See the driving directions above. The first 2 to 3 miles can be muddy and difficult, especially with a loaded bicycle. After that the trail is higher, drier, and easier. There are several creeks to ford. The trail gains about 900 feet elevation in about 15 miles. Strong bikers can do this round trip in a day, but most will want to allow two days, plus time to explore. The Kotsina ATV trail can also be biked or hiked. Ask the National Park Service for more information (see location and contact information in the appendix).

52 | KENNECOTT MINES

Erie Mine
Round trip: 8 miles (from Kennicott)
Hiking time: 4–7 hours
High point: 2,800 feet
Total elevation gain: 800 feet

Jumbo Mine
Round trip: 8 miles (from Kennicott)
Hiking time: 7–8 hours
High point: 5,750 feet
Total elevation gain: 2,750 feet

Bonanza Mine
Round trip: 8 miles (from Kennicott)
Hiking time: 7–8 hours
High point: 6,050 feet
Total elevation gain: 3,050 feet

Best: June–September
Map: Trails Illustrated "Wrangell–St. Elias National Park and Preserve"
Agency: Wrangell–St. Elias National Preserve

Historic buildings of the Kennecott Copper Corporation and nearby once-boisterous town of McCarthy sit beside the Kennicott Glacier. High above, on precipitous mountain slopes, mines once disgorged precious blue-green ore onto aerial trams for transporting to the mill 4,500 feet below. Abandoned wagon roads leading to three of the mines, Erie, Jumbo, and Bonanza, are trails into history.

The Kennecott copper deposit, which became the Bonanza Mine, was

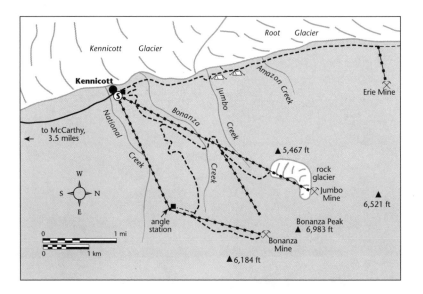

reportedly found in 1900 by two prospectors looking for a horse pasture. They mistook the distant outcropping of malachite (copper carbonate) for green grass. Nearby Jumbo Mine tapped the largest deposit in the area, producing 70,000 tons of 70-percent copper ore (with 20 ounces of silver per ton). The entire production of the Kennecott mines assayed an average of 13 percent copper. A honeycomb of more than 70 miles of layered tunnels connects the Erie, Jumbo, Bonanza, and Mother Lode Mines. When the rich veins played out and the mines closed in 1938, the towns died. Through the years, Alaskans who prefer a more remote lifestyle have been reclaiming the settlements. New summertime activity came with the area's designation as Wrangell–St. Elias National Preserve and the subsequent arrival of tourists. Sixty miles of gravel access road limits the number of visitors, however.

Driving directions. Drive to mile 82.6 of the Richardson Highway (86 miles north of Valdez and 219 miles east of Anchorage). Turn east onto Edgerton Highway and continue 33 miles to Chitina. Expect no gas or groceries beyond here. Follow the main road through Chitina and cross the Copper River bridge. The 59-mile, primitive gravel McCarthy Road begins here and follows the bed of the old Copper River and Northwestern Railroad, which carried ore from Kennecott to Cordova from 1911 to 1938. The road is not recommended for large camper vehicles or trailers. Allow 2½ hours to drive the rough road, and beware of flat tires; railroad spikes churned up by road graders are a threat. The road terminates at the Kennicott River. Although residents take vehicles across winter ice, there is no automobile bridge. Park at the river, for a fee, or park near the National

Mount Blackburn and Root Glacier from Erie Mine trail (Gayle Nienhueser)

Park Service Day Use Area ¾ mile before the river and walk the last bit. An alternate access to McCarthy is to fly to the airstrip, just outside of town. Planes can be chartered in the Chitina or Glennallen–Gulkana areas, or take the Wednesday or Friday mail plane from Gulkana (see Ellis Air Taxi in Appendix for contact information).

Rent bicycles or arrange commercial raft trips at the river. Information about and arrangement for shuttle service into McCarthy and Kennicott can be obtained at the parking lot by the river.

Cross the Kennicott River on footbridges and walk or bike the gravel road east, up a small rise, to an intersection and the McCarthy/Kennicott Historical Museum. This is an old red railroad depot well worth a visit. The left fork of the road goes to Kennicott, 4 miles away. The right fork leads quickly into McCarthy.

Be sure to visit the McCarthy Lodge, built in the early 1900s, which is full of relics and old photographs. The Kennicott Glacier Lodge in Kennicott, of recent construction, also is filled with memorabilia. Ask about the two spellings of Kennicott. If camping near McCarthy, please find a spot near the Kennicott River. Clear Creek, which you cross as you walk into McCarthy, supplies drinking water to the residents; be careful not to contaminate it. Please remember that *all* structures and land in McCarthy and some in Kennicott are privately owned—do not enter buildings, take relics, or use old lumber for firewood.

To reach the mines, walk or bicycle the road north from the museum to Kennicott or take the ground shuttle operated by Wrangell Mountain Air or Kennicott Glacier Lodge. In Kennicott, cross the bridge over National Creek and proceed on flat ground on the main street through town. Follow this old wagon road about 5 minutes (by foot) beyond the end of town to a fork.

Erie Mine

The walk toward Erie Mine is on an easy, mostly level trail with great glacier and mountain views. At the fork, take the left-hand trail, which goes straight, paralleling the Kennicott Glacier, and leads in the direction of Erie Mine. In a few minutes cross Bonanza Creek on a plank bridge. About a mile out, the trail heads uphill briefly to cross Jumbo Creek on a footbridge. Shortly after Jumbo Creek there are several possible campsites and a metal food and trash container. About ¼ mile farther is an access trail to Root Glacier, which joins Kennicott Glacier below you. The trail has now become a narrow footpath through low shrubs. In late June, blue lupine grace the trailside and frame the glacier and mountains in the distance. In another mile the trail crosses the dry, rocky outwash plain of Amazon Creek, then regains the top of the lateral moraine. In places the moraine is eroding and taking pieces of the trail with it. Exposure may bother some hikers occasionally. About 4 miles from Kennicott an old cable crosses the trail. This was the cable for the tram to Erie Mine, high above on the mountainside. Stop here for a picnic lunch and enjoy the view of the white Root Glacier, the Stairway Icefall to the north, and the majestic white mountains: Blackburn (16,390 feet) and Regal (13,845 feet). The continuing trail is soon buried beneath a steep rockslide. It is difficult and dangerous to climb down to the glacier here. Head back toward Kennicott and take a side trip to the glacier via the access trail you passed on your way in. For walking on the glacier, crampons and ice ax are recommended; the ice can be slippery and, with occasional water holes and bottomless tubes eroded from the ice by water, can be dangerous. A guided trip can be arranged in Kennicott and includes the use of crampons and ice ax.

Jumbo Mine

At the fork just outside Kennicott, go right, and switchback uphill toward Jumbo and Bonanza Mines. This route comes close to the top of the mill building, the centerpiece of Kennicott, which makes a nice overlook. The main route continues toward the mines. After about an hour of steady but leisurely climbing, when the main trail makes a very sharp switchback to the right, an obscure, overgrown, hard-to-find trail goes left through the alders. Look hard; the trail goes more or less straight ahead toward Bonanza Creek from the outside of the turn. The first part of this Jumbo Mine trail, an old wagon track, was seriously overgrown by alders at the time of this writing. The trail bed should be clear. The trail leads to Jumbo Mine, high in a cirque at 5,750 feet. The main road continues to Bonanza Mine, a good alternative if you miss the trail.

The side trail to Jumbo Mine crosses Bonanza Creek about ½ mile after it leaves the main trail, and the alders continue on the other side for a short distance. Then the trail breaks out of the alders, and the old wagon track provides generally good walking. Just before Jumbo Creek, scree slides cover the trail, and it is necessary to cross short stretches of steep scree slope. At about 4,700 feet the trail climbs up a massive rock glacier. Water and a possible campsite are at the lower end of the glacier. Follow the remnants of the old track up the rock glacier as it bears right into the cirque below Bonanza Peak (elevation 6,983 feet). Here, if you are lucky, an old building still stands, leaning eerily.

Bonanza Mine

Follow the directions, above, for Jumbo Mine, but stay on the main trail instead of taking the obscure turnoff to Jumbo Mine. At an intersection near an old tram, take the left fork; the right-hand trail leads to a private cabin at an "angle station" (where the tram cable turned a corner). The upper part of the trail parallels Bonanza Creek and passes a waterfall. Camping is possible near the falls, the first plentiful water source along the trail. In July the slopes are rife with wildflowers. The buildings at Bonanza Mine (elevation 5,950 feet) are mostly collapsed, but the views are spectacular and well worth the climb. The most incredible of the views is from the ridge above the collapsed buildings (6,050 feet).

Because the slope faces south, the climbs to Jumbo and Bonanza Mines can be very hot on a sunny day. Carry plenty of water.

Other Hikes

Stop at the National Park visitor center in Copper Center or Chitina, or check the Park website (see Appendix) for information on other hiking options in the area, all more difficult than those described here. Ask about Nikolai Ridge. This several-day trip with a spectacular destination requires crossing McCarthy Creek, which can be difficult and dangerous.

53 | WORTHINGTON GLACIER OVERLOOK

Round trip: 2 miles
Hiking time: 2–3 hours
High point: 3,400 feet
Total elevation gain: 1,200 feet
Best: late June–September
Map: USGS Valdez A5
Agency: Alaska Division of Parks and Outdoor Recreation

This short hike follows the lateral moraine of Worthington Glacier, offering impressive views of the deeply crevassed glacier below and of the alpine meadows and mountain wilderness of the Thompson Pass area. This informal trail, created simply by the passage of feet, is a perfect leg-stretcher for the more adventurous visitors to Worthington Glacier and gives a hint of the thrill of mountaineering. Those bothered by exposure will want to stick

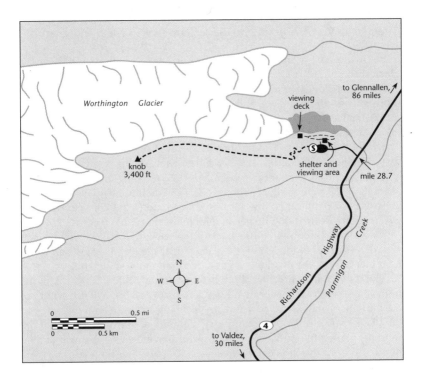

Lateral moraine of Worthington Glacier, late June (Gayle Nienhueser)

to the lower part of this trail or to the short, paved flatland trail near the glacier face.

Don't let cloudy or misty weather cancel the hike; the blue of the ice is more intense on gray days, and the mountains are more mysterious. This glacial landscape is recognized as a National Natural Landmark. Like many other Alaskan glaciers, Worthington is receding.

Driving directions. The trailhead is located on the Richardson Highway, 33 miles from Valdez and 273 miles from Anchorage. Coming from Valdez the entrance is 2 miles past milepost 27. Coming from the north, the entrance is 0.3 mile south of milepost 29. (The distance between mileposts 27 and 29 is 2.3 miles.) Follow a 0.4-mile side road west to the Worthington Glacier State Recreation Site parking lot (elevation 2,200 feet).

Find a gravel footpath at the back of the parking lot, near the bus-stop sign. Up the trail to the left of the glacier, near the icefall, stands a prominent black knob, the overlook, a good destination for skilled hikers.

The trail leads uphill, steeply in places, through alder, to the top of the highest gravel ridge or moraine. Keep left at several forks. Once on top of the moraine, you will notice that many feet have beaten a path to the top of the black knob ahead. On a sunny day, a couple of places to the left of the moraine make a fine spot for a picnic. If children are along, watch that they don't approach the cliffs above the glacier. Carry water with you.

The more adventurous can continue to parallel the glacier edge, climbing the moraine as far as is comfortable. The trail is frequently exposed, requiring sure footing and boots with good traction. On rainy days, particularly, the moraine can be slippery; a fall could be serious, perhaps fatal. However, with caution, this little hike is one of the most delightful in southcentral Alaska.

Walking on the glacier itself should be undertaken only by trained and properly equipped mountaineers.

From the parking lot a short, paved, wheelchair-accessible trail offers an alternative leg-stretcher. This trail leads to the right, toward the glacier face. It passes restrooms and a kiosk, then leads to a viewing platform in front of the glacier and just above the lake at the glacier's face. An 1,800-foot loop side trail takes visitors closer to the lake and ends up near the viewing platform. Snow may linger on parts of this trail into July even though the moraine trail is snow free.

Camp at Blueberry Lake State Recreation Site, at mile 24 of the Richardson Highway. If the grade seems too steep at Worthington, look for a flatter but unmarked trail at the back of the Blueberry Lake campground loop (1.5 miles round trip). It leads to a valley overlook along an old telegraph line. The whole Thompson Pass area offers good, easy hiking above tree line on heather and smooth bedrock. The area is exceptionally scenic in autumn when tiny tundra leaves burn a brilliant red.

54 | HISTORIC VALDEZ TRAIL

One way: 8 miles
Hiking time: 4–5 hours
High point: 985 feet
Total elevation gain: northbound 725 feet, southbound 435 feet
Best: mid-May–mid-October
Maps: USGS Valdez A5, A6 SE
Agency: Alaska Division of Mining, Land, & Water

Take a walk into history through Keystone Canyon, along the route used by seekers of gold more than 100 years ago. The Historic Valdez Trail climbs the mountainside above the south end of Keystone Canyon, and then traverses the west side of the canyon several hundred feet above the Lowe River. After the first initial climb at the south end, it's an easy walk on a mostly level trail through a thick forest of Sitka spruce with occasional glimpses of spectacular waterfalls plunging down canyon walls and misty mountains looming overhead. Access points every 2 to 3 miles make several variations possible.

Built in 1899 by the U.S. Army, this trail offered the first glacier-free, year-round, all-American land route to Alaska's Interior. At first it was a pack trail for horses and dogs. A telegraph line connecting Eagle (Fort Egbert) and Valdez came next. In 1905 work began on widening part of the trail so that it could be used by wagons, and by 1916 the first adventurous motorists were using the road. When the Richardson Highway was built in the bottom of the canyon after World War II, alders reclaimed the historic trail. Recently the Valdez Trail Association, a small group of dedicated volunteers, has reopened the trail.

Driving directions. To find the south end of the trail, drive to mile 11.8 of the Richardson Highway (about 16 miles from downtown Valdez) and turn west (left coming from Valdez) on the old Richardson Highway Loop. Drive 0.3 mile and find the trail on the left, marked by a trail sign. Park in a small clearing across the road from the trail. (The east end of the old Richardson Highway Loop is at mile 12.5 of the Richardson Highway. The trail begins about 0.4 mile from that intersection.)

Moving north, there are three more access points along the Richardson Highway:

- Mile 13.8, at Bridal Veil Falls. The trail section known as the Goat Trail begins at the south end of a pullout.
- Mile 16.5, at Bear Creek. A short side road lies 0.2 mile east of the Lowe River bridge, just east of a cabin with a sign for Keystone Adventures. Where the side road ends at the hillside, find the access trail on the right. It is marked by a sign on a tree about 10 feet in, but the sign may be hard to see in midsummer.
- Mile 18. The trail begins in a large pullout with a pay phone. Find the trail about 50 yards west of the phone.

This trail description assumes that you start at the southern end. The initial section of the trail is locally known as "The Pack Trail." This section was cleared using only hand tools, to keep alive the original spirit of 1899. For a little over ½ mile the trail climbs through coastal rainforest of Sitka spruce and northern hemlock laced with devil's club, dwarf dogwood, and ferns. The tall trees, providing some shelter, make this a good hike for a rainy day. Some of the Sitka spruce are 3 feet in diameter, large for southcentral Alaska, and may be as much as 200 years old. Interpretive signs along the way tell the story of the trail's history. After the trail levels out, it crosses a small stream where the 100-year-old trail work can be seen in the rockwork. Old telegraph wire still lines the trail in many spots and may trip unwary hikers.

Yes, those black piles in the trail are bear scat so remember to make noise. Openings in the forest provide occasional views of the Lowe River valley, Meteorite Mountain, and Keystone Canyon and its waterfalls.

After a little over a mile the trail descends gradually into the valley of Horsetail Falls Creek, parallels the creek upstream, crosses the stream on a small footbridge, and then heads down valley to an overlook of Horsetail Falls. The vegetation changes in this area, losing the hemlock and adding more birch, currants, and salmonberry. By midsummer the trail could be overgrown if not maintained or used frequently.

As the trail descends toward Bridal Veil Falls, it reaches a very steep section with loose gravel. A rope strung along the trail provides handholds for the descent.

Approximately 2.3 miles from the trailhead, the Pack Trail reaches an intersection with the wagon road that was built on top of the original trail. This section is known as "The Goat Trail." A side trail to the right leads 0.2 mile to the parking lot at Bridal Veil Falls.

To continue the hike, turn left onto the Goat Trail. At first the trail is much more open than the Pack Trail, allowing views of rocky cliffs and cloud-swathed, snow-streaked mountains above as the sound of waterfalls fades in the distance. Later, alder and tall grasses crowd the old roadbed, except for a narrow footpath in the center. Look for the occasional old telegraph pole or length of wire. In places the trail hugs the sheer, flower-studded cliffs and in places it traverses a narrow ledge with a steep drop off. Though the path is good, there is some exposure.

About 1.8 miles from the intersection with the Pack Trail, the Goat Trail reaches Snowslide Gulch where large, dramatic avalanches often leave snow lingering well into July and sometimes all summer. A bridge was completed here in 2001, but it may be vulnerable to avalanches. The creek is too deep and fast to cross safely without the bridge. In early summer it

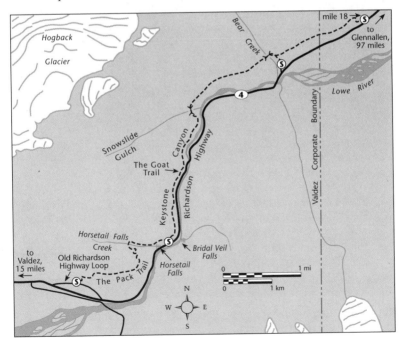

Viewpoint on the Goat Trail; painting Bridal Veil Falls, June (Helen Nienhueser)

may be possible to cross Snowslide Gulch on hard-packed snow. (Use extreme caution: evaluate the thickness of the snow, the amount of water underneath, the condition of the surface, and where you would land if you broke through.) Contact the Valdez Parks and Recreation Department for information on current trail conditions (see Appendix).

After crossing Snowslide Gulch, follow the old wagon road about 2 miles, out of Keystone Canyon to Bear Creek. The first part of this trail north of Snowslide Gulch was widened to allow access for heavy equipment during bridge construction. About ¼ mile north on this wide section, the trail splits. The wide trail continues down to the Lowe River. The narrower trail to the left continues approximately 1.75 miles to the Bear Creek Bridge. Follow the narrower trail. At Bear Creek, the historic steel-span bridge, constructed by the Army during World War II, has been resurfaced to provide a safe crossing for hikers. About 100 yards beyond the bridge watch for a narrow trail to the right that leads to the Bear Creek trailhead near the Richardson Highway.

The trail from Bear Creek continues to follow the old wagon road for another 1½ miles through woods of cottonwood, alder, and Sitka spruce. Wild cucumber, fireweed, goats beard, and cow parsnip join the devil's club and grasses lining this part of the trail. At one point the trail crosses a recent avalanche area. The downed trees on either side of the trail are testament to the power of these winter snow slides and warn hikers against use of the trail in winter. This part of the trail is locally known as the "Dutch Flats" section.

Currently the trail leaves the old wagon road and heads for mile 18 of the Richardson Highway shortly after the avalanche area and a stretch where rows of mature cottonwoods line the trail.

The annual avalanches that sweep down Snowslide Gulch keep the hillside bare of trees. Therefore locals use Snowslide Gulch as a relatively brush-free route to alpine valleys above.

55 | SHOUP BAY

Round trip: 22 miles
Hiking time: 8–10 hours one way; allow 2–3 days
High point: 1,000 feet
Total elevation gain: 1,000 feet
Best: June–September
Map: USGS Valdez A7
Agencies: Shoup Bay State Marine Park and City of Valdez

A new, primitive trail, built by Alaska State Parks, offers hikers a spectacular walk above Port Valdez into beautiful Shoup Bay with stunning views of

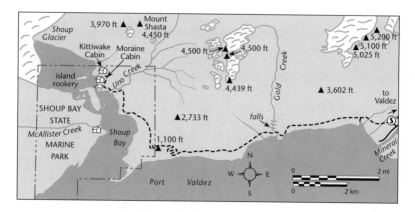

Shoup Glacier and the iceberg-strewn lagoon at its toe. Two public-use cabins and good campsites await hikers on the shores of Shoup Bay Lagoon at trail's end. The first part of the trail, to Gold Creek, is easy and offers the option of a day hike out of Valdez. The trail becomes increasingly rugged beyond Gold Creek. Hikers choosing the full trip should be experienced and in good condition.

Driving directions. The trailhead is located west of Valdez, where Egan Drive dead-ends. Drive west through Valdez on Egan Drive to Mineral Creek, about 1 mile from Hazelet Avenue. Cross the creek and follow West Egan Drive until it ends, in a little over a block. A small parking lot and trailhead bulletin board are on the left.

The first mile or so of the trail is wide, relatively level, and quite easy. After crossing a bridge, the trail winds through woods to a broad, wildflower-dotted meadow and great views of Port Valdez. After 20 to 30 minutes, a side trail to the left leads to a gravel beach that makes a fine destination for a short hike. Beyond the beach access, the trail narrows and may at times be overgrown and wet in rainy weather. In several places the trail crosses small streams; Gore-Tex boots and gaiters will keep feet dry.

After 1 to 1½ hours, the trail descends steeply to the broad, green, fan-shaped delta of Gold Creek, 3.5 miles from the trailhead. At the foot of the hill the trail forks. The left fork leads into thick spruce woods to a campsite with a latrine and food storage locker. Be prepared for a healthy mosquito population here in June and July! The right fork leads across a massive footbridge over Gold Creek and onward toward Shoup Bay.

Beyond the bridge the trail heads upward through the spruce forest. Follow the main trail out of the spruce trees and up and down across the hillside above Port Valdez. About a mile beyond Gold Creek the trail enters a large, east-facing gully, and begins climbing. As it reaches the top, the hiker is rewarded with the first views of the mountains west of Shoup Bay.

The trail continues across the mountainside and eventually begins to

Shoup Glacier and Shoup Bay Lagoon, June (Helen Nienhueser)

climb uphill through a green tunnel of alder, then up four switchbacks, to the high point at about 1,000 feet. The trail then goes through a small pass and past a possible (undeveloped) campsite near a small stream.

Suddenly the trail rounds a corner to a spectacular view of Shoup Glacier and Bay. A short distance farther is a nice rock for sitting and a sign that says it is 3 miles to the cabins. It is a very difficult 3 miles. From here the trail descends steeply for 1,000 feet, through alder, traversing a steep, rocky hillside. It is often muddy and slippery. Snow may linger across the trail into July. In one spot, a wooden stairway leads down a cliff. Farther down, a chain affixed to the cliff provides handholds and angle iron set into the rock provides footholds. At one point, where the trail is less than 100 yards above the bay, the way abruptly turns inland and climbs upward across bedrock. At this turn, an old route plunges downhill to the Bay. Do not go downhill here!

The trail winds through rock escarpments until it reaches Uno Creek, a large stream, just below a thundering waterfall. A right fork goes uphill to the waterfall. Follow the left fork downhill. When the trail dead-ends at the creek, look for rock cairns. Follow them downstream and cross the creek where it braids out into channels just before entering the Bay. Water levels may be anywhere from ankle to knee deep (see "Stream Crossings" in the Introduction). Beware of icebergs and shifting sandbars near the mouth of the creek.

On the west side of the creek the continuing trail is marked by cairns. It is now an easy ½ mile walk to the camping area and Kittiwake and Moraine public-use cabins. The camping area is undeveloped except for a latrine and a bear-resistant food storage locker. To rent a cabin, contact the Department of Natural Resources Public Information Center or check the Alaska State Parks' website (see Appendix). A third cabin, at McAllister Creek, is accessible only by boat. The Moraine Cabin may be rented to the U.S. Fish and Wildlife Service for research from June though August.

Water is available from Uno Creek and sometimes from a stream in a small canyon just north of the Kittiwake Cabin. The trail to the small canyon starts from the gravel beach north of Kittiwake Cabin and is marked by cairns. Get water when you cross Uno Creek so you don't have to backtrack if the other stream is not flowing. Boil or filter the water.

Linger here a day to enjoy the spectacular scenery. Out in the lagoon more than 9,000 breeding pairs of noisy, blacklegged kittiwakes populate a small island rookery. Glaucous-winged gulls occupy the top of the island. Harbor seals, eagles, porcupines, and bears are occasional visitors here. An option for the return is to prearrange a pick-up from one of the charter boat operators in Valdez.

Do not attempt this trail in winter due to severe avalanche hazard. The first 3 to 6 miles of the trip can be done beginning in mid-May, but snow is likely at the cabins and camping area at that time. Snow is probable on the last 3 miles of the trail until mid-June, depending on the previous winter's snowfall. The trip can also be done into October; the first snow usually falls about mid-October.

Other hikes in the Valdez area are trails at Mineral Creek and Solomon Gulch. Pick up trail guides at the Valdez Visitors Information Center.

APPENDIX

LAND MANAGERS

Alaska Department of Fish and Game
333 Raspberry Road
Anchorage, AK 99518
(907) 267-2342
(Kachemak Bay State Critical
    Habitat Area)

Alaska Division of Mining, Land, & Water
Southcentral Region
550 West 7th Avenue, Suite 900
Anchorage, AK 99501
(907) 269-8552

Alaska Division of Parks and Outdoor Recreation (Alaska State Parks)
State cabin rental information
(907) 269-8400
www.alaskastateparks.org

Chugach State Park
Potter Section House
Mile 115 Seward Highway
HC52, Box 8999
Indian, AK 99540
(907) 345-5014
(907) 345-6982 (fax—for trip plans)
chugach_state_park@dnr.state.ak.us

Homer Ranger Station
P.O. Box 3248
Homer, AK 99603
(907) 235-7024

Kenai Area Office
P.O. Box 1247
Soldotna, AK 99669
(907) 262-5581
(Shoup Bay State Marine Park)

Matanuska-Susitna/Copper Basin Area Office
Finger Lake State Recreation Area
HC32, Box 6706
Wasilla, AK 99654
(907) 745-3975

Chugach National Forest (U.S. Forest Service)
3301 C Street, Suite 300
Anchorage, AK 99503
(907) 271-2500
TDD (907) 271-2282
www.fs.fed.us/r10/chugach
Cabin reservations: (877) 444-6777.
This is a private company under
contract to the Forest Service. It
operates 7 A.M. to 8 P.M. Alaska
time.
www.reserveusa.com

Glacier District Office
Forest Station Road, Mile 0.5
Alyeska Highway
P.O. Box 129
Girdwood, AK 99587
(907) 783-3242

Seward District Office
P.O. Box 390
Seward, AK 99664
(907) 224-3374

Fort Richardson Military Reservation
Military Police (907) 384-0823 or Military Fish and Wildlife Office (907) 384-0830 (Call to be sure military land is open.)

Kenai Fjords National Park
P.O. Box 1727
Seward, AK 99664
(907) 224-3175
(907) 224-2132 (recording)
KEFJ_Superintendant@nps.gov
www.nps.gov/kefj/

Kenai National Wildlife Refuge
P.O. Box 2139
Soldotna, AK 99669
(907) 262-7021
www.r7.fws.gov/nwr/kenai

Wrangell–St. Elias National Park and Preserve
Mile 106.4 Richardson Highway
P.O. Box 439
Copper Center, AK 99573
(907) 822-5234
www.nps.gov/wrst

ADDITIONAL INFORMATION SOURCES
Alaska Avalanche School
Alaska Mountain Safety Center
9140 Brewsters Drive
Anchorage, AK 99516
(907) 345-3566

Alaska Department of Natural Resources
Public Information Center
550 West 7th Avenue, Suite 1260
Anchorage, AK 99501
(907) 269-8400
TDD 269-8411
pic@dnr.state.ak.us

Alaska Department of Transportation and Public Facilities
P.O. Box 196900
Anchorage, AK 99519-6900
Numbers to call for highway and road conditions:
(907) 273-6037 (recording)
(907) 269-0760 main number, Maintenance Division
(907) 745-2159 Matanuska-Susitna District (for Petersville Road)
www.dot.state.ak.us (Whittier tunnel information)

Alaska Travel Industry Association
(907) 929-2200
Ask for the "Vacation Planner," a publication listing names, addresses, and phone numbers of businesses and services of interest to the traveler (e.g., car rental, guide services).
www.travelalaska.com
www.adventuresalaska.com

Alaska Public Lands Information Center
605 West Fourth Avenue
Anchorage, AK 99501
(907) 271-2737
TDD (907) 271-2738
www.nps.gov/aplic

Alaska Wilderness Recreation and Tourism Association
2207 Spenard Road, Suite 201
Anchorage, AK 99508
(907) 258-3171 (Ask for the Alaska Ecotourism Directory.)
info@awrta.org
www.awrta.org

Anchorage Convention and Visitors Bureau
(907) 276-4118
www.anchorage.net

Cooperative Extension Service
2221 East Northern Lights Boulevard, #118
Anchorage, AK 99508-4242
(907) 786-6300
www.uaf.edu/coop-ext

Eagle River Nature Center
32750 Eagle River Road
Eagle River, AK 99577
(907) 694-2108
www.ernc.org

Homer Chamber of Commerce
201 Sterling Highway
(907) 235-7740
Homer, AK 99603
www.homeralaska.org

Valdez Parks and Recreation Department
(907) 835-2531

PUBLIC TRANSPORTATION
Check yellow pages for current listings.

Alaska Direct Bus Line (Anchorage)
(907) 277-6652; (800) 770-6652
www.alaskadirect@tokalaska.com
Service between Anchorage, Glennallen, Tok, and intermediate points

Alaska Marine Highway (state ferry)
605 West Fourth Avenue, Anchorage
(907) 272-4482; (800) 642-0066
www.state.ak.us/ferry

Service between Whittier and Valdez and between Seward and Homer via Kodiak

Alaska Railroad
(907) 265-2494 (Anchorage)
www.alaskarailroad.com
Service from Anchorage to Girdwood to Seward, Anchorage to Talkeetna, Talkeetna to Hurricane and points between

Anchorage Public Transit, "The People Mover" (City Bus)
700 West Sixth Avenue, Anchorage
(907) 343-6543
www.peoplemover.org

Backcountry Connection, Glennallen
(907) 822-5292 or (866) 582-5292 (toll free in Alaska)
bakcntry@alaska.net
www.alaska-backcountry-tours.com
Scheduled van service between Glennallen and McCarthy

Ellis Air Taxi
P.O. Box 106
Glennallen, AK 99588
(907) 822-3368
Mail plane to McCarthy from Glennallen or Anchorage

Miller's Landing
P.O. Box 81
Seward, AK 99664
(907) 224-5739
miland@ptialaska.com
www.millerslandingak.com
Water taxi for Caines Head

Parks Highway Express
(888) 600-6001 (toll free)

www.alaskashuttle.com
Serves all points on the Parks, Glenn, and Richardson Highways

Seward Bus Lines
Box 1338
Seward, AK 99664
Anchorage (907) 563-0800; Seward (907) 224-3608; Homer (907) 235-2252
Serves Seward, Homer, Anchorage, and points between

Susitna Expeditions
(907) 892-6916
(800) 891-6916 (in Alaska)
kayaker@mtaonline.net
www.susitnaexpeditions.com
Shuttle service between Kesugi Ridge trailheads

CANOE, KAYAK, AND OUTDOOR GEAR RENTALS AND MAP SALES
Check the yellow pages for current listings.

Anchorage
Recreational Equipment, Inc. (REI)
1200 West Northern Lights Boulevard
Anchorage, AK 99503
(907) 272-4565
Canoes, camping equipment, maps

Alaska Mountaineering and Hiking (AMH)
2633 Spenard Road
Anchorage, AK 99503
(907) 272-1811
www.alaskamountaineering.com
Kayaks, maps

U.S. Geological Survey
Earth Science Information Center
4230 University Drive
Anchorage, AK 99508
(907) 786-7011
http://mapping.usgs.gov/

Soldotna (Kenai Peninsula)
The Fishin' Hole
139B Warehouse Street
Soldotna, AK 99669
(907) 262-2290
info@TheFishinHoleAlaska.com

The Sports Den
44176 Sterling Highway
Soldotna, AK 99669
(907) 262-7491

Sterling (Kenai Peninsula)
Alaska Canoe and Campground
35292 Sterling Highway
Sterling, AK 99672
(907) 262-2331
alaskacanoe@yahoo.com
Canoes, shuttle service, mountain bikes, camping equipment

Weigner's Backcountry Guiding
P.O. Box 709
Sterling, AK 99672
(907) 262-7840
weigner@alaska.net

Eklutna Lake
Lifetime Adventures
P.O. Box 1205
Palmer, AK 99645
(800) 952-8624
info@lifetimeadventures.net
www.lifetimeadventures.net
Kayaks, mountain bikes; may offer shuttle to/from south end of lake

Willow (North of Anchorage)
Nancy Lake Resort
P.O. Box 114
Willow, AK 99688
(907) 495-6284
Canoes and car-top carriers

Tippecanoe Rentals
South Rolly Lake Campground,
Nancy Lake Recreation Area
P.O. Box 288
Willow, AK 99688
(907) 495-6688
www.paddlealaska.com
Canoes available at Lynx Lake Loop
trailhead and other locations

CONSERVATION AND OUTDOOR ORGANIZATIONS

Alaska Center for the Environment
897 G Street, Suite 100
Anchorage, AK 99501
(907) 274-3621
www.akcenter.org

Alaska Conservation Alliance
750 West 2nd Avenue, Suite 109
Anchorage, AK 99501
(907) 258-6171
unite@akvoice.org
www@akvoice.org

Alaska Conservation Foundation
441 West 5th Avenue, Suite 402
Anchorage, AK 99501-2340
(907) 276-1917
www.akcf.org

Alaska Mountain and Wilderness Huts Association
3039 Alder Circle
Anchorage, AK 99508-3256
(907) 279-4663
www.alaskahuts.org

Alaska State Parks Foundation
P.O. Box 245001
Anchorage, AK 99524-5001

Alaska Quiet Rights Coalition
P.O. Box 202592
Anchorage, AK 99520
(907) 566-3524
quietrights@yahoo.com
www.quietrights.org

Arctic Bicycle Club, Mountain Bikers
P.O. Box 244302
Anchorage, AK 99524
(907) 566-0177
www.arcticbike.org

Knik Canoers and Kayakers
P.O. Box 101935
Anchorage, AK 99510
(907) 566-1554

Mountaineering Club of Alaska
Box 102037
Anchorage, AK 99510
www.mcak.org
Meets at 7:30 P.M. third Wednesday
of each month (First United Meth-
odist Church, 9th Avenue and G
Street) in Anchorage

National Audubon Society
308 G Street, #217
Anchorage, AK 99501
(907) 276-7034

National Outdoor Leadership School (NOLS)
P.O. Box 981
Palmer, AK 99645
(907) 745-4047
alaska@nols.edu
www.nols.edu

National Parks and Conservation Association
750 West Second Avenue, Suite 205
Anchorage, AK 99501
(907) 277-6722

Nordic Skiing Association of Anchorage/Nordic Ski Club
203 West 15th Avenue, Suite 204
Anchorage, AK 99501-3504
(907) 276-7609
Recording: (907) 248-6667

nordski@alaska.net
www.alaska.net/~nsaa

Sierra Club
201 Barrow Street, Suite 101
Anchorage, AK 99501
(907) 276-4048

The Wilderness Society
430 West Seventh Avenue, Suite 205
Anchorage, AK 99501
(907) 272-9453

INDEX

Helen D. Nienhueser moved to Alaska in 1959 after traveling north for summer camp work during college. She homesteaded, raised a family, was active in the early days of the Mountaineering Club of Alaska, helped to put the Alaska Center for the Environment on its feet, and for many years planned state land selections and land use with the Alaska Department of Natural Resources. Now retired, she is busier than ever making sure her granddaughters get time in the backcountry, working as a catalyst for a major urban park in midtown Anchorage, traveling for adventure, and pursuing various public policy issues in Anchorage and statewide.

Co-author Helen Nienhueser with husband, Gayle Nienhueser, at the Shoup Bay trailhead (Trip 55), June 2000

John Wolfe Jr. has been hiking in southcentral Alaska since he was a small child and his parents (including co-author Helen Nienhueser) took him hiking for early editions of this book. Now he tramps the trails and ridges with wife, Gretchen Nelson, and coaxes his own young children into getting out. He has guided on Denali but loves simple peak scrambles in the Chugach Mountains. He is an environmental planner for an Anchorage consulting firm and is founder of the nonprofit Alaska Mountain and Wilderness Huts Association. He became co-author beginning with the fourth edition in 1994.

Co-author John Wolfe Jr. (second from left) with wife, Gretchen Nelson (left), brother, Dave Wolfe, and sister-in-law, Lynn Palmquist, on the divide between Lost Creek and Trail Creek (Trip 50), July 2000

THE MOUNTAINEERS, founded in 1906, is a nonprofit outdoor activity and conservation club, whose mission is "to explore, study, preserve, and enjoy the natural beauty of the outdoors . . . ." Based in Seattle, Washington, the club is now the third-largest such organization in the United States, with 15,000 members and five branches throughout Washington State.

The Mountaineers sponsors both classes and year-round outdoor activities in the Pacific Northwest, which include hiking, mountain climbing, ski-touring, snowshoeing, bicycling, camping, kayaking and canoeing, nature study, sailing, and adventure travel. The club's conservation division supports environmental causes through educational activities, sponsoring legislation, and presenting informational programs. All club activities are led by skilled, experienced volunteers, who are dedicated to promoting safe and responsible enjoyment and preservation of the outdoors.

If you would like to participate in these organized outdoor activities or the club's programs, consider a membership in The Mountaineers. For information and an application, write or call The Mountaineers, Club Headquarters, 300 Third Avenue West, Seattle, WA 98119; 206-284-6310.

The Mountaineers Books, an active, nonprofit publishing program of the club, produces guidebooks, instructional texts, historical works, natural history guides, and works on environmental conservation. All books produced by The Mountaineers Books fulfill the club's mission.

Send or call for our catalog of more than 500 outdoor titles:

The Mountaineers Books
1001 SW Klickitat Way, Suite 201
Seattle, WA 98134
800-553-4453
mbooks@mountaineersbooks.org
www.mountaineersbooks.org

THE MOUNTAINEERING CLUB OF ALASKA, founded in 1958, is a non-profit outdoor organization with the following purposes:
- To promote the enjoyment of hiking, climbing, and exploration of the mountains;
- To teach and encourage safety;
- To assist in the prevention of waste and unnecessary destruction of the natural scene.

The Mountaineering Club meets at 7:30 P.M. on the third Wednesday of every month at the First United Methodist Church at the corner of 9th Avenue and G Street in downtown Anchorage. New members and guests are welcome. The club sponsors classes and a regular schedule of hikes and climbs. For more information contact:

Mountaineering Club of Alaska
P.O. Box 102037
Anchorage, AK 99510
www.mcak.org